Despatches from the Crimea

Sir William Howard Russell

Despatches from the Crimea

WILLIAM HOWARD RUSSELL

Edited with an Introduction by Nicholas Bentley

—

Foreword by Martin Bell

Frontline Books, London

Naval Institute Press, Annapolis, Maryland

Despatches from the Crimea

This edition published 2008 by Frontline Books, an imprint of Pen & Swords Books Limited, 47 Church Street, Barnsley, S. Yorkshire S70 2AS

Published and distributed in the United States of America and Canada by the Naval Institute Press, Beach Hall, 291 Wood Road, Annapolis, Maryland 21402-5034
www.navalinstitute.org

British Library Cataloguing-in Publication Data

Russell, William Howard, Sir, 1820–1907
Russell's despatches from the Crimea, 1854–56
1. Crimean War, 1853–1856 – Sources 2. Great Britain –
History, Military – 19th century – Sources
I. Title II. Bentley, Nicolas
947'.0738

Frontline edition
ISBN: 978-1-84415-708-2

NIP edition
ISBN: 978-1-59114-200-3

Library of Congress Control Number: 2007933199

Printed and bound in Great Britain by Biddles Ltd, King's Lynn

CONTENTS

ILLUSTRATIONS

(Positioned between pp 144 and 145)

MAPS

Foreword

William Howard Russell was of all war reporters probably the one most admired by those who came after him. We envy his access and his courage – not only the courage to report from the front lines of so many and bloody encounters, but to tell inconvenient truths about the appalling hardships suffered by an ill-provided army.

These days there is much academic theorising – maybe too much – about the political effects of war reporting, especially in television. First it was called the CNN effect. Then for a while the BBC effect. It involves governments taking actions, whether to engage in armed conflict or to withdraw from it, which without the pressures of television they would not have taken. These despatches remind us that there was once a *Times* effect: Russell would not be silenced. He brought down a government.

He was *with* the Army but not *of* it. That remains the crucial relationship in our time as in his.

Set to one side those war reporters – and they exist today as they always did – who are what the Army calls 'Walts' (Walter Mittys) and for whom soldiering is the career that they wish to have had. They will always be so embarrassingly onside as to be (in my view) short of the authority and credibility that mark the best of what Russell called the 'luckless tribe' of which he was in a very real sense the founding father. For the rest of us, soldiers and journalists are, quite simply different sorts of people. The journalists' instinct is to publish and be damned; the soldiers' is to censor and be safe.

There are two permanent sources of tension between them. One is the reporting of defeats and of casualties. The other relates to operational security – plans, capabilities and troop movements. Russell was not the last, but was one of the first, to be accused of endangering the lives of the soldiers whose battles he reported. Prince Albert called him 'that miserable scribbler'. And a former Secretary of the Army wrote 'I trust the Army will lynch *The Times* correspondent'. Occasionally, copies of Russell's newspaper despatches filtered back to the Crimea, having not been greatly appreciated backin London. He wrote:

> *I was honoured by a great deal of abuse for telling the truth. But I could not tell lies to 'make things pleasant'. There was not a single man in the camp who could put his hand upon his heart and declare that he believed one single casualty had been caused to us by information communicated to the enemy by me or any other newspaper correspondent.*

And his Editor stood by him, which took courage of a different sort.

William Howard Russell was not only the first but I would say – with the possible exceptions of George Steer of *The Times* and James Cameron of the *News Chronicle* – the most distinguished of our kind, or at least the British section of it. He was also, indirectly, the cause of the profession's peculiar scourge of censorship. Because of the impact he had, the idea took hold that reporters in war zones should not be free to tell the truth as they saw it – whether because it was politically embarrassing or operationally dangerous. After the death in the Crimea of Lord Raglan, the new commander-in-chief, Sir William Codrington, issued an order authorising the ejection of any correspondent who published news of value to an enemy. By the time that it reached London the war in the Crimea was over. But censorship both formal and informal has been with us ever since – by diktat at the point of transmission, by exclusion and denial of access, or more subtly by the modern practice of 'embedding'.

Look carefully through these remarkable dispatches, note Russell's sympathy with the soldiers whose ordeal he chronicles, and you may conclude that he was actually the original 'embeed'. He spoke of the soldiers alongside him as 'our' forces and their encampments as 'our' encampments. There was none of the studied distancing that those who came later, myself included, tried to observe in the cause of objectivity. But still, he stood apart from them.

He was, as all of us are to this day, a creature of his time. He wrote in a consciously ornate and literary idiom. He was appalled by what he saw, but only semi-detached from it. He thought it deplorable, for instance, that the officers should have to share the Crimean hardships of the other ranks. We today would be disturbed if they did not. Although he antagonised the high command, and at one point even had his tent cut down, he was careful to exonerate the generals in the field. 'The officers at Gallipoli were not to blame,' he wrote, 'the persons really culpable were those who sent them out without a proper staff and without the smallest foresight or consideration.' Time and again he made the contrast between the neglected British and the well-provided French.

Russell never knowingly underwrote. He described the Battle of Inkerman, a confused collision of armies fighting at bayonet point, as 'the bloodiest struggle ever witnessed since war cursed the earth'. He couldn't be everywhere, and wasn't. But events he couldn't see for himself he found others to describe for him. What comes over in his accounts is the sense of participation and being there, the *first-handness* of it all.

This is what distinguishes him from so much of the war reporting of a century and a half later. His heirs and successors are for the most part more prudent and more constrained. The armies they are alongside impose certain rules on them and access is more easily denied. Those who choose to work unilaterally, without accreditation to an armed force, are at increasing risk of being blown away. Even a satellite dish can be seen by an army in the field as evidence of 'belligerent activity'. The dangers are actually greater now than they were in Russell's time.

War reporting is therefore less authentic. Especially in the world of television, journalists have to a significant extent withdrawn from the field of battle. They have found a way of copying each other's material and folding it into their own reports. They stand on the rooftops of hotels and in front of palm trees in fortified areas, answering questions from unknowing anchor people and broadcasting *as if* from the front lines without actually being there. Rooftop journalism is a retreat from reality. William Russell would not have understood it.

Rereading his despatches, I am struck by the conflicting impressions of how much has changed and how much stays the same. The methods of transmission, from satellite dishes to mobile phones, would have baffled the *Times* man considerably. Indeed the hero of the Crimea was scooped by younger rivals in the Franco-Prussian war, who found a faster means of getting their copy to London.

The technology advances, but human nature remains obstinately the same. The qualities required of a good war reporter are just as they ever were: courage, resourcefulness, cunning, an understanding of the military and a way with words which does not diminish, but sharpens, under the coincident pressures of danger and deadlines. William Howard Russell possessed them all. We have much to learn from what he did and how he did it.

MARTIN BELL, 2008

Introduction

Journalists are sometimes inclined to imagine that the destinies of nations are governed by the powers of the press and hence indirectly by their own efforts. Fortunately this is seldom true. Among the very small number of journalists by whom such power has in fact been exerted is William Howard Russell, who for more than twenty years was a special correspondent of The Times. *During the Crimean War it was due to Russell's despatches from the scene more than to any other single factor that the British government's mishandling of affairs, and the gross negligence of the War Office in particular, came to light and that the resignation of Lord Aberdeen's cabinet was brought about. This timely event, had it been delayed even for a little while longer, must have resulted inevitably in a disaster to the British army far worse than any that the Russians had succeeded in inflicting upon it. It was not merely from a shortage of guns and ammunition that the army suffered, though these were scarce enough; it also lacked such simple necessities as clothing, fuel, medical supplies and, not least important, encouragement from an efficient and determined administration at home. It was the indignation aroused in Britain by the state of affairs revealed through Russell's despatches that saved the army from annihilation through sheer neglect in the bone-piercing cold and freezing mud of the Crimea.*

Russell's despatches, though often far from objective, were not deliberately sensational. There was no need for them to be, the facts spoke for themselves. Besides, the news value of an indisputable fact was worth more to Russell than any purple patch of supposition; and if, for reasons of policy, information was temporarily withheld from the press, he did not try to hide his ignorance by elaborate obscurity. He was easily moved to pity or indignation and reacted accordingly, with the result that his judgements were sometimes thought to be unduly harsh, sometimes too hasty. But however deeply his criticisms were resented, his honesty of purpose was beyond question. If nowadays his sentiments occasionally seem a trifle heroic or his style flowery, it should be remembered that they did not seem so at the time. And in an age of journalism debased by ignorant perversions or stemming from the influence of Time *magazine's syntactical rape, it is satisfying to read the reports of a journalist who has a solid respect for the usage and common forms of the English language. Only occasionally is a lapse noticeable, no doubt owing to speed or the difficult circumstances in which many of the despatches were written.*

It was not Russell's aim, or indeed his mission, to write a history of the war; nor would he have been fitted by temperament to make the dispassionate assessment of complex policies and motives that such a task would have involved. He was essentially, as at heart a war correspondent must be, a man of action, not an historian. His purpose was to give readers at home a perspective from which to view the progress and conduct of the war. This he did by writing an account of day-to-day events as he saw them, describing the scenes and circumstances, the forces, strategies and personalities involved.

There was little in Russell's early life to indicate the gifts that were later to bring him honours and world-wide fame. He was born on March 28, 1820, *in a rural district of County Dublin. His parents were both of what would then have been called humble birth. He was educated first at Dr Geoghegan's academy in Dublin and then at Trinity College, but failed to take a degree. He did manage, however, to acquire what was undoubtedly a good deal more useful to him in later life – a sound and invincible love of the classics.*

His association with The Times *began under the legendary Delane in* 1841, *when he was asked to report on the Irish elections. At that time he had had practically no experience of writing for the press beyond contributing some fugitive pieces to the Dublin* Evening Mail. *Thereafter he combined intermittent journalism with reading for the English bar and for a short time he also taught mathematics at Kensington Grammar School. Later, he joined* The Times *as a parliamentary reporter and began to spend much of his time, as had Dickens a few years earlier, in the press gallery at the House of Commons.*

It was in 1850, *the year in which he was called to the bar – after ten years spent in reading for it – that he was given his first assignment as a war correspondent, reporting on the conflict between Schleswig-Holstein and Denmark. Four years later he was sent by Delane to the Crimea.*

In his reports from Gallipoli and Varna, the Bulgarian Black Sea port used by the Allies as a springboard for the Crimea, he began to give his readers some idea of the inadequacies and unnecessary hardships from which the army was already suffering. At headquarters these reports created furious resentment. This reaction was understandable, but it was unjust. Russell saw clearly, and made it apparent, that the conditions of which he complained were often not so much the fault of anyone on the spot as of the departmental chiefs and the politicians at home. But the Commander-in-Chief, Lord Raglan, felt that Russell's criticisms reflected on his conduct of affairs and as a result when Russell reached the Crimea he found himself ostracized by the authorities. Not only was he denied the normal facilities given to a journalist, but even the means of drawing rations. To add to his troubles he had accidentally lost his baggage and so for a while was forced to rely on acquaintances for clothes, rations and accommodation. It is not difficult to believe that he made acquaintances easily. He was a man of great personal charm, of good humour, and of considerable courage. Thackeray is said to have remarked that he would give a guinea any day to have Russell sitting with him for dinner at the Garrick Club.

The restrictions placed on him by the authorities did not deter Russell from trying to get at the truth and reporting it. His tenacity as much as his enquiring mind, his observant eye, and the power of his descriptive writing compel one's admiration. His was not merely the tenacity of a journalist who scents a scoop, or of one whose professional pride refuses to let him acknowledge himself defeated by authority: it was the tenacity of a man whose imagination had been seared by the sight of incredible suffering and whose conscience had been jolted by a strong suspicion that much of that suffering could have been avoided. He was appalled by the state of affairs that he discovered, the more so because it was obvious that those who suffered most were completely innocent, and he was determined that so far as it lay in his power to get matters put right he would do so, regardless of any man's rank or reputation.

This was easier said than done. Even Delane was reluctant at first to give full credit to the reports that Russell sent him. But when he eventually became convinced that these reports were not exaggerated, Delane brought the full weight and authority of The Times *to bear against the government. Unable to defend itself against the attack, the government was forced to resign. Russell was vindicated. But what was far more important to him was that henceforth the British soldier ceased to be an isolated and helpless victim of departmental incompetence and ministerial indifference.*

Between the ending of the war in 1856 and his retirement from the position of special correspondent in 1882, Russell reported on the closing stages of the Indian Mutiny, on the American Civil War, the Seven Weeks' War between Prussia and Austria, the Franco-Prussian war, the Zulu War of 1879, and the Egyptian campaign against Arabi Pasha in 1882. in 1895 he was awarded a knighthood in recognition of his services to journalism.

Earlier he had contested Chelsea unsuccessfully as a Conservative candidate for Parliament, and in 1860 had founded the Army and Navy Gazette, *of which he remained editor and part-proprietor till his death in London on February 10, 1907. The esteem in which he was held both by the public and his profession is marked by the memorial to him in St Paul's Cathedral.*

Russell's name is synonymous with the personal integrity, the professional discipline, and the untiring energy of mind and body which characterize that very small company of dedicated men who may be truthfully described as great journalists.

The final version of his Crimean despatches was published in 1858. With the benefit of hindsight Russell made some minor changes and additions, but left unaltered a few passages in which changes of tense occur. It is impossible to tell whether this was done intentionally, so these passages have been left as they were in the original version. Its length is enormous and the problems that arise in trying to condense it are not easy to overcome. Russell was with the army from the time it embarked at Southampton in September 1854 until the proclamation of peace just two years and five weeks later. He went everywhere, he saw everything, he knew everybody, and his despatches are crammed with detail. A certain amount of this detail, however, has become superfluous with the passage of time. Ordnance statistics, the composition of military units, changes of staff, lists of casualties, stores, equipment, and so on, are typical of his precise and thorough methods of reporting, but are hardly likely to be of interest nowadays to anyone except the military historian. Most references of this sort have therefore been omitted from the present version, as have a number of polemical passages relevant only in the context of their time. Also omitted are several of Russell's lengthy recapitulations of the strategic situation: these have been briefly summarized, and a number of descriptive passages shortened but not otherwise altered. There is one major omission – an account of an extended tour of the whole Crimean area, which Russell made shortly after the proclamation of peace. This is in the nature of a meditation on some of the main events of the war. None of these omissions affect in any way the continuity of Russell's narrative and leave unimpaired his perspective of the war as a whole.

Where necessary, a linking commentary, distinct from the body of the text, has been provided, and in order to conform with modern practice some changes have been made in the author's punctuation and use of italics.

CHRONOLOGY

	1854
February 23	British advance contingents sail for Gallipoli in anticipation of hostilities.
March 28	Britain and France declare war.
May 30	The Allies establish themselves at Varna in Bulgaria.
September 7	The allied armies sail for Russia and on September 14 land unopposed at Eupatoria.
September 20	The Russians defeated in the Battle of the Alma.
September 26	The British encamp at Balaklava.
October 25	The Battle of Balaklava and charge of the Light Brigade.
November 26	The Russians repulsed at the Battle of Inkerman.
	1855
May 23	Allied troops destroy the Russian base at Kertsch on the Sea of Azov.
June 7	The Mamelon captured by French forces.
June 17	Attacks on the Redan and Malakoff beaten off with severe allied losses.
August 16	The Russians defeated in the Battle of the Tchernaya.
September 8	The British again defeated in an attack on the Redan.
	The Malakoff captured by French troops.
September 9	Evacuation of Sebastopol by the Russians.
	1856
February 28	The armistice is announced.

PRINCIPAL OFFICERS ENGAGED IN THE CAMPAIGN

BRITISH

Lord Raglan, *Commander-in-Chief*
Sir George Brown, *Light Division*
H.R.H. the Duke of Cambridge, *First Division*
Sir de Lacy Evans, *Second Division*
Sir Richard England, *Third Division*
The Hon. Sir George Cathcart, *Fourth Division*
Sir Colin Campbell, *the Highland Brigade*
Lord Lucan, *Cavalry Division*
The Earl of Cardigan, *Light Cavalry Brigade*
Brigadier-General Scarlett, *Heavy Cavalry Brigade*
Sir John Burgoyne, *superintendent of the Royal Engineers*
General Richard Airey, *Quartermaster-General*
Sir James Simpson, *successor to Lord Raglan as Commander-in-Chief*
Sir William Codrington, *successor to Sir James Simpson*
Vice-Admiral Sir James Dundas, *commander of the English fleet*
Rear-Admiral Sir Edmund Lyons, *second-in-command to Admiral Sir James Dundas*

FRENCH

Marshal St Arnaud, *Commander-in-Chief*
General Canrobert, *successor to Marshal St Arnaud*
General Pelissier, *successor to General Canrobert*
General Bosquet, *Second Division*
Prince Napoleon, *Third Division*

TURKISH

His Excellency Omar Pasha, *Commander-in-Chief*
Suleiman Pasha

RUSSIAN

Prince Mentschikoff, *Commander-in-Chief*
General Gortschakoff

GLOSSARY

ABATTIS: a defence formed by felled trees placed with their boughs pointing outwards.

APPROACH: any form of excavated work running towards the enemy's position (see PARALLEL).

ATTACK: an offensive base occupied by the combat troops of an army during a siege.

BANQUETTE: a fire-step or raised runway along the bottom of a trench.

CARTOUCH: a cartridge; also the waterproof container for cartridges.

CURTAIN: a connecting wall between two bastions.

CANISTER: small cast-iron shot packed into cartridges.

ENFILADE: to fire from the flank or from an oblique angle.

EPAULEMENT: a bank of earth erected as a protection against enemy fire from the flank.

FASCINE: long pieces of brushwood bound together for use in revetting trench walls or parapets.

FOUGASSE: a small explosive mine, often loaded with stones.

GABION: an earth-filled wicker cylinder used for strengthening defence works.

GRAPE: small cast-iron balls connected together for firing from a gun.

MANTLET: a protective screen made of rope matting, iron, steel or timber, for use by gunners while in action.

MITRAILLE: miscellaneous metal fragments used as filling for a shell; also shot fired collectively from multi-barrelled small arms.

MINIÉ: a rifle with a grooved bore for firing a lead bullet instead of a ball, as fired by a smooth-bored musket.

PARADOS: the rear parapet of a trench.

PARALLEL: a trench running parallel with the enemy's position, so formed as to connect the several approaches directed towards a besieged place.

ROUND SHOT: a solid iron ball, weighing from 6 to 68 lb. and capable of causing heavy damage or casualties.

SAP: a covered trench forming the farthest extremity of an approach or a parallel under excavation.

SCARP: the sloping side of a ditch below the wall of a fortification.

TRAVERSE: a barrier of earth erected across a trench to prevent its being enfiladed; also, a partition wall inside a fortification.

VEDETTE: a mounted sentry in advance of an outpost.

WOOLBAG: a large sack filled with wool for use in surmounting an abattis or filling in a ditch.

I

A Rendezvous in the Dardanelles

In British history there are few situations more ironical than that which resulted from our participation in the Crimean War, when Britain, defender of the faith, found herself at the same time defender of the Faithful. To explain how this singular state of affairs came about would involve unravelling what Russell describes as 'a mass of verbiage . . . wrapped up in endless coatings of manifestos, protocols and despatches . . .' The immediate reasons put forward by Russia and the Allies to justify their taking up arms against each other were, on the one hand, the defence of an oppressed religious minority, and on the other, resistance to a threat of territorial aggression. How much truth was there in these claims?

As regards Russia, Tsar Nicholas I, as self-appointed guardian of the interests of Greek Orthodoxy in Turkey, professed to see in the attitude of the Sublime Porte a threat to the members of the Orthodox Church living there. To Britain, no less a champion of minorities than the Tsar, this seemed merely a specious excuse for Russia to encroach on the shores of the Bosphorus and perhaps even the Dardanelles. By something rather less than a coincidence, Britain's decision to stand firm in defence of the independence of these territories was matched by an equally resolute determination to prevent Russia from dominating the land route to India by gaining a position of strategic advantage in the Eastern Mediterranean. France no less than England was apprehensive of the possible consequences of such a situation, and in Napoleon III had a leader who has been described as 'too much a Bonaparte not to wish to revenge 1812 . . . too uncertain of his new throne not to welcome a successful war'. Whatever may be said for the claims of either side, it is probable that in the diplomatic skirmishes that preceded the war, as in most negotiations that precede war, a little more forbearance and heart-searching and less greed, stiff-necked pride and patriotic hysteria would have saved the day. But these were considerations hardly to be expected from a paranoic despot, a cabinet of feeble and aristocratic English gentry, and a parvenu dictator filled with apprehensions about the security of his regime. The day was consequently lost, and on March 28, 1854, Britain declared war on Russia.

A month earlier advance contingents of the army had left England for Gallipoli in readiness for an expected Russian attack on Turkey. Seldom can an army have gone forth to fight so ill-prepared, knowing so little of the strength or circumstances of its opponent, or being so blind to the probable consequences of its ignorance. As always, it was the soldiers, not the politicians, who took the rap. Through an act of snobbish folly unequalled in the history of British politics, command of the army was given to Lord Raglan, then aged sixty-five, who had spent the previous thirty-nine years behind a desk at the War Office. Of active service he had had no experience since Waterloo, where he had lost his right arm. In the intervening period his knowledge of warfare and of the needs of a fighting army had grown somewhat out-of-date, though upon these vital subjects his ideas were less corroded than those of the British cabinet, or indeed of some of his own staff. Lord Raglan however, was courageous, fair-minded and immensely conscientious. If devotion to duty had been all that a commander-in-chief required, no one could have been better fitted to occupy that position. But more was needed than devotion – a great deal more. A Marlborough or a Wellington – and Raglan was decidedly not of their stamp – would have had his work cut out to overcome the enormous difficulties that resulted from the army's state of unpreparedness. It is fair to say that Raglan did his best according to his lights and died in attempting to do far more than he could possibly have achieved. That he should ever have been given the task when others far better suited to it were available, or that out of mistaken loyalty he should have accepted it, were errors of judgement for which the army and the nation were soon forced to pay a terrible price.

Few people seem to have suspected that there was anything wrong with the army, least of all those whose business it was to acquaint themselves with the facts. Certainly, no suspicion of the true state of affairs could have occurred to the crowds that gathered along the barrack railings in Birdcage Walk and in front of Buckingham Palace in the early hours of February 27 to watch the Scots Guards set out for Gallipoli. The morning was dark and cold, but by five o'clock thousands were already waiting to see the troops. At half-past six, the Queen and Prince Albert, with members of the Royal Family, stepped out on to the balcony. Bell's Weekly Messenger *gave its readers this description of the scene:*

*'Precisely at seven o'clock the barrack gates were thrown open, and the Guards commenced their march in slow time . . . down Birdcage Walk, and into the esplanade in front of the Palace. At the head of the column marched the splendid regimental band, playing, "*O *Where, and* O *Where is my Highland laddie gone?" the plaintive and rather melancholy air of which gave, for the moment, an impression of solemnity to the whole scene which well became the occasion. But this feeling was only momentary, as the instant the troops began to pass in front of the Palace, the crowd outside the railings commenced such deafening cheers as quite drowned the notes of the whole band.*

'Amid such marks of enthusiasm the regiment steadily pursued its way . . . In front of the Palace the whole force presented arms as one man – the colours were lowered – the officers saluted – the band tried to play "God Save the Queen", but were fairly hushed by the cheers of the crowd . . . When the men had "recovered arms", they took off their bearskin caps and gave three deafening cheers . . . waving their muskets, and tossing their huge caps high into the air . . .

'After this . . . the regiment again marched forward tolerably quiet, though as each company passed the Royal party, the same scene of vociferous cheering was renewed on a small scale. At length the regiment emerged upon the Mall . . . at the National Gallery, round St Martin's Church and in Trafalgar-Square, crowds had gathered which greeted the troops as they swept into the Strand with a cheer which was tremendous . . .'

A week earlier the departure of the Grenadier and Coldstream Guards had aroused similar scenes of enthusiasm. Russell, recalling the occasion after the war was over, added: 'To that march, in less than one year, there was a terrible antithesis. A handful of men – wasted and worn and badly clad – crept slowly down from the plateau of Inkerman, where their comrades lay thick in frequent graves, and sought the shelter of the hillside of Balaklava till they could recover their strength, and be ready for battle once more.'

The Guards sailed from Southampton in three troopships early on the morning of Thursday, February 23.

They ran past the Needles at 8.15, and were soon bowling along with a fresh breeze on the bow in weather which sailors, by some strange perversity of the usual terms relating to the state of the atmosphere, denominated 'moderate and fine'. The breeze was, with all deference to naval authority, strong and boisterous, but, with the excitement and novelty of the situation, the mind ruled the stomach, and the men evinced the usual degree of anxiety as to the time for eating and drinking, which shows that the nastiest and most anti-gastric of all maladies had not seized them. The crews of the ships busied themselves swinging hammocks for the men. Fourteen inches is man-of-war allowance, but eighteen inches were allowed for the Guards. The hammocks were not strictly luxurious: they consisted of the usual canvas, one blanket, and the military overcoat for those that liked to use it. Knapsack-stowing was wondrous work for the time, but even it palled after an hour or so, and there was nothing but looking at seagulls, smoking pipes, watching each other smoke, and 'wondering if they were going to be sick'.

Good beef, the domestic pudding of sea life—consisting of large quantities of flour and infinitesimally small portions of plums, compressed by culinary skill into adamantine hardness, and excellent bread, with pea-soup every second day, formed very substantial pieces of resistance to the keen appetites of the men. Half a gill of rum to two of water was served out once a day to each man. On the first day it appeared that in the fullness of his heart and emptiness of his stomach Jack Firelock was rather too liberal on board one of the ships to his brother Jack Tar, and gave him an extra allowance. On the next occasion of serving grog, the very big and ponderous Sergeant-Major of the Grenadiers, anxious to prevent such a proof of affection from one service to the other, presided over the grog-tub, and is reported to have delivered the following oracular order, 'Men served – two steps to the front, and swallow!'

On Friday, the long-swell from the westward began to tell upon the troops. The figureheads plunged deeply into the waters and the heads of the poor soldiers hung despondingly over gunwale, portsill, stay, and mess-tin, as their bodies bobbed to and fro with the swaying, creaking, tumbling tabernacle in which they were encamped. It was satisfactory to see that the paroxysms of the complaint were more characterized by resolute torpor and a sullen determination 'to do or die' than by the ecstatic misery of the Frenchman, or the prostrate inanity of the German. At night they brightened up, and when the bugle sounded at nine o'clock nearly all were able to crawl into their hammocks for sleep. On Sunday all the men had to a great extent recovered; and when at half-past ten the ship's company and troops were mustered for prayers, they looked as fresh as could be expected under the circumstances – in fact, as the day advanced, they became as lively as ever, and the sense of joyfulness for release from the clutches of their enemy was so strong that they cheered a grampus which blew close alongside, in reply to a stentorian demand for 'three cheers for the jolly old whale!'

After a voyage lasting ten days, the Guards reached Malta and were followed at intervals by other British and French troops.

On the 28th of March 800 Chasseurs de Vincennes, some Zouaves, and more infantry and horses arrived from France. The Zouave (an object of some curiosity to all) wears a sort of red fez cap with a turban of white or green rolled round it to protect the head; a jacket of blue cloth with red facings, decorated with some simple ornaments and open in front, so as to display the throat. Round his waist a broad sash is folded several times, so as to keep up the ample pantaloons and to support the back. The pantaloons, of scarlet cloth, fit closely over the hips, and then expand to the most Dutchman-like dimensions, till they are gathered just below the knee in loose bagging folds, so that they look almost like a kilt. From the knee to the ankle the leg is protected by greaves made of stout, yellow-embroidered leather (with black stripes), laced down the back and descending to the ankle, where it is met by a white gaiter which nearly covers the shoe. The whole costume is graceful, easy and picturesque. The men (natives of France, and not Arabs, as many suppose) are generally smart young fellows, about five feet six inches in height, burnt to a deep copper tint by the rays of an African sun, and wearing the most luxuriant beards, moustaches and whiskers; so that it is somewhat hard to believe these fierce-looking warriors can be Europeans.

Another vessel arrived yesterday with Zouaves from Africa and the usual freight of horses, and the streets were full of men in scarlet-and-blue uniforms walking arm and arm together in uncommunicative friendliness, their conversation being carried on by signs, such as pointing to their throats and stomachs to express the primitive sensations of hunger and thirst. In most cases our men saluted the foreign officers as if they were their own and the greatest cordiality existed amongst them.

Directly the declaration of war reached Malta, the embarkation of troops for Gallipoli was carried on with unremitting assiduity, and the excitement produced in the island was almost indescribable. Crowds of people assembled on the shores of the harbours and lined the quays and public landing-places, the crash of military music being almost drowned in the enthusiastic cheers of the soldiers; the leave-taking by the officers and men of their wives and families formed a painful contrast to the joy which otherwise so generally prevailed. As the vessels moved slowly from their buoys, dense masses of people lined the batteries, and yet denser crowds of soldiers the forts, cheering their comrades as the vessels glided along, the cheers from one fort being taken up by the troops in the others, and as joyously responded to from those on board.

The voyage to Gallipoli was uneventful and one day passed very much like another.

The men ate and drank, and then walked on deck till they were able to eat and drink again, and so on till bed time. In the course of the day many small birds fluttered on the yards, masts and bulwarks, plumed their little jaded wings, and after a short rest, impelled by an inscrutable instinct, launched themselves once more across the bosom of the deep. Some of them were common titlarks, others little greyish buntings, others yellow and black fellows. They were agreeable visitors, and served to afford much entertainment to Jack and the soldiers. Three of the owls and a titlark were at once introduced to each other in a cage, and the ship's cat was thrown in by way of making an impromptu 'happy family'. Pussy obstinately refused to hold any communication with the owls – they seemed in turn to hate each other, and all evinced determined animosity towards the unfortunate titlark, which speedily languished and died.

After dinner, when the band had done playing, the men of the Sappers assembled on the quarter-deck and sang some glees excellently well, while the Rifles in another part of the ship had a select band of vocal performers of their own, who sang comic and sentimental songs amid very great applause.

After four days at sea, during which the weather steadily deteriorated, Russell's ship, the 'Golden Fleece' ran for shelter into Vatika Bay in the southern Peloponnesus and anchored there for the night.

Some time afterwards the 'Cape of Good Hope' and a French screw-steamer also ran into the bay for shelter and anchored near us. This little flotilla evidently alarmed the inhabitants very much, for the few who were fishing in boats fled to shore. No doubt the apparition in the bay of such a force, flying the tricolor and the union jack, and so hastily assembled, frightened the people. They could be seen running to and fro along the shore like ants when their nest is stirred.

At dusk our bands played the popular dance music of the day, and the mountains of the Morea, for the first time since they rose from the sea to watch the birth of Venus, echoed the strains of 'God Save the Queen'. The people lighted bonfires, as if by way of signal, upon the hills, but the lights soon died out. Our vocalists reassembled, and sang glees or fine vigorous choruses together and the night passed very pleasantly in smooth water and on an even keel.

At six o'clock on Tuesday morning the 'Golden Fleece' left her her snug anchorage. The Greek coast trending away to the left showed rugged masses of mountains capped by snowy peaks, and occasionally the larger towns – clusters of white specks on the dark purple of the hills – were visible; but before evening the ship, having run safely through all the terrors of the Aegean and its islands, dashed right away for the entrance to the Dardanelles.

On Wednesday morning smooth seas greeted the ship as she steamed by Mitylene. At 9.30 [p.m.] the ship passed the Castles of the Dardanelles. She was not stopped nor fired at, but as she ran up higher the sentinels on the European side screeched horribly and showed lights, and seemed to execute a convulsive *pas* of fright or valour on the rocks. The only reply was the calm sounding of the tattoo on the bugles – the first time that the blast of English light infantry trumpets broke the silence of those antique shores. After midnight we arrived at Gallipoli and anchored for the night. No one took the slightest notice of us, nor was any communication made with the shore.

Early on Thursday morning a boat came off from the shore with two commissariat officers and an interpreter. They informed us that the Consul had gone up the Dardanelles to look for us, but that he would return in the course of the day, and added the unwelcome news that horses were not to be had at any price, that provisions were not very cheap, and that the French, being the first comers, had got hold of the best part of the town, and of the best quarters as well. After the necessary arrangements had been made, the troops were disembarked and marched out to encamp eight and a half miles north of Gallipoli at a place called Bulair.

Take the most dilapidated outhouses of farmers' yards in England – remove rickety old wooden tenements of the Borough – catch up any seedy, cracked, shutterless structures of planks and tiles that have escaped the ravages of time in our cathedral towns – carry off sheds and stalls from Billingsgate, bring them all to the European side of the Dardanelles, and having pitched on a bare round hill, sloping away to the water's edge with scarcely tree or shrub, tumble them higgledy piggledy on its declivity; let the roadway be very narrow, of varying breadth, according to the bulgings and projections of the houses, and filled with large round slippery stones, here and there borrow a dirty gutter from a back street in Boulogne – let the houses in parts lean across to each other so that the tiles meet, or that a few planks thrown across from over the doorways unite and form a sort of arcade – steal some Irish round towers – surround them with a light gallery about twelve feet from the top, put on a large extinguisher-shaped roof, paint them all white, and having thus made them into minarets, clap them down into the maze of buildings; transport the ruins of a feudal fortress from Northern Italy and put it into the centre of the town, with a flanking tower extending to the water's edge – erect a few buildings of wood by the waterside to serve as café, custom-house, and government stores – and, when you have done this, you have to all appearance imitated the process by which Gallipoli was created.

To fill it up you must, however, catch a number of the biggest breeched, longest bearded, dirtiest, and stateliest old Turks; provide them with pipes and keep them smoking all day on little wooden stages or platforms about two feet from the ground by the water's edge or up the main streets, as well as in the shops of the bazaar (one of the arcades already described); see that they have no slippers on, nothing but shawl turbans, fur-lined flowing coats and bright-hued sashes round the waist, in which are to be stuck silver-sheathed yataghans and ornamented Damascus pistols; don't let them move more than their eyes, or express any emotion at the sight of anything except an English lady; then gather a noisy, picturesque and active crowd of fez-capped Greeks in baggy blue breeches, smart jackets, sashes, and rich vests – of soberly-dressed Armenians – of intellectual-looking Jews, with keen flashing eyes – Chasseurs de Vincennes, Zouaves, British riflemen, *vivandières*, Sappers and Miners, Nubian slaves, camel-drivers, commissaries, officers and sailors, and direct them in streams through the streets round the little islets in which the smoking Turks are harboured, and you will do much to populate the place.

It will be observed that women are not mentioned in this description, but children were not by any means wanting – on the contrary, there was a glut of them, in the Greek quarter particularly, and now and then a bundle of clothes in yellow leather boots, and covered at the top with a piece of white linen, might be seen moving about, which you will do well to believe contained a woman neither young nor pretty. Dogs, large, savage, tailless, hairy, and curiously-shaped, prowled along the shore and walked through the shallow water, in which stood a herd of bullocks and buffaloes waiting till the araba, or cart, was ready for them.

In truth, it is a wretched place – picturesque to a degree, but horribly uncomfortable. The French came first, and like all first comers, they were the best served. When the 'Golden Fleece' arrived on Thursday night there was no pilot to show her where to anchor and it was nearly an hour ere she ran out her cable. No one came off to her, for it was after midnight, and there was something depressing in this silent reception of the first British army that ever landed on the shores of these straits. When morning came the tricolor was floating right and left and the blue coats of the French were well marked on shore, the long lines of bullock-carts stealing along the strand towards their camp making it evident that they were taking care of themselves.

It was at this point that the negligence and inefficiency that were to have such disastrous consequences for the British army began to have effect. Although it had long been decided that Gallipoli was to be their venue, no preparations whatever had been made to receive the troops, except for the sending out of two commissariat officers, without staff or interpreters, who had arrived a few days earlier.

These officers could not speak the language, nor were they furnished with any facilities for making themselves intelligible; their proceedings, therefore, in all matters of purchase, hire, or contract, were necessarily very slow, and, considering the pressure of the French demands, it is very wonderful they were so successful. However, the English Consul [Mr Calvert] was, fortunately, a man of energy; he came to Gallipoli and found the French had literally got hold of the town. Mr Calvert went to the Turkish Council, reminded them that there were British troops yet to come, and succeeded in having half of the quarters in the town reserved for him for their use. Next day he visited and marked off the houses; but on his return the French authorities said they had made a mistake as to the portion of the town they had handed over to him, and he of course had to yield and give them up. They had the Turkish part of the town close to the water, with an honest and favourable population; the English had the Greek quarter, further up the hill, and perhaps the healthier, with dexterous tradesmen and a population which hated them bitterly and regarded them as foes quartered on them for force of arms.

On Saturday [April 8] the troops were landed and sent to their quarters. The force consisted of only some thousand and odd men, and, small as it was, it had to lie idle for two days and a half watching the seagulls, or with half-averted eye regarding the ceaseless activity of the French, the daily arrival of their steamers and the admirable completeness of all their arrangements in every detail – hospitals for the sick, bread and biscuit bakeries, waggon trains for carrying stores and baggage – every necessary and every comfort, indeed, at hand, the moment their ships came in.

The camps in the neighbourhood of Gallipoli extended and increased in numbers every day, and with the augmentation of the allied forces, the privations to which the men were at first exposed became greater, the inefficiency of our arrangements more evident, and the excellence of the French commissariat administration more strikingly in contrast. Amid the multitude of complaints which met the ear from every side, the most prominent were charges against the commissariat; but the officers at Gallipoli were not to blame. The persons really culpable were those who sent them out without a proper staff and without the smallest foresight or consideration. Early and late these officers might be seen toiling amid a set of apathetic Turks and stupid araba drivers, trying in vain to make bargains and give orders in the language of signs, or aided by interpreters who understood neither the language of the contractor nor contractee. And then the officers of a newly arrived regiment rushed on shore, demanded bullock-carts for the luggage, guides, interpreters, rations, etc., till the unfortunate commissary became quite bewildered. The French had a perfect baggage train and carried off all their stores and baggage to their camps the moment they landed, while the English were compelled to wait till a proper number of araba carts had been collected, instead of having an organized administration and military train department to do what was required.

The men suffered exceedingly from cold. Some of them, officers as well as privates, had no beds to lie upon. None of the soldiers had more than their single regulation blanket. They therefore reversed the order of things and dressed to go to bed, putting on all their spare clothing before they tried to sleep. The worst thing was the continued want of comforts for the sick. Many of the men labouring under diseases contracted at Malta were obliged to stay in camp in the cold, with only one blanket under them, as there was no provision for them at the temporary hospital.

There can be no disguising the fact that the French got on much better than we did because they bullied the natives where we tried to carry our point by soft sawder. The French Commandant de Place posted a tariff of all articles which the men were likely to want on the walls of the town, and regulated the exchanges like a local Rothschild. A Zouave wanted a fowl; he saw one in the hand of an itinerant poultry merchant and he at once seized the bird and, giving the proprietor a franc – the tariff price – walked off with the prize. The Englishman, on the contrary, more considerate and less protected, was left to make hard bargains, and generally paid twenty or twenty-five per cent more than his ally.

One fact will show the reckless way in which the French treated their allies. At a short distance was a burial-ground with its white headstones shining brightly in the sun amid the greensward. Right through the centre of this a fatigue party from a French regiment drove a road to their camp, while horror-stricken Greeks, Moslems, and Jews stood by with upraised eyes and arms. There is no people on earth who pay such reverence to the departed as these Orientals, and it is scarcely possible to imagine what their feelings must have been as they saw these stout, active little men, with pipe in mouth, shovelling away the bones and skulls of their ancestors, to some favourite air of a popular camp opera. Whether any official notice was taken of this act or not it is impossible to say, but in the English general orders the greatest stress was laid on treating the Turks with proper respect, and both officers and men were strictly enjoined to pay every deference to 'the most ancient and faithful of our allies.' They bought everything they wanted, but on going for a walk into the country one might see the fields dotted by stragglers from the French camp, tearing up hedgestakes, vines and sticks for fuel, and looking out generally with eyes wide open for the *pot au feu*. The few wretched sheds which were dignified with the names of 'shops' were rendered all but useless by the number of holy days kept by the Greek Church, for the bulk of the shopkeepers being members of that body, there were closed shutters in the bazaar at this season four days out of the seven.

With the exception of the *vivandières*, the French brought no women whatever with them. Will it be credited that the Malta authorities, acting, of course, on orders from home, had the egregious folly to send out no less than ninety-seven women to this desolate and miserable place, where men were hard set to live? The General, however, did not seem inclined to let them land, and this indiscretion was not repeated. The Lieutenant-General commanding the division was evidently actuated by a sincere desire to do all in his power for the comfort of the men, but he was also determined to secure their efficiency according to the light that was in him. If Sir George Brown had his way, the whole race of bears'-grease manufacturers and pomade merchants would have scant grace and no profit. His hatred of hair amounted to almost a mania. 'Where there is hair there is dirt, and where there is dirt there will be disease.' That is an axiom on which was founded a vigorous war against all capillary adornments, and in vain engineers, exposed to all weathers, and staff officers, exhibit sore and bleeding lips; they must shave, no matter what the result is. The stocks,[1] too, were ordered to be kept up, stiff as ever. On the march of the Rifles to their camp at least one man fell out of the ranks senseless; immediate recovery was effected by the simple process of opening the stock. The General would not allow the little black pouches hitherto worn on the belt by officers. They are supposed to carry no pockets, and are not to open their jackets; and the question they very naturally ask is, 'Does the General think we are to have no money?' The new orders contained stringent

[1] Close-fitting leather neckbands worn inside the tunic collar.

regulations about baggage, etc. The order which gave the greatest dissatisfaction was that which provided that each officer must carry his own tent. They were warned to provide mules for that purpose, and to carry their baggage, but mules were not to be had at any price. For close shaving, tight stocking, and light marching, Lieutenant-General Sir George Brown was the general. A kinder man to the soldiers, or one who looked more to their rights, never lived, and no 'but' need be added to this praise, although he exhibited more of the *fortiter* than the *suaviter* in his mode of communicating with the officers under him.

The allied armies lost no time in erecting strong defence works across the narrow neck of the Chersonese peninsula,[1] *on which Gallipoli is situated, in order to hamper any advance that might be attempted by the Russians from the north-east.*

Whilst part of the army was engaged in these works, arrangements were made for the reception of English regiments in the Bosphorus. These regiments were the first which landed at Scutari[2] – a place then about to acquire a sad notoriety as the headquarters of death and sickness and an immortal interest as the principal scene of the devoted labours of Florence Nightingale. The huge barracks were given up to the men just as they had been left by the Turkish troops, and they were inhabited in every nook and corner by legions of fleas and less active but more nauseous insects. It was late in the day when the regiment arrived at quarters, and several officers lay for the night in the guard-room, which had an open brazier of charcoal to keep warmth in it. The day was bitterly cold; Constantinople and Pera[3] black-looking and desolate, contrasted with the white hills behind them, all covered with deep snow; and the Asiatic mountains in the distance had an Alpine, wintry aspect, which gave a curious shock to our notions of an Oriental spring. At night we could scarcely sleep,

[1] Both the Gallipoli and the Crimean peninsulas were known at this time by the same name.

[2] Scutari lies on the southern shore of the Bosphorus, about a mile across the water from Istanbul.

[3] That part of the city situated on the northern side of the Golden Horn.

and at dawn began to receive visits from Turks, who were kind enough to see if they could relieve us of anything they thought we did not want. A few days exhausted all the sights of Stamboul and Pera and the snow began to tumble on one's head from the housetops and the mud to surge over one's boots, so I was very glad to return even to Gallipoli, where I recovered my old quarters.

Provisions at this time were dear, but in sufficient quantity, for the country began to feel the pressure of the demand from without and the pashas were indefatigable in providing for the wants of the army as far as possible. Every day long strings of camels laden with skins of coarse strong wine, raki and corn, might be seen stalking along the dusty roads and filing through the dingy bazaar, and wild-looking countrymen with droves of little shaggy ponies trooped in hour after hour to sell the produce they carried and the beasts that bore it. They were corrupted already and had quite lost the simplicity of their mercantile notions. Instead of piastres, they began to demand lire, shillings, pounds and Napoleons, and they displayed ingenuity in the art of selling horses and doctoring them that would have done honour to Yorkshiremen. Wine, which was formerly two or three piastres (4d or 5d) a bottle as an outside price, soon sold for 1s 6d or 2s. Meat was bad and dear, the beef being very like coarse mahogany; the mutton was rather better, but very lean. Milk was an article of the highest luxury and only to be seen on the tables of the great; and the sole attempt at butter was rancid lard packed in strong-smelling camel's-hair bags. It was really wonderful that no Englishman had sufficient enterprise to go out to Gallipoli with a stock of creature comforts and camp necessaries. There was scarcely an article of common use in England which could not be disposed of at very considerable profit.

The bazaar, a narrow lane, twisting and twining through the town, presented a curious scene from an early hour in the morning till sunset. This lane was lined on each side by wretched wooden houses, with the 'front parlours' open to the street; overhead was a covering of loose planks and staves of wood about twelve feet above the ground, and through the chinks and holes in this roof the sun-light fell brightly in patches on the variegated crowd below. So numerous are the holy days of the Greek Church that on an average three-fourths of these parlours were closed every day, so that the number of shops open was comparatively small. Around those in a condition to carry on traffic there are assembled in their picturesque costumes motley groups of camp-followers, Jews, Armenians, Greeks of the islands, Zouaves, Africans, riflemen, Sappers, chasseurs, artillerymen, and soldiers' wives, engaged in varied purchases and intricate monetary arrangements. As change is very scarce, there was great difficulty in obtaining articles of small value, and a sum of 19s. was occasionally made up in piastres, half-piastres, gold pieces of 5, 10, 20 and 50 piastres each, francs, soldi, lire, halfpence, sixpences, and zwanzigers, collected at several shops up and down the street. Towards evening, when raki and wine have done their work, the crowds became more social and turbulent and English and French might be seen engaged in assisting each other to preserve the perpendicular, or toiling off to their camps laden with bags of coffee, sugar, rice and large bottles of wine. At sunset patrols cleared the streets, taking up any intoxicated stragglers they might find there or in the cafés, and when the brief twilight had passed away the whole town was left in silence and in darkness, except when the barking and yelping of the innumerable dogs which infested it woke up the echoes, and now and then the challenge of a distant sentry, or the trumpet-calls of the camp fell on the ear.

There being little to do in Gallipoli at this time, Russell took the opportunity of exploring the countryside.

There is a rich sylvan look about the scenery, for at a distance the hills across the straits appear to be dotted with verdant lawns and plantations. The villages built in the recesses of the hills and in the little bays and creeks of the straits, surrounded by all the enchantment of distance, looked clean and picturesque, the dark groves of cypress casting into bright relief the whitewash of the houses and the tall shafts of minarets standing out gracefully from the confused mass of roofs, gables, masts, yards and sails by the seaside.

The land round Gallipoli on the European side of the straits is more bleak and more level. Indeed, for miles around the town and all the way across to the Gulf of Saros the country very much resembles the downs about Brighton. It is nearly as destitute of wood or plantations. The soil, which is light but deep and rather sandy, produces excellent crops, but bears no trees, except a few figs and olives. The vines are abundant and the grape yields a rich, full and generous wine which is highly esteemed. Into the soil, which is just scratched up by ploughs rather inferior to those described by Virgil 1,800 years ago, the dejected, wretched rayahs were at the time of which we are now writing busied throwing the corn and barley seed: and as the slow steers or huge lumbering buffaloes paced along the furrows, they were followed by a stately army of storks which marched gravely at the very heels of beast and ploughman and engaged themselves busily in destroying the grubs and larvae. On all the heights around glistened the white tents of French or English, and here and there the eye rested upon their serrated lines on the slope of some pleasant valley, or lighted on the encampment of some detached party posted in a recess of the hills. Faint clouds of dust, through which might be seen the glistening of steel and dark masses of uniform, blurred the landscape here and there and betrayed the march of troops along the sandy roads, which were exactly like those worn by the tramp of men and horses through Chobham-common.

It was arranged at about this time that certain regiments should be sent on to Scutari to join the British troops already there, and on May 6 they began to leave.

Soon after daybreak the tents of the Rifle Brigade, the 50th Regiment and the 93rd Regiment were struck and the whole encampment was broken up. The mass of baggage belonging to these regiments was enormous. The trains of buffalo and bullock carts, of pack-horses and mules, and of led-horses, which filed along the road seemed sufficient for the army of Xerxes. For seven or eight miles the teams of country carts, piled up with beds and trunks and soldiers' wives and tents, were almost unbroken, and now and then an overladen mule tumbled down, or a wheel came off, and the whole line of march became a confused struggle of angry men and goaded cattle. It so happened that two French battalions were moving out to fresh quarters, and it became perceptible at a glance that *pro rata* they carried much less impedimenta than our regiments. There is difficulty in accounting for this, but it may be that the absence of women and the small kit of the French officers went far to account for it. Frenchmen live in their uniform, while everybody knows no real British soldier is quite happy without his mufti. He must have his wideawake and shooting-jacket, and dressing-gown and evening dress, and a tub of some sort or other, a variety of gay shirting, pictorial and figurative, while the Gaul does very well without them.

On May 2, a few days before the troops departed, Lord Raglan arrived at Gallipoli, and was followed a week later by Marshal St Arnaud. Their arrival coincided with news that the Russian army had advanced into northern Bulgaria. It was clearly necessary that the situation should be discussed with Omar Pasha, commander-in-chief of the Turkish Army, and shortly afterwards the three generals had a meeting at the Bulgarian Black Sea port of Varna. Omar Pasha's plan was for an Anglo-French army to pin down the Russian forces on the eastern bank of the Danube while he advanced across the river towards Bucharest, so as to menace their right flank.

He placed great reliance on the position of Varna. A general at the head of a large army could paralyse the whole Russian invasion when once he had got his men into the neighbourhood of this place, aided, as he must be, by the fleets. He might from that point move on Shumla [Kolarovgrad] and on the passes of the Balkan with equal ease; he could attack the right flank or the left flank of the Russians, or, by landing in their rear, covered by the fleet, he might break up their position in front of the Danube and frustrate all their plans of campaign. With similar facility he could have sent an army across to the Asiatic shores of the Black Sea to aid the Turkish army, or to attack the forces of the Caucasus, or could direct his attention to the Crimea, so as to make an attempt on Sebastopol.

Omar Pasha's plan was accepted by both the allied generals and on May 23 they returned to Scutari. News arrived, as they were about to leave, that the Russians had begun to bombard Silistria on the Danube, some seventy miles from Bucharest.

2

Gallipoli to Varna

ON THE RETURN OF THE GENERALS, ARRANGEMENTS FOR moving from Scutari were pushed forward with great vigour. Reinforcements arrived; Lord Cardigan and other officers made their appearance, and a fleet of some thirty vessels, steamers and transports, was anchored off the barracks and camp. The quarters in which Lord Raglan then lived seemed to be endowed with enormous centripetal and centrifugal forces, for generals, brigadiers, colonels of regiments, commissary officers and aides-de-camp were flying to and from them every moment of the day, as fast as their horses could carry them. Yenikeui, where the French Marshal resided, presented symptoms of extraordinary excitement. The Sappers were busily engaged fitting up horse-boxes on board the transports, all the stores required for the troops having been previously put on board. The Sea of Marmora was covered with the white sails of transports and store-ships making way against the current, and the little wharf and landing-place at Scutari were alive with men working hard in loading boats with casks of provisions or munitions of war, while the air was shrill with the creaking and screaming of the wheels of buffalo carts toiling up and down the steep ascent to the barracks.

In strange contrast to all this life and activity, the natives idled on the shore, scarcely raising their heads to look at what was passing around them, or taking a very unobtrusive and contemplative interest in the labours of the soldiery, as, chibouque in mouth, they watched them from their smoking-perches in front of the cafés of the town, or of the sutlers' booths pitched along the shore. Lord Raglan's quarters seemed to be an especial resort for them. The house, a low wooden building two storeys high, very clean, and neatly painted and matted within, was situated on the beach about three-quarters of a mile from the barracks. In front was a tolerably spacious courtyard with high walls, well provided with little stone boxes for the sparrows and swallows to build in, and inside this court a small stud of horses, belonging to the aides and officers on duty, might be seen constantly pacing about. Directly opposite to the entrance of the court was a wooded knoll with a few gravestones peering above the rich grass, and a Turkish fountain in front of a group of pine-trees, usually surrounded by water-carriers, was placed in the foreground.

Groups of Turks, Greeks and Armenians were generally to be seen reclining at the foot of these trees, gazing listlessly into the courtyard, while they carried on monosyllabic conversations at long intervals between the puffs of tobacco smoke. The beach, which somewhat resembled that at Folkestone at high water, was bounded by a tolerable road, a favourite walk of women and children, but these animated bundles of bright-coloured clothing scarcely deigned to look at the men in uniforms or to turn their heads at the jingle of sword and spur. In the stagnant water which ripples almost imperceptibly on the shore there floated all forms of nastiness and corruption, which the prowling dogs, standing leg-deep as they wade about in search of offal, cannot destroy. The smell from the shore was noisome, but a few yards out from the fringe of buoyant cats, dogs, birds, straw, sticks – in fact, of all sorts of abominable flotsam and jetsam, which bob about on the pebbles unceasingly – the water became exquisitely clear and pure. The slaughter-houses for the troops, erected by the sea-side, did not contribute, as may readily be imagined, to the cleanliness of this filthy beach, or the wholesomeness of the atmosphere.

On a slope rising up from the water's edge the camp of the brigade of Guards was pitched; a kind of ravine about a quarter of a mile wide divided it from the plateau and valley at the back of the barracks, in which were pitched the camps of the other regiments. Clumps of tall shady trees were scattered here and there down towards the water's edge, under which a horde of sutlers had erected sheds of canvas and plank for the sale of provisions, spirits and wines, combined with a more wholesome traffic in cakes, Turkish sweetmeats, lemonade and sherbet. The proprietors were nearly all Smyrniotes or Greeks from Pera, not bearing the highest character in the world. The regular canteens established within the lines were kept by a better class of people under the surveillance of the military authorities.

Syces, or grooms, with horses for sale, rode about at full speed through the lanes and pathways leading to the camp, but the steeds they bestrode were generally small bony animals with mouths like a vice, stuffed out with grass and green food and not worth a tithe of the prices asked for them. These gentry were kept at arm's length and were not allowed to come within the lines. All this scene, so full of picturesque animation – these files of snowy tents sweeping away tier after tier over hillock and meadow, till they were bounded by the solemn black outlines of the forest of cypress – this constant play and glitter of bayonet and accoutrement as the numerous sentries wheeled on their beaten tracks – this confused crowd of araba drivers, match sellers, fruit and cigar and tobacco vendors, of hamals or porters, of horse-dealers and gaily-dressed rogues of all nations, afterwards disappeared as if by magic in a few hours and left no trace behind, except the barren circle which marked where the tent once stood and the plain all seared and scorched by the camp-fires.

Among the most amusing specimens of the race must be reckoned some Jew and Armenian money-changers – squalid, lean, and hungry-looking fellows – whose turbans and ragged gabardines were ostentatiously dirty and poverty-stricken – who prowled about the camp with an eternal raven-croak of, 'I say, John, change de monnish – change de monnish,' relieved occasionally by a sly tinkle of a leathern purse well filled with dollars and small Turkish coin. They evaded the vigilance of the sentries, and startled officers half asleep in the heat of the sun by the apparition of their skinny hands and yellow visages within the tent, and the cuckoo-cry, 'I say, John, change de monnish.'

Immediately on Lord Raglan's return, the various generals of brigade visited him and received instructions to prepare for active operations, and several transports were detached from the fleet to proceed up to the Black Sea with stores. The brigade orders for the Guards were distinguished by a great novelty. They were ordered to appear the following day on parade without: Muskets? – No. Coatees? – No. Epaulettes? – No. Cartouch-boxes? – No. Boots? – No. In fact, Her Majesty's Guards were actually commanded to parade WITHOUT STOCKS! This great boon was granted to the Guards to celebrate Her Majesty's birthday, and never since they were formed did the regiments give three more ringing, thundering cheers than issued from their throats on that occasion, when they marched on the ground as erect and upright as ever, but not 'caught by the wind-pipe,' to be inspected by Lord Raglan.

A few days later, the Light Division, which was to play a vital and a gallant part in the Crimea, embarked for Varna.

The little army consisted of about 6,500 men. The morning was fine, but a little too hot. The men were in excellent spirits, and as they marched over the dusty plain to the landing-places they were greeted with repeated peals of cheering from the regiments of the other divisions. The order and regularity with which they were got on board the boats, and the safety and celerity with which they were embarked – baggage, horses, women and stores – were creditable to the authorities and to the discipline and good order of the men themselves, both officers and privates.

The scenery of the Bosphorus has much the character of a Norwegian fiord. For thirteen miles, the waters escaping from the Black Sea, in one part compressed by swelling hillocks to a breadth of little more than a mile, at another expanding into sheets of four times that breadth, gush along in a blue flood, like the Rhône as it issues from the Lake of Geneva, till they mingle with the Sea of Marmora, passing in their course by a succession of beautiful groupings of wood and dale, ravine and hillside, covered with the profusest carpeting of leaf and blade, while kiosk and pleasure-ground, embrasured bastion and loopholed curtain, gay garden, villa, mosque and noble mansion, stud the banks in unbroken lines from the very foot of the forts which command the entrance up to the crowning glory of the scene, where the imperial city of Constantine, rising in many-coloured terraces from the verge of the Golden Horn, confuses the eye with its masses of foliage, of red roofs, divers-hued walls, gables and fretwork, surmounted by a frieze of snow-white minarets with golden summits and by the symmetrical sweep of St Sophia. The hills strike abruptly upwards to a height varying from 200 feet to 600 feet and are bounded at the foot by a line of quays which run along the European side almost without interruption from Pera to Bujukderé, about five miles from the Black Sea.

The kiosks and residences of the pashas, the imperial palaces of the Sultan, and the retreats of opulence, line these favoured shores; and as the stranger passes on, in steamer or caique, he may catch a view of some successful plunderer of a province, some hoary pasha, or unscrupulous ex-governor, sitting cross-legged in his garden or verandah, smoking away, and each looking so like the other that they might all pass for brothers. The windows of one portion of these houses are mostly closely latticed and fastened, but here and there a bright flash of a yellow or red robe shows the harem is not untenanted. These dwellings succeed each other the whole length of the Bosphorus quite as numerously as the houses on the road from Hyde Park Corner to Hammersmith; and at places such as Therapia and Bujukdére they are dense enough to form large villages, provided with hotels, shops, cafés, and lodging-houses. The Turks delight in going up in their caiques to some of these places and sitting out on the platforms over the water, while the chibouque or narghile confers on them a zoophytic happiness; the greatest object of Turkish ambition is to enjoy the pleasures of a kiosk on the Bosphorus. The waters abound in fish, and droves of porpoises and dolphins disport on its surface, plashing and playing about, as with easy roll they cleave their way against its rapid flood, or gambolling about in the plenitude of their strength and security, till a sword-fish takes a dig at them and sets them off curvetting and snorting like sea-horses. Hawks, kites, buzzards, and sea-eagles are numerous, and large flocks of a kind of gregarious petrel of a dusky hue with whitish breasts, called by the French '*âmes damnées*', and which are said never to rest on land, keep constantly flying up and down close to the water.

It was five o'clock ere the last steamer, which had to wait for the transports, got under way and night had set in before they reached the entrance of the Black Sea. As they passed the forts (which are pretty frequent towards the Euxine), the sentries yelled out strange challenges and burned blue lights, and blue lights answered from our vessels in return. Two lights shone, or rather bleared hazily on either bow – they marked the opening of the Bosphorus into the Euxine. We shot past them and a farewell challenge and another blue halo showed the sentries were wide-awake. We were in the Black Sea, and, lo! sea and sky and land were at once shut out from us! A fog, a drifting, clammy, nasty mist, bluish-white and cold and raw, fell down upon us like a shroud, obscured the stars and all the lights of heaven and stole with a slug-like pace down yard and mast and stays, stuck to the face and beard, rendered the deck dark as a graveyard and forced us all down to a rubber and coffee. This was genuine Black Sea weather.

The shore was not far off on our port quarter, but had it been within a quarter of a mile it would have been equally invisible. In the morning the same haze continued drifting about and the line of land was marked by a bank of white clouds and the edge of the sea horizon was equally obscured.

The bulk of the convoy arrived and cast anchor in Varna Bay before the evening, and the disembarkation of the troops was conducted with admirable celerity. The French assisted with the most hearty goodwill. Of their own accord the men of the Artillery and the Chasseurs came down to the beach, helped to load buffalo carts, and set to work at once to thump the drivers, to push the natives out of the way, to show the road, and, in fact, to make themselves generally useful.

With great difficulty Russell eventually succeeded in finding quarters at Aladyn, near the British camp, and was at last given permission, in consequence of instructions from home (issued, no doubt, through the intervention of his editor, Delane) to draw rations for himself, his servant and his horse.

I had been a few days at Aladyn, and never were tents pitched in a more lovely spot. When the morning sun had risen it was scarcely possible for one to imagine himself far from England. At the other side of the lake which waters the meadows beneath the hill on which the camp was placed was a range of high ground finely wooded, with short crisp grass between the clumps of forest timber. The open country was finely diversified, with abundance of wood and water all around. Long lines of storks flew overhead or held solemn reviews among the frogs in the meadows. As for the latter, their concerts by day and night would delight the classical scholar who remembered his Aristophanes and who could test the accuracy of the chorus. Eagles soared overhead, looking out for dead horses, and vultures, kites and huge buzzards scoured the plains in quest of vermin, hares or partridges. Beautiful orioles, a blaze of green and yellow, gaudy woodpeckers, apiasters, jays and grosbeaks, shrieked and chattered among the bushes, while a lovely little warbler in a black cap and red waistcoat with bluish facings, darted about after the flies, and when he had caught and eaten one, lighted on a twig and expressed his satisfaction in a gush of exquisite music. Blackbirds and thrushes joined in the chorus, and birds of all sorts flitted around in multitudes. The commonest bird of all was the dove, and he was found so good to eat that his cooing was often abruptly terminated by a dose of No. 6.

On the first morning of my visit, as I rode from the camp, a large snake, about eight feet long and as thick as my arm, wriggled across the path; my horse plunged violently when he saw him, but the snake went leisurely and with great difficulty across the sandy road; when he gained the grass, however, he turned his head round, and darted out a little spiteful-looking tongue. He was of a dark green, mottled with white, had a large head of a lighter hue, and protuberant, bright eyes. Jackals were said to abound, but probably the wild dogs were mistaken for them. There were traditions in camp concerning roe deer in the hill forests, and the sportsmen found out the tracks of wild boars through the neighbouring hills. Huge carp abounded in the lake, and very fine perch, enormous bream and pike might be had for the taking, but tackle, rods and lines were very scarce in the camp. There were no trout in these waters, but perch and pike took large flies very freely, whenever the angler could get through the weeds and marshy borders to make a cast for them.

But where are the natives all this time? – come, here is one driving an araba – let us stop and look at him. He is a stout, well-made and handsome man, with finely-shaped features and large dark eyes; but for all that there is a dull, dejected look about him which rivets the attention. There is no speculation in the orbs which gaze on you, half in dread half in wonder; and if there should be a cavass or armed Turk with you, the poor wretch dare not take his look away for a moment, lest he should meet the ready lash or provoke some arbitrary act of violence. His head is covered with a cap of black sheepskin with the wool on, beneath which falls a mass of tangled hair which unites with beard and whisker and moustache in forming a rugged mat about the lower part of the face. A jacket made of coarse brown cloth hangs loosely from the shoulders, leaving visible the breast, burnt almost black by exposure to the sun. Underneath the jacket is a kind of vest, which is confined round the waist by several folds of a shawl or sash in which are stuck a yataghan or knife, and a reed pipe-stick. The breeches are made of very rudely manufactured cloth, wide above and gathered in at the knee; and the lower part of the leg is protected by rags, tied round with bits of old string, which put one in mind of the Italian bandit in a state of extreme dilapidation and poverty.

If you could speak with this poor Bulgarian, you would find his mind as waste as the land around you. He is a Christian, after a fashion, but he puts far more faith in charms, in amulets, and in an uncleanly priest and a certain saint of his village, than in prayer or works. He believes the Turks are his natural masters, that he must endure meekly what they please to inflict, and that between him and Heaven there is only one power and one man strong enough to save him from the most cruel outrages, or to withstand the sovereign sway of the Osmanli – and that power is Russia and that man is the Czar. His whole fortune is that wretched cart, which he regards as a triumph of construction; and he has driven those lean, fierce-eyed buffaloes many a mile, from some distant village, in the hope of being employed by the commissariat, who offer him what seems to him to be the most munificent remuneration of 3s 4d a day for the services of himself, his beasts and araba. His food is coarse brown bread, or a mess of rice and grease flavoured with garlic, the odour of which has penetrated his very bones and spreads in vapour around him. His drink is water, and now and then an intoxicating draught of bad raki or sour country wine. From whatever race he springs, the Bulgarian peasant hereabouts is the veriest slave that ever tyranny created, and as he walks slowly away with downcast eyes and stooping head by the side of his cart, the hardest heart must be touched with pity at his mute dejection and hate the people and the rule that have ground him to the dust.

The people were so shy it was impossible to establish friendly relations with them. The inhabitants of Aladyn, close to the camp at the borders of the lake, abandoned their houses altogether. Not one living creature remained out of the 350 or 400 people who were there on our arrival. Their houses were left wide open, and such of their household goods as they could not remove, and a few cocks and hens that could not be caught, were all that was left behind. The cause generally assigned for this exodus was the violence of a few ruffians on two or three occasions, coupled with groundless apprehension of slaughter-houses there. Certainly the smell was abominable. Diarrhoea broke out in the camp soon after my arrival and continued to haunt us all during the summer. Much of this increase of disease must be attributed to the use of the red wine of the country, sold at the canteens of the camp; but as the men could get nothing else they thought it was better to drink than the water of the place. There were loud complaints from officers and men on this score, and especially on account of the porter and ale they were promised not being dealt out to them. It was evident that some wholesome drink ought to have been provided for the men to preserve [them] from the attacks of sickness in a climate where the heat was so great and the supply of pure water inadequate. Many of the officers rode into Varna, bought salt, tobacco, tea, and spirits, and brought it out in saddlebags, either to distribute gratuitously or at cost price to their men. This was an immense boon.

On June 25 news was received that the Russian army besieging Silistria had been defeated by the Turks and was in full retreat. A force of cavalry led by Lord Cardigan, commanding the Light Brigade, was immediately sent forward to make a reconnaissance, but although an extensive search of the area was made, no sign was seen of the Russians, except for a few Cossacks.

It may readily be believed that the news of the Russian retreat caused a profound sensation. The prominent feeling among the men was one of disappointment, lest they should lose the chance, 'after coming so far, of having one brush with the Russians'.

3

Cholera

A COUNCIL OF WAR WAS HELD ON JULY 18TH AT VARNA, at which Marshal St Arnaud, Lord Raglan, Admiral Hamelin[1], Admiral Dundas, Admiral Lyons and Admiral Bruat were present, and it was resolved that the time had come for an active exercise of the power of the allied forces by sea and land. The English Cabinet, urged probably by the English press, had despatched the most positive orders to Lord Raglan to make a descent in the Crimea and to besiege Sebastopol.

There was only one drawback to the successful descent of the allied armies on Russian soil: they had not the faintest idea where to land or what the terrain would be like when they got there. Nevertheless, it was now decided that the operation must go ahead and two days after the meeting of the generals, Sir George Brown and General Canrobert set off on a mysterious mission aboard HMS 'Fury'.

Of course, the object of this expedition was kept a dead secret; but it was known, nevertheless, that they went to explore the coast in the neighbourhood of Sebastopol in order to fix upon a place for the descent. On the 21st, the 1st Division of the French army struck their tents and broke up their camp outside Varna. They took the road which led towards the Dobrudscha, which they were to reconnoitre as far as the Danube.

The result of this expedition was one of the most fruitless and lamentable that has ever occurred in the history of warfare. The

[1] Commander of the French Naval forces, his second-in-command being Admiral Bruat.

French Marshal, terrified by the losses of his troops, which the cholera was devastating by hundreds in their camps at Gallipoli and Varna, resolved to send an expedition into the Dobrudscha, where there were – as Colonel Desaint, chief of the French topographical department, declared on his return from an exploration – about 10,000 Russians, two regiments of regular Cavalry, 10 sotnias of Cossacks, and 35 pieces of artillery. Marshal St Arnaud, who was confident that the expedition for the Crimea would be ready by the 5th of August, imagined that by a vigorous attack on these detached bodies of men he might strike a serious blow at the enemy, raise the spirits and excite the confidence of the allies, remove his troops from the camp where they were subject to such depressing influences, and effect all this in time to enable them to return and embark with the rest of the army. The 1st Division was commanded by General Espinasse, and started on the 21st for Kostendji [Constanta]; the 2nd Division, under General Bosquet, marched on the 22nd towards Bajardik [Dobrici], and the 3rd Division, under Prince Napoleon, followed next day and served as a support to the 2nd. All the arrangements were under the control of General Yusuf.[1]

The 1st Division reached Kostendji on the 28th of July. They found that the whole country had been laid waste by fire and sword – the towns and villages burnt and destroyed, the stock and crops carried off. On that night, just ere the French broke up their camp in order to set out on this march, the cholera declared itself among them with an extraordinary and dreadful violence. Between midnight and eight o'clock next morning nearly 600 men lay dead in their tents. At the same moment the division of Espinasse was stricken with equal rapidity and violence at Kerjelouk. All that night men suffered and died, and on the 31st of July General Yusuf made his appearance at Kostendji with the remains of his haggard and horror-stricken troops, and proceeded towards Mangalia in his death march. On the 1st August General Canrobert, who had returned from his reconnaissance, arrived at Kostendji from Varna, and was horrified to find that his camp was but a miserable hospital, where the living could scarcely bury the remains of their comrades. He could pity and

[1] A celebrated Algerian general, who was in command of 3,000 Bashi-Bazouks.

could suffer, but he could not save. That day and the next the pestilence redoubled in intensity, and in the midst of all these horrors food fell short, although the General had sent most urgent messages by sea to Varna for means of transport and for medicine and the necessaries of life. The 2nd and the 3rd Divisions were also afflicted by the same terrible scourge, and there was nothing left for the Generals but to lead their men back to their encampments as soon as they could, leaving behind them the dead and the dying. The details of the history of this expedition, which cost the French more than 7,000 men, are among the most horrifying and dreadful of the campaign.

We return to Varna, where we find the same awful plague developing itself with increasing strength and vigour. All the months of June and July I had been living in camp at Aladyn and Devno, with the Light Division, making occasional excursions into Varna or over to the camps of the other divisions; and although the heat was at times very great indeed, there were no complaints among the men, except that diarrhoea began to get common about the beginning of July. On the 20th, as I expected there would be a move down to Varna and wanted to get some articles of outfit, I rode down there with some officers. Up to this time there had been no case of cholera in the Light Division; but early on Sunday morning, 23rd, it broke out with the same extraordinary violence and fatal effect which had marked its appearance in the French columns, and the camp was further broken up forthwith and the men marched to Monastir, nine miles further on towards the Balkans.

In Varna the inhabitants suffered from the pestilence as much as the troops. Many of them fled from the town and encamped near the neighbouring villages. Turks and Greeks suffered alike, and perished 'like flies', to use their own image.

On July 28, Sir George Brown and the officers who had accompanied him, returned from their reconnaissance of the Crimean coast, having decided that Eupatoria, some forty miles north of Sebastopol, looked a likely spot for a landing.

The Commission returned after a cruise in which they had been enabled to count the very guns of Sebastopol. The 'Fury' stood off the port quietly at night, and about two o'clock ran in softly and stopped within 2,000 yards of the batteries. There she remained till six o'clock in the morning. As the General was counting the guns, an officer observed a suspicious movement in the muzzle of one, and in a moment afterwards a shot roared through the rigging. This was a signal to quit, and the 'Fury' steamed out of the harbour as fast as she could; but the shot came after her still faster. A shell burst close to her and one shot went through her hull; fortunately no one was hurt. In the course of their reconnaissance they coasted slowly along the west face of the shore from Eupatoria southwards, and at the mouth of the Katscha discovered a beach, which the English and French generals decided on making the site of their landing.

Signs of a move soon became unmistakeable. The next day the Turkish fleet and the transports which had been lying in the Bosphorus left their anchorage for Varna, carrying with them pontoons and siege guns, and it began to be rumoured that we should really do something ere the winter came on. There were, however, divided counsels and *timides avis*. Admiral Dundas and Admiral Hamelin were notoriously opposed to the descent on the Crimea, and Marshal St Arnaud did not like to attack Sebastopol, nor was Sir George Brown very sanguine of success. The force of the Russians in the Crimea was supposed to be upwards of 55,000 men, but considerable reinforcements might have been sent there, of which we knew nothing. We could not, between French and English, at this time have sent a greater army than 42,000 or 43,000 men to the Crimea; and, speaking merely in reference to strategic considerations, there appeared to be some rashness in attempting the reduction of such a fortress as Sebastopol with an army inferior in force to that of the enemy inside and outside the walls – an army liable to be attacked by all the masses which Russia could direct, in her last extremity, to defend the 'very navel of her power' – unless the fleet was able to neutralize the preponderance of the hostile army and place our troops upon equal terms. An assault on Sebastopol, an attempt to carry it by storm or by *coup de main*, at first sight, was out of the question, according to the opinion of most of our officers. It was not impregnable, either from the quality of the works or natural position, and, like all such fortresses, it could not but fall before the regular uninterrupted continuance and progress of sap and mine and blockade. The result showed, however, that the usual conditions of a siege were not complied with in this case; and the character of the expedition, which was at first a dashing, sudden onslaught, was, perhaps inevitably, changed by the course of events.

The cholera prevailed at Varna and in the camps, but its attacks were not so fatal as at first. The hospital was full, and numerous as our medical staff was and unremitting as were our medical officers in doing all that skill and humanity could suggest for the sufferers, there were painful cases in which the men did not procure the attention they required till it was too late.

The French losses from cholera were frightful. Convinced that there was something radically wrong in the air of the hospital at Varna, the French cleared out of the building altogether, and resolved to treat their cases in the field. The hospital had been formerly used as a Turkish barrack. It was a huge quadrangular building, like the barracks at Scutari, with a courtyard in the centre. The sides of the square were about 150 feet long, and each of them contained three floors, consisting of spacious corridors, with numerous rooms off them of fair height and good proportions. About one-third of the building was reserved for our use; the remainder was occupied by the French. Although not very old, the building was far from being in thorough repair. The windows were broken, the walls in parts were cracked and shaky, and the floors were mouldering and rotten. Like all places which have been inhabited by Turkish soldiers for any time, the smell of the buildings was abominable. Men sent in there with fevers and other disorders were frequently attacked with the cholera in its worst form and died with unusual rapidity, in spite of all that could be done to save them. I visited the hospital and observed that a long train of carts filled with sick soldiers were drawn up by the walls. There were thirty-five carts, with three or four men in each. These were sick French soldiers sent in from the camps and waiting till room could be found for them in the hospital. A number of soldiers were sitting down by the roadside and here and there the moonbeams flashed brightly off their piled arms. The men were silent; not a song, not a laugh. A gloom, seldom seen among French troops, reigned amid these groups of grey-coated men and the quiet that prevailed was only broken now and then by the moans and cries of the poor sufferers in the carts. Observing that about fifteen arabas without any occupants were waiting in the square, I asked a *sous-officier* for what purpose they were required. His answer, sullen and short, was – 'Pour les morts – pour les Français décédés, Monsieur.'

On the night of August 10th, a great fire broke out at Varna, which utterly destroyed more than a quarter of the town. The sailors of the ships, and the French and English soldiery stationed near the town, worked for the ten hours during which the fire lasted with the greatest energy; but as a brisk wind prevailed, which fanned the flames as they leapt along the wooden streets, their efforts were not as successful as they deserved. The fire broke out near the French commissariat stores, in a spirit shop. The officers in charge broached many casks of spirits and as the liquid ran down the streets a Greek was seen to set fire to it. He was cut down to the chin by a French officer and fell into the fiery torrent. The howling of the inhabitants, the yells of the Turks, the clamour of women, children, dogs, and horses, were appalling. Marshal St Arnaud displayed great vigour and coolness in superintending the operations of the troops, and by his exertions aggravated the symptoms of the malady from which he had long been suffering. The French lost great quantities of provisions, and we had many thousand rations of biscuit utterly consumed. In addition, immense quantities of stores were destroyed – 19,000 pairs of soldiers' shoes and an immense quantity of cavalry sabres, which were found amid the ruins fused into the most fantastic shapes. To add to our misfortunes the cholera broke out in the fleets in Varna Bay and at Baltschik with extraordinary virulence. The 'Friedland' and 'Montebello' suffered in particular – in the latter upwards of 100 died in twenty-four hours.

The conduct of many of the men, French and English, seemed characterized by a recklessness verging on insanity. They might be seen lying drunk in the kennels, or in the ditches by the road-sides, under the blazing rays of the sun, covered with swarms of flies. They might be seen in stupid sobriety gravely paring the rind off cucumbers of portentous dimensions and eating the deadly cylinders one after another to the number of six or eight, till there was no room for more; or frequently three or four of them would make a happy bargain with a Greek for a large basketful of apricots, scarlet pumpkins, water melons, wooden-bodied pears, greengages and plums, and then retire beneath the shade of a tree, where they divided and ate the luscious food till nought remained but a heap of peel, rind, and stones. They then diluted the mass of fruit with raki, or peach brandy, and would straggle home or to sleep as best they could. It was no wonder, indeed, that cholera throve and fattened among us.

In the second week in August it assumed such an alarming character that both Admirals, French and English, resolved to leave their anchorage at Baltschik and stand out to sea for a cruise. On Wednesday the 16th, the 'Caradoc' which left Constantinople with the mails for the fleet and army the previous evening, came up with the English fleet under Admiral Dundas. The 'Caradoc' was boarded by a boat from the 'Britannia',[1] and the officer who came on board communicated the appalling intelligence that the flag-ship had lost seventy men since she left Baltschik and that she had buried ten men that morning. Upwards of 100 men were on the sick list. Some of the other ships had lost several men, but not in the same proportion.

After the great fire on the night of the 10th, the cholera seemed to diminish in the town itself and the reports from the various camps were much more favourable than before. It was found, indeed, that the plan of wide open encampments answered in checking disease. The British army was scattered broad-cast all over the country, from Monastir to Varna, a distance of twenty-six or twenty-seven miles. The Duke of Cambridge's division had marched in from Aladyn and was encamped towards the south-western side of the bay. It appeared that notwithstanding the exquisite beauty of the country around Aladyn, it was a hot-bed of fever and dysentery. The same was true of Devno, which was called by the Turks 'the Valley of Death'; and had we consulted the natives ere we pitched our camps, we assuredly

[1] The flagship of Admiral Dundas.

should never have gone either to Aladyn or Devno, notwithstanding the charms of their position and the temptations offered by the abundant supply of water and by the adjacent woods. Whoever gazed on the rich meadows, stretching for long miles away, and bordered by heights on which dense forests struggled all but in vain to pierce the masses of wild vine, clematis, dwarf acacia and many-coloured brushwoods, might well have imagined that no English glade or hill-top could well be healthier or better suited for the residence of man. But these meadows nurtured the fever, the ague, dysentery, and pestilence in their bosom – the lake and the stream exhaled death, and at night fat unctuous vapours rose fold after fold from the valleys and crept up in the dark and stole into the tent of the sleeper and wrapped him in their deadly embrace. So completely exhausted was the Brigade of Guards after a short encampment that these 3,000 of the flower of England had to make two marches in order to get over the distance from Aladyn to Varna, which was not more than ten miles.

The Highland brigade was in better condition, but even the three noble regiments which composed it were far from being in good health or in the spirits in which they set out for Varna. The Light Division had lost 110 or 112 men. The Second Division had suffered somewhat less. The little cavalry force had been sadly reduced by death, and the Third Division, which had been encamped to the north-west of Varna, close outside the town, had lost upwards of 100 men. The ambulance corps had been completely crippled by the death of the drivers and men belonging to it. In truth, it may be taken as an actual fact that physically and morally each division of the army had been weakened by nearly one regiment.

Horrors occurred here every day which were shocking to think of. Walking by the beach one might see some straw sticking up through the sand, and on scraping it away with his stick, be horrified at bringing to light the face of a corpse which had been deposited there with a wisp of straw around it, a prey to dogs and vultures. Dead bodies rose up from the bottom in the harbour and bobbed grimly around in the water or floated in from sea and drifted past the sickened gazers on board the ships – all buoyant, bolt upright, and hideous in the sun. One day, the body of a French soldier, who had been murdered (for his neckerchief was twisted round the neck so as to produce strangulation, and the forehead was laid open by a ghastly wound which cleft the skull to the brain), came alongside the 'Caradoc' in harbour and was with difficulty sunk again.

But the armies of the allies were about to enter upon the career of active warfare and to escape from a spot fraught with memories of death unredeemed by a ray of glory. It was no secret that in the middle of July a council of generals and admirals had, by a majority, overcome the *timides avis* of some, and had decided upon an expedition to the Crimea in compliance with the positive orders of the English Cabinet and with the less decided suggestions of the Emperor of the French. That project had been arrested by the sickness and calamities which had fallen on the French and English armies, but it had not been abandoned.

At a Council of War, held at Marshal St Arnaud's quarters on the 24th of August, the final decision was taken.

Preparations for the departure of the armies were immediately put in hand. The camps were struck and men and horses, guns and ammunition, stores and equipment began to converge on Varna. The embarkation of the thousands of troops, English, French and Turkish, with all their impedimenta, from the small port was a prodigious undertaking, but by September 6 it was complete and the ships were standing out to sea. At half-past four the next morning the signal was given, by the firing of three guns in 'Agamemnon', for the ships to proceed to their rendezvous.

Their progress was slow. The convoy continually hove to while reconnaissance vessels steamed ahead on the look-out for Russian ships and it was not until just after dawn on September 12 that the Crimean coastline became visible.

On the afternoon of the next day, the huge fleet, consisting of 600 vessels, with more than 50,000 men on board, and protected by 3,000 guns of the combined British, French and Turkish fleets, was steaming slowly towards Eupatoria.

4

The Invasion

IT WAS A VAST ARMADA. NO PEN COULD DESCRIBE ITS effect upon the eye. Ere an hour had elapsed it had extended itself over half the circumference of the horizon. Possibly no expedition so complex and so terrible in its means of destruction, with such enormous power in engines of war and such capabilities of locomotion, was ever yet sent forth by any worldly power. The fleet, in five irregular and straggling lines, flanked by men-of-war and war steamers, advanced slowly, filling the atmosphere with innumerable columns of smoke, which gradually flattened out into streaks and joined the clouds, adding to the sombre appearance of this well-named 'Black' Sea. The land was lost to view very speedily beneath the coal clouds and the steam clouds of the fleet, and as we advanced not an object was visible in the half of the great circle which lay before us, save the dark waves and the cold sky.

Not a bird flew, not a fish leaped, not a sail dotted the horizon. From time to time signals were made to keep the stragglers in order and to whip up the laggards, but the execution of the plan by no means equalled the accuracy with which it had been set forth upon paper and the deviations from the mathematical regularity of the programme were very natural. The effect was not marred by these trifling departures from strict rectilinearity, for the fleet seemed all the greater and the more imposing as the eye rested on these huge black hulls weighing down upon the face of the waters and the infinite diversity of rigging which covered the background with a giant network.

On the morning of the 11th September, signal was made to the transports to steer to Eupatoria. For the whole day we ran very quietly on this course without any incident worthy of notice. The night closed in very darkly. The lightning flashed in sheets and forked streams every two or three minutes from heavy masses of cloud behind us and the fleet was greatly scattered. Our course was rather hazardous at times, and so many steamers were steering across us that great care was required to steer clear of them in the dark. The moon, which would otherwise have aided us, was quite obscured by banks of clouds.

During the night the expedition altered its course slightly to the eastward, and stood in more directly towards the land. The night was fine, but the sharpness of the air told of the approach of winter. Two heavy showers of hail, which fell at intervals in the morning, covered the decks with coatings of ice a couple of inches thick, but the sun and the broom soon removed them. Early in the morning of the 12th, just after dawn, a dark line was visible on our port side, which became an object of interest and discussion, for some maintained it was land, others declared it was cloud-land. The rising sun decided the question in favour of those who maintained the substantiality of the appearance. It was indeed the shore of the Crimea.

The impression as we drew near was that the coast presented a remarkable resemblance to the dunes of La Belle France. The country was flat, but numerous herds of cattle were to be seen in the plains and salt marshes and the farmhouses became more frequent as we proceeded.

Eupatoria lies on a spit of sand and for a long time we imagined that it was defended by heavy works, for the solid stone houses close by the sea-coast were so increased by refraction and lifted up so high that they looked like forts. Towards the south side were innumerable windmills, and several bathing boxes gaily painted along the beach gave an air of civilization to the place, in spite of the old Turkish minarets which peered above the walls in a very dilapidated state. At a quarter-past three the expedition anchored off the town at the distance of two or three miles.

A British and a French officer, with an interpreter, put off in a boat, carrying with them a flag of truce, and called on the town governor to surrender, which he did with rather bad grace. The allied generals decided that enough had been accomplished for one day and that the fleets should stand by along the coast until eight o'clock the next morning, when the landing would begin.

The place selected for landing was a low strip of beach and shingle forming a sort of causeway between the sea and a stagnant salt-water lake about one mile long and half a mile broad. When we first arrived its borders and surface were frequented by vast flocks of wild fowl. The causeway was not more than two hundred yards broad, leading by a gentle ascent to a plateau dotted with tumuli or barrows, such as are seen in several parts of England. Towards the sea this plateau presented a precipitous face of red clay and sandstone, varying in height from a hundred to a hundred and fifty feet, and it terminated by a descent almost to sea-level at the distance of nearly two miles from the shores of the lake. Thence towards the south there was a low sandy beach. This low coast stretched along as far as the eye could reach, till it was lost beneath the base of the mountain ranges over Sebastopol. The country inland was covered with cattle, with grain in stack, with farm-houses. The stubble fields were covered with wild lavender, southernwood, and other fragrant shrubs, which the troops collected for fuel, and which filled the air with an aromatic perfume. As we cruised down towards Eupatoria, we could see the people driving their carts and busy in their ordinary occupations.

Now and then some Cossacks were visible, scouring along the roads to the interior. The post carriage from Sebastopol to Odessa also was seen rolling leisurely along, and conveying, probably, news of the great armament with which the coast was menaced.

Daybreak gave promise of a lovely morning. The vast armada, which had moved on during the night in perfect order, studded the horizon with a second heaven of stars, and covering the face of the sea with innumerable lights, advanced parallel with the coast till it gradually closed in towards the shore.

At seven a.m. most of the fleet were inshore near their prescribed positions. As the expedition drew up in lines parallel to the beach, the French fleet passed us under steam, and extended itself on our right, and ran in close to shore below the cliffs of the plateau. Their small war steamers went much nearer than ours were allowed to do, and a little after seven o'clock the first French boat put off from one of the men-of-war; not more than fifteen or sixteen men were on board her. She was beached quietly on shore at the southern extremity of the red cliff. The crew leaped out, formed into a knot on the strand, and seemed busily engaged for a few moments over one spot of ground, as though they were digging a grave. Presently a flag-staff was visible above their heads, and in a moment the tricolor was run up to the top, and fluttered out gaily in the wind, while the men took off their hats, and no doubt did their '*Vive l'Empereur!*' in good style. The French were thus the first to take possession of the Crimea.[1]

The most scrutinizing gaze at this moment could not have detected a hostile uniform along the coast. The French admiral fired a gun shortly after eight o'clock, and the disembarkation of their troops commenced. In little more than an hour they got 6,000 men on shore. Their whole force to be landed consisted of 23,600 men. Our army amounted to 27,000 men.

The instant the French had landed a regiment, a company was pushed on to reconnoitre. As each regiment followed in column, its predecessors deployed and advanced in light marching order *en tirailleur*, spreading out like a fan over the plains. It was most curious and interesting to observe their progress, and to note the rapid manner in which they were appropriating the soil. In about an hour after their first detachment had landed their advanced posts were discernible between three and four miles from the beach, like little black specks moving over the corn-fields, and darkening the highways and meadow paths.

[1] It seems to have been a sort of passion with the French to be 'the first' to do everything – or was it a passion with our generals to be second? Our allies were first at Gallipoli, first at Varna, first in the Crimea – all our attacks depended on them. They attacked first at the Alma, and when they turned the Russian right our attack was to take place. They also attacked first in the two great assaults, and our assaults were made to depend on the success of their demonstrations. WHR.

In our fleet the whole labour and responsibility of the disembarkation rested with Sir E. Lyons. About nine o'clock one black ball was run up to the fore of the 'Agamemnon', and a gun was fired to enforce attention to the signal. This meant, 'Divisions of boats to assemble round ships for which they are told off, to disembark infantry and artillery'. In an instant the sea was covered with a flotilla of launches, gigs, cutters, splashing through the water, some towing flats, others with horse floats plunging heavily after them. They proceeded with as great regularity as could be expected to their appointed ships and the process of landing commenced. Up to this moment not an enemy was to be seen; but as the boats began to shove off from the ships, five horsemen slowly rose above the ridge on the elevated ground, to the right of the strip of beach which separated the salt-water lake from the sea in front of us. Two of these men appeared to be officers. The others were irregular cavalry. After a while four of them retired to one of the tumuli inland opposite the French fleet. The other retained his position and was soon the cynosure of all neighbouring eyes. The Russian was within about 1,100 yards of us and through a good telescope we could watch his every action. He rode slowly along by the edge of the cliff, apparently noting the number and disposition of the fleet and taking notes with great calmness in a memorandum book. He wore a dark green frock-coat, with a little silver lace, a cap of the same colour, a sash round his waist, and long leather boots. His horse, a fine bay charger, was a strange contrast to the shaggy rough little steeds of his followers. There they were, 'the Cossacks', at last! – stout, compact-looking fellows, with sheep-skin caps, uncouth clothing of indiscriminate cut, high saddles, and little fiery ponies, which carried them with wonderful ease and strength. Each of these Cossacks carried a thick lance some fifteen feet in length and a heavy-looking sabre. At times they took rapid turns by the edge of the cliff in front of us – now to the left, now to the rear, of their officer, and occasionally they dipped out of sight over the hill. Then they came back, flourishing their lances, and pointed to the accumulating masses of the French on their right, not more than half a mile from them, on the shore, or scampered over the hill to report progress as to the lines of English boats advancing to the beach. Their officer behaved very well. He remained for an hour within range of a Minié rifle, and when the 'Highflyer' stood in close to shore, while he was coolly making a sketch in his portfolio of our appearance, we all expected she was going to drop a shell over himself and his little party.

Meantime, the English boats were nearing the shore in irregular groups; a company of the 7th Fusileers landed first on the beach to the left of the cliffs; then came a company of the 2nd Battalion of the Rifle Brigade: a small boat from the 'Britannia' had, however, preceded the Fusileers and disembarked some men on the beach, who went down into the hollow at the foot of the cliffs. The Russian continued his sketching. Suddenly a Cossack crouched down and pointed with his lance to the ascent of the cliff. The officer turned and looked in the direction. We looked too, and, lo! a cocked hat rose above the horizon. Another figure, with a similar head-dress, came also in view. The first was Sir George Brown (Light Division) on foot; the second we made out to be the Assistant Quartermaster-General Airey. Sir George had landed immediately after the company of the Fusileers on their right, and having called attention to the ground where he wished the Light Division to form, he walked on towards the cliff on rising ground on the right of the salt-water lake. It was evident the Russian and the Cossack saw Sir George, but that he did not see them. A picket of Fusileers and Riflemen followed the General at a considerable interval. The Russian got on his horse, the Cossack followed his example, and one of them cantered to the left to see that the French were not cutting off their retreat, while the others stooped down over their saddle-bows and rode stealthily, with lowered lances, towards the Englishmen.

Sir George was in danger, but he did not know it. Neither did the Russians see the picket advancing towards the brow of the hill, for our General was not alone; Sergeant Maunsell and two privates of the 23rd had followed him as he advanced towards the hill; and they had not gone very far when Sir George ordered one of them to go back, and tell the officer commanding the company to advance and extend his men along the brow of the hill. Sir George was busy scanning the country, and pointing out various spots to the Quartermaster-General. Suddenly they turned and slowly descended the hill – the gold sash disappeared – the cocked hat was eclipsed – Cossacks and officers dismounted and stole along by the side of their horses. They, too, were hid from sight in a short time. In about five minutes two or three tiny puffs of smoke rose over the cliff, and presently the faint cracks of a rifle were audible. In a few minutes more the Cossacks were visible, flying like the wind on the road towards Sebastopol.

When we landed, we heard that Sir George Brown, whose sight is very indifferent, had a near escape of being taken prisoner. He was the first to land, and pushed on without sending vedettes or men in front, though he took the precaution, very fortunately, to bring up a few soldiers with him. The Cossacks made a dash when they were within less than a hundred yards. The General had to run, and was only saved from capture by the fire of the Fusileers. The first blood spilt in this campaign was that of a poor boy, an arabajee, who was wounded in the foot; and our first capture consisted of fourteen arabas, in which were found abundance of delicious fruit and stores of firewood. The Cossacks beat the drivers to hasten them in taking the bullocks out of the carts, nor did they desist in their attempts till one of them was badly hit and our men were close at hand. The drivers at once came in to us when the Cossacks rode off. Meantime, swarms of boats were putting off from the various ships to carry the English troops to land.

By twelve o'clock, that barren and desolate beach, inhabited but a short time before only by the seagull and wild-fowl, was swarming with life. From one extremity to the other, bayonets glistened and red coats and brass-mounted shakoes gleamed in solid masses. The air was filled with our English speech and the hum of voices mingled with loud notes of command. Very amusing was it to watch the loading and unloading of the boats. A gig or cutter, pulled by eight or twelve sailors, with a paddle-box boat, flat, or Turkish pinnace in tow would come up alongside a steamer or transport in which troops were ready for disembarkation. The officers of each company first descended, each man in full dress. Over his shoulder was slung his haversack, containing what had been, ere it underwent the process of cooking, four pounds and a-half of salt meat, and a bulky mass of biscuit of the same weight. This was his ration for three days. Besides this, each officer carried his greatcoat, rolled up and fastened in a hoop round his body, a wooden canteen to hold water, a small ration of spirits, whatever change of underclothing he could manage to stow away, his forage-cap, and, in most instances, a revolver. Each private carried his blanket and greatcoat strapped up into a kind of knapsack, inside which was a pair of boots, a pair of socks, a shirt, and, at the request of the men themselves, a forage-cap; he also carried his water canteen, and the same rations as the officer, a portion of the mess cooking apparatus, firelock and bayonet of course, cartouch box and fifty rounds of ball-cartridge for Minié, sixty rounds for smooth-bore arms.

As each man came creeping down the ladder, Jack helped him along tenderly from rung to rung till he was safe in the boat, took his firelock and stowed it away, removed his knapsack and packed it snugly under the seat, patted him on the back, and told him 'not to be afeerd on the water'; treated 'the sojer', in fact, in a very kind and tender way, as though he were a large but not very sagacious 'pet', who was not to be frightened or lost sight of on any account, and did it all so quickly, that the large paddle-box boats, containing 100 men, were filled in five minutes. Then the latter took the paddle-box in tow, leaving her, however, in charge of a careful coxswain, and the same attention was paid to getting the 'sojer' on shore that was evinced in getting him into the boat; the sailors (half or wholly naked in the surf) standing by at the bows and handing each man and his accoutrement down the plank to the shingle, for fear 'he'd fall off and hurt himself'. Never did men work better than our blue-jackets; especially valuable were they with horses and artillery; and their delight at having a horse to hold and to pat all to themselves was excessive. When the gun-carriages stuck fast in the shingle, half a dozen herculean seamen rushed at the wheels, and soon spoked it out with a run and landed it on the hard sand. No praise can do justice to the willing labour of these fine fellows. They never relaxed their efforts as long as man or horse of the expedition remained to be landed, and many of them, officers as well as men, were twenty-four hours in their boats.

At one o'clock most of the regiments of the Light Division had moved off the beach over the hill, and across the country towards a village, to which the advanced parties of the French left had already approached. Up to three o'clock we had landed 14,200 men, and two batteries of artillery. Many of the staff-officers, who ought to have been mounted, marched on foot, as their horses were not yet landed. Generals might be seen sitting on powder barrels on the beach, awaiting the arrival of 'divisional staff horses', or retiring gloomily within the folds of their macintosh. Disconsolate doctors too were there, groaning after hospital panniers – but too sorely needed, for more than one man died on the beach. During the voyage several cases of cholera occurred: 150 men were buried on the passage from Varna, and there were about 300 men on board not able to move when we landed. The beach was partitioned off by flagstaffs with colours corresponding to that of each division, in compartments for the landing of each class of man and beast; but it was, of course, almost beyond the limits of possibility to observe these nice distinctions in conducting an operation which must have extended over many square miles of water.

After a short time the country people began to come in, and we found they were decidedly well inclined towards us. Of course they were rather scared at first, but before the day was over they had begun to approach the beach and to bring cattle, sheep and vegetables for sale. Their carts, or rather arabas, were detained, but liberally paid for; and so well satisfied were the owners, that they went home, promising increased supplies tomorrow. The men were apparently of pure Tartar race, with small eyes very wide apart, the nose very much sunk, and a square substantial figure. They generally wore turbans of lambswool and jackets of sheepskin with the wool inwards. They spoke indifferent Turkish and were most ready with information respecting their Russian masters, by whom they had been most carefully disarmed. A deputation of them waited on Lord Raglan to beg for muskets and powder to fight the Muscovite.

They told us that the ground round Sebastopol had been mined for miles, but such rumours are always current about a fortress to be defended. They said, too, that the cholera had been most fatal at Sebastopol, that 20,000 of the troops and seamen were dead, and that the latter had been landed to man the forts. They estimated the force between us and Sebastopol at about 15,000 men, and the garrison at 40,000 more. On the whole, the information we at first obtained was most encouraging, and the favourable disposition of the people and their willingness to furnish supplies were advantages which had not been expected.

Few of those who were with the expedition will forget the night of the 14th of September. Seldom or never were 27,000 Englishmen more miserable. No tents had been sent on shore, partly because there had been no time to land them, partly because there was no certainty of our being able to find carriage for them in case of a move. Towards night the sky looked very black and lowering; the wind rose, and the rain fell in torrents. The showers increased about midnight, and early in the morning fell in drenching sheets which pierced through the blankets and great-coats of the houseless and tentless soldiers. Let the reader imagine some of these old generals and young lords and gentlemen exposed hour after hour to the violence of pitiless storms, with no bed but the reeking puddle under the saturated blankets, or bits of useless waterproof wrappers, and the twenty-odd thousand poor fellows who could not get 'dry bits' of ground, and had to sleep, or try to sleep, in little lochs and water courses – no fire to cheer them, no hot grog, and the prospect of no breakfast – let him imagine this, and add to it that the nice 'change of linen' had become a wet abomination, which weighed the poor men's kits down, and he will admit that this 'seasoning' was of rather a violent character – particularly as it came after all the luxuries of dry ship stowage. Sir George Brown slept under a cart tilted over. The Duke of Cambridge (First Division), wrapped in a waterproof coat, spent most of the night riding about among his men. Sir de Lacy Evans (Second Division) was the only general whose staff had been careful enough to provide him with a tent. In one respect the rain was of service: it gave the men a temporary supply of water; but then it put a fire out of the question, even if enough wood could have been scraped together to make it. The country was, however, quite destitute of timber.

During the night it blew freshly from the west, a heavy sea tumbled into the bay and sent a high surf upon the beach, which much interfered with the process of landing cavalry and artillery on the 15th. Early in the day signal was made to the steamers to get up steam for Eupatoria, and it was no doubt intended to land the cavalry and artillery there, in consequence of the facility afforded by a pier and harbour; but towards noon the wind went down, and the swell somewhat abated. Several valuable animals were drowned in an attempt to land some staff horses. Lord Raglan lost one charger, and another swam off seaward and was only recovered two miles from the shore. Some boats were staved and rendered useless, and several others were injured by the roll of the surf on the beach; nor did the horse boats and flats escape uninjured. Operations went on slowly, and the smooth days we had wasted at sea were bitterly lamented.

The work was, however, to be done, and in the afternoon orders were given to land cavalry. For this purpose it was desirable to approach the beach as close as possible and a signal to this effect was made to the cavalry steamers. The 'Himalaya' immediately commenced discharging her enormous cargo of 390 horses and nearly 700 men. The horses were so accustomed to an existence of unstable equilibrium in slings, and to rapid ascents and descents from the tight ropes, that they became comparatively docile. Besides this, they were very tired from standing for fourteen days in one narrow box, were rather thin and sickly, and were glad of change of air and position.

Before the disembarkation had concluded for the day, signal was made for all ships to 'land tents'. Subsequently the order was countermanded, and the tents which had been landed were sent back to the ships again. The miseries of the night before were indeed too great to be lightly incurred. Our French allies, deficient as they had been in means of accommodation and stowage and transport, had yet managed to land their little scraps of tents the day they disembarked, whilst our poor fellows were soaked through and through, their blankets and greatcoats saturated with wet, and without any change of raiment, the French close at hand, and the Turks, whose tents were much more bulky than our own, were lying snugly under cover. The most serious result of the wetting was, however, a great increase in illness among the troops.

Throughout the next two days huge fatigue parties were at work disembarking and distributing stores and equipment to the various divisions, including rather late in the day, a supply of tents: but there was still, as there had been from the start of the expedition, an acute shortage of medical supplies and doctors. Only the siege train, consisting of heavy artillery and other materials that would be needed in the event of such an operation, remained on board the ships standing off shore, the intention being to land this equipment at the mouth of the river Belbek, close to Sebastopol.

During the daytime Cossacks were seen reconnoitering the British outposts, and at night the sky was reddened by the glare of burning villages which they had set on fire to prevent them from falling into the Allies' hands. On September 17th some friendly Tartars – most of them seemed to fraternize as soon as they found that prompt payment would be given for whatever provisions they had to sell – brought news that an army of 15,000 Russians was encamped on the river Alma, about twelve miles further south.

5

Skirmishing

AT THREE O'CLOCK IN THE MORNING THE CAMP WAS roused by the reveille, and the 50,000 sleepers woke into active life. The boats from the ships lined the beach to receive the tents which were again returned to the ships. The English commissariat officers struggled in vain with the very deficient means at their disposal to meet the enormous requirements of an army of 26,000 men for the transport of baggage, ammunition, and food; and a scene, which to an unpractised eye seemed one of utter confusion, began and continued for several hours, relieved only by the steadiness and order of the regiments as they paraded previous to marching.

The French, in advance on our right, were up betimes, and the camp fires of the allied armies, extending for miles along the horizon, and mingling with the lights of the ships, almost anticipated morning. Six thousand Turkish infantry, under Suleiman Pasha, moved along by the sea-side; next to them came the divisions of Generals Bosquet, Canrobert, Forey, and Prince Napoleon. Our order of march was about four miles to the left of their left wing, and as many behind them.

The right of the allied forces was covered by the fleet, which moved along with it in magnificent order, darkening the air with innumerable columns of smoke, ready to shell the enemy should they threaten to attack our right, and commanding the land for nearly two miles from the shore.

It was nine o'clock in the morning ere the whole of our army was ready for marching. The day was warm, and our advance was delayed by the wretched transport furnished for the baggage, an evil which even at that time threatened to be more severely felt in any protracted operations. Everything not absolutely indispensable was sent on board ship. At last the men fell in and the march of the campaign began. On the extreme right and much in advance, next the sea, was the 1st Division of the French army.

The country beyond the salt lake, near which we were encamped, was entirely destitute of tree or shrub, and consisted of wide plains, marked at intervals of two or three miles with hillocks and long irregular ridges of hills running down towards the sea. It was but little cultivated, except in the patches of land around the unfrequent villages built in the higher recesses of the valleys. Hares were started in abundance, and afforded great sport to the soldiers whenever they halted, and several were fairly hunted down among the lines. All oxen, horses, or cattle had been driven off by the Cossacks. The soil was hard and elastic, and was in excellent order for artillery.

After a march of an hour a halt took place for fifty minutes, during which Lord Raglan, accompanied by a very large staff, Marshal St Arnaud and a number of French officers, rode along the front of the columns. The men of their own accord got up from the ground, rushed forward, and column after column rent the air with three thundering English cheers. It was a good omen. As the Marshal passed the 55th Regiment, he exclaimed, 'English, I hope you will fight well today!' The troops presented a splendid appearance. The effect of these grand masses of soldiery descending the ridges of the hills, rank after rank, with the sun playing over forests of glittering steel, can never be forgotten by those who witnessed it. At last, the smoke of burning villages and farm-houses announced that the enemy in front were aware of our march. It was melancholy to see the white walls of the houses blackened with smoke – the flames ascending through the roofs of peaceful homesteads – and the ruined outlines of deserted hamlets. Many sick men fell out and were carried to the rear. It was a painful sight – a sad contrast to the magnificent appearance of the army in front, to behold litter after litter borne past to the carts with the poor sufferers who had dropped from illness and fatigue.

Presently, from the top of a hill, a wide plain was visible, beyond which rose a ridge darkened here and there by masses which the practised eye recognised as cavalry. On the left of the plain lay a large village in flames; right before us was a neat white house unburnt, though the outhouses and farm-yard were burning. This was the Imperial Post-house of Bouljanak, just twenty miles from Sebastopol and some of our officers and myself were soon busily engaged in exploring the place.

The house was deserted and gutted. Only a picture of a saint, bunches of herbs in the kitchen, and a few household utensils were left; and a solitary pea-hen stalked sadly about the threshold, which soon fell a victim to a revolver. A small stream [the Bouljanak] ran past us, which was an object of delight to our thirsty soldiers, who had marched more than eight miles from their late camp. After a short halt for men and horses by the stream, over which the post-road was carried by a bridge which the enemy had left unbroken for the passage of our artillery, the army pushed on again. The cavalry pushed on in front, and on arriving about a mile beyond the post-house we clearly made out the Cossack Lancers on the hills in front. Lord Cardigan (Light Cavalry Brigade) threw out skirmishers in line, who covered the front at intervals of ten or twelve yards from each other. The Cossacks advanced to meet us in like order, man for man, the steel of their long lances glittering in the sun. They were rough-looking fellows, mounted on sturdy little horses; but the regularity of their order and the celerity of their movements showed that they were regulars and by no means despicable foes. As our skirmishers advanced, the Cossacks halted at the foot of the hill.

Lord Cardigan was eager to try their strength and permission was given to him to advance somewhat nearer; but as he did so, dark columns of cavalry appeared in the recesses of the hills, and it became evident that if our men charged up such a steep ascent their horses would be blown, and that they would run a risk of being surrounded and cut to pieces by a force of three times their number. Lord Lucan (Cavalry Division) therefore ordered the cavalry to halt, gather in their skirmishers, and retire slowly. None of the infantry or artillery could be seen, as they had not yet topped the brow of the hill. When our skirmishers halted, the Cossacks commenced a fire of carabines from their line of vedettes, which was quite harmless. Few of the balls came near enough to let the whiz be heard. I was riding between the cavalry and the skirmishers, with Lieutenant-Colonel Dickson, RA, when suddenly the Russians, emboldened by our halt, came over the brow of the hill, and slowly descended the slope in three solid squares, the centre one of which advanced nearer than the others.

'Now,' said Dickson, 'we'll catch it. These fellows have guns, and mean mischief.' I, in my ignorance, conceived that it would be a very pleasant thing to look at, whatever they meant. We had offered them battle, and they had lost their chance, for our cavalry now turned round and rode quietly towards the troops. Our skirmishers, who had replied smartly to the fire of the Cossacks, but without effect, retired and joined their squadrons. At every fifty paces our cavalry faced about to receive the Cossacks if they prepared to charge. Suddenly one of the Russian cavalry squares opened: a spirt of white smoke rose out of the gap and a round shot, which first pitched close to my horse and covered me with dirt, tore over the column of our cavalry behind and rolled away between the ranks of the riflemen in the rear just as they came in view of the cavalry. In another instant a second shot knocked over a horse, taking off his rider's leg above the ankle. Another and another followed, tearing through our ranks.

All this time our cavalry were drawn up as targets for the enemy's guns, and had they been of iron they could not have been more solid and immoveable. The Russian gunners fired admirably; they were rather slow, but their balls came bounding along, quite visible as they passed. After some thirty rounds from the enemy, our artillery, having cleared their front, opened fire. The first gun fired the shell with so true an aim that it was seen to burst right over a Russian gun, and apparently to shut it up. Our round shot ploughed up the columns of the cavalry, who speedily dispersed into broken lines, wheeling round and round with great adroitness to escape the six and nine-pound balls. All our shells were not so successful as the first, but one, better directed than the rest, burst right in the centre of a column of light infantry, which the Russians had advanced to support their cavalry. Our fire then became so hot, the service of the guns so quick, that the enemy retired in about fifteen minutes after we opened on them.

It is impossible to form an accurate notion of the effect of our fire, but it must have caused the Russians a greater loss than they inflicted upon us. We lost six horses, and four men were wounded. One of the wounded men rode coolly to the rear with his foot dangling by a piece of skin to the bone and told the doctor he had just come to have his leg dressed. Another wounded trooper behaved with equal fortitude and refused the use of a litter to carry him to the rear, though his leg was broken into splinters. It was strange, in visiting the scene where the horses lay dead, that the first feeling produced on the spectator, when the horror of seeing the poor animals ripped open by shells from chest to loin, as though it were done by a surgeon's knife, had subsided, was that Sir E. Landseer, in his picture of 'War', must have seen one of the animals before us—the glaring eye-ball, the distended nostril, the gnashed teeth, being all true to life.

When the Russians had retired beyond the heights, orders were given to halt and bivouac for the night, and our tired men to set to work to gather fuel. So ended the affair of the Bouljanak.

Lord Cardigan was, it is said, anxious to charge, but he received most positive orders from Lord Lucan not to do so, and it will be seen that had his Lordship charged he would have anticipated all the disastrous part of Balaklava and none of its glory. As our skirmishers retired and formed, the Cossacks raised a derisive yell, but did not attempt to pursue or molest them. When the enemy disappeared, the troops fell back and rested on the Bouljanak for the night.

As soon as the rations of rum and meat had been served out, the casks were broken up and the staves used to make fires for cooking, aided by nettles and long grass. At night the watch-fires of the Russians were visible on our left and front. It was cold and dreary and if I could intrude the recital of the sorrows of a tentless, baggage-less man wandering about in the dark from regiment to regiment in hope of finding his missing traps,[1] I might tell a tale amusing enough to read, the incidents of which were very distressing to the individual concerned. The night was damp, the watch-fires were mere flashes, which gave little heat, and barely sufficed to warm the rations; but the wanderer was lucky enough to get a lodging on the ground beside a kindly colonel, who was fortunate enough to have a little field-tent with him, and a bit of bread and biscuit to spare after a march of ten miles and a fast of ten hours.

All night arabas continued to arrive, and soldiers who had fallen out or got astray came up to the sentries to find their regiments. Sir George Brown, Sir de Lacy Evans, the Brigadier-Generals, and staff-officers, went about among their divisions and brigades ere the men lay down, giving directions for the following day, and soon after dusk the regiments were on the ground, wrapped up in great-coats and blankets, to find the best repose they could after the day's exertions. It was much regretted that our cavalry force was so miserably deficient, for if we had been even two to three we could readily have disposed of the vapouring lancers on the hill, who had irritated the men very much by their derisive cries when our skirmishers retired.

All night we could see the Russian position on the Alma clearly defined by the watch-fires, which illuminated the sky for four miles. A heavy dew fell, but the night was clear, and many a debate did we hold as to the strength of the enemy – of the ground they occupied – of their qualities as soldiers – ere we laid down to rest. It was by no means sure that the Russian cavalry might not beat up our quarters, and there is every reason to be thankful that they gave us a quiet night, for an alarm on the part of an enemy who knew the ground might have greatly distressed us, at little risk to them. But their cavalry all through the war acted with more caution than valour.

[1] They were thrown out of the commisariat araba in which they had been placed by order of the Commisariat-General and were abandoned to the Cossacks, so I never saw them again. It was found necessary to make room for some of the reserve ammunition which had been stowed in arabas that broke down on the march. WHR.

6

Alma

Some hours earlier Lord Raglan had conferred with Marshal St Arnaud, who had produced a plan of attack which had as its ultimate objective a threat to Sebastopol from the rear.

This plan was that 'the English army should execute "a turning movement" on the Russian right, whilst its attention was seriously drawn on its left by a French division, and that the bulk of the army should make a powerful effort to force the Russian centre'.

The allied armies were to advance on a front some four miles wide and after crossing the river Alma were to storm and capture the steep heights which lay immediately beyond its southern bank. Under General Bosquet the French Second Division, supported by Turks and guns of the French fleet, and with the sea-coast on its right flank, was to turn the Russians' left which, in the belief that it was inaccessible because of the steepness of the ascent, they had left undefended by artillery. At the opposite (eastern) end of the front, the British Light Division, with the First Division in support, was to turn the Russians' left flank. The main attack, by both British and French troops, was to be made in the centre.

Although subsequent events suggest that Lord Raglan may have had some doubts about the feasibility of this plan, he nevertheless promised Marshal St Arnaud the full co-operation of the British. Strategically, the operation no doubt sounded simple enough – partly because no British reconnaissance had been made and consequently no proper estimate formed of the probable hazards. Had this elementary precaution been taken, it would have shown that the odds against the Allies achieving their objective were enormous. And when the time came, the British were not ready. The French advance had been timed to begin at five a.m., the British two hours later: yet it was not until after ten o'clock that they were in a position to start. The French, who had begun operations according to plan, had by that time been halted, with the inevitable result that confusion developed not only upon the flanks but also in the centre where the two armies were supposed to advance side by side.

A further cause of misunderstanding, no doubt, was Lord Raglan's peculiar reticence about the plan. Not even Sir de Lacy Evans (the only general in his army who had ever commanded a division in the field, and whose Second Division was to be the spearhead of the attack in the centre) was told what the plan was. Lord Raglan's reason for this omission is hard to guess: or rather, it is difficult to disentangle the most likely reason from a complex of probabilities. He was not used to having to make prompt decisions, much less to discuss their implications with subordinates: his army had had little rest during the previous twenty-four hours, and although he may have seemed aloof towards his troops, he was at all times very much concerned about their condition: also, it was known that his feelings towards the French were not exactly warm, nor did he show much confidence in their abilities; finally, his appreciation, if it ever existed, of General Evans's considerable campaign experience was successfully concealed. M. de Bazancourt, the French historian, quoted by Russell, had his own views on Raglan's failure to acquaint his officers with the Allied plan: 'Lord Raglan appears to have allowed his strong political feelings and his very aristocratic prejudices to have influenced his judgment: and I believe that, with one exception . . . Lord Raglan never invited Sir de Lacy Evans to his table till the evening after the Alma.'

Shortly before day-break, Sir de Lacy Evans was visited by the French chiefs, General Canrobert and Prince Napoleon, from whom he learnt for the first time what Lord Raglan's intentions were. According to the plan on which Lord Raglan had agreed with Marshal St Arnaud, the British Second Division, with two French divisions (that of Prince Napoleon being on Sir de Lacy's right) were to attack the centre, while the whole of the rest of the British forces were to try to turn the enemy's right flank.

Not long before the battle began Lord Raglan announced to Sir de Lacy that although there would be no objection to his keeping in touch with

Prince Napoleon, or regulating his movements according to those of the Prince, he was not to accept orders from anyone except Lord Raglan himself. This, as Sir de Lacy knew from his conversation with the French chiefs, was not their understanding of the arrangements that had been agreed upon. Accordingly he asked that a message should be sent immediately to acquaint them with this change of plan. This was done and an officer appointed to act as liaison between the French chiefs and Sir de Lacy. Whether any consideration was given to the way in which this officer was to perform his duties at the height of a battle over exceptionally difficult terrain and in which the commanders might easily become widely separated, we do not know. It can only be said that it seems highly unlikely.

At eleven o'clock Bosquet received the order to march, which was countermanded soon afterwards, as he was too far in advance, and whilst the halt took place, that active and able general made a reconnaissance, the first of the day, of the enemy's position, and discovered two passes to the heights in front—one a mere path on the mountain side, close to the sea; the second to the left of that path, running from the village of Almatamak and ascending the heights by a very narrow ravine. It was plain that infantry could get up, but it seemed very doubtful if guns could be brought up the second of these passes to the heights, and the first was utterly impracticable for artillery.

It appears somewhat strange that no other reconnaissance was made of the Russian position by the other generals. They did not reconnoitre the Alma, nor did they procure any information respecting the strength of the enemy or of the ground they occupied. They even concerted their plan before they had seen the enemy at all, relying on the bravery of the troops not only to force the Russians from their lines, but, if necessary, to swim or to ford a stream of unknown depth, with steep rotten banks, the bridges across which might, for all they knew, have been destroyed by the enemy.

Nevertheless, the French infantry, after moving towards the mouth of the river, managed to scale the steep cliffs on its opposite bank.

It would seem very bad generalship on the part of Prince Menschikoff to have permitted them to establish themselves on the plateau, if we did not know now that it was part of his plan to allow a certain number of battalions to gain the edge of the cliffs, and then, relying on the bayonet, to send heavy masses of infantry against them and hurl them down into the Alma and the ravines which run towards its banks.

In spite of the enormous difficulties the French also managed to get their artillery on to the heights, from which they proceeded to enfilade the Russians.

On hearing the first guns of Bosquet's artillery, the French, in the centre and in the left, deployed and advanced, covered by a number of riflemen. The 1st Zouaves at once rushed to the front, driving before them a line of Russian riflemen and skirmishers placed among the orchard trees and rivers which skirted the deep banks of the Alma and availing themselves of the branches of these trees to swing themselves across the narrow stream into which others plunged up to the waist.

A furious battle followed, in which the Russians, partly through their bad generalship, partly owing to some 'happy chances' were eventually forced to retreat.

Marshal St Arnaud, riding up to the Generals, congratulated them on the day, and directed them to proceed to the aid of the English. Thanks be to the valour of our soldiers – thanks be to Heaven – we required no French aid that day. We received none, except that which was rendered by one battery of French artillery of the reserve which fired a few rounds on some broken Russian columns.

Such, in brief, was the French version of the part they had played. What of the British? It had been agreed between Lord Raglan and Marshal St Arnaud the night before that the French, forming the right wing, should advance at 5.30 a.m., the British, forming the left, at 6, and the French in the centre, half an hour later. Yet in spite of Lord Raglan's assurances the British did not begin to advance until ten o'clock.

The reason of the extraordinary delay in executing our plan of attack has never yet been explained. The distance between the Bouljanak and the Alma is barely six miles. Were we five hours marching six miles? That Lord Raglan was brave as a hero of antiquity, that he was kind to his friends and to his staff, that he was unmoved under fire, and unaffected by personal danger, that he was noble in manner, gracious in demeanour, of dignified bearing I am ready to admit; that he had many and great difficulties to contend with I believe; but that this brave and gallant nobleman had lost, if he ever possessed, the ability to conceive and execute large military plans – and that he had lost, if he ever possessed, the faculty of handling great bodies of men, I am firmly persuaded.

It was about ten o'clock ere the British line moved towards the Alma.

A gentle rise in the plain enabled us to see their position for some time after we moved, but the distance was too great for details. The order in which our army advanced was in columns of brigades, our left protected by a line of skirmishers, of cavalry, and of horse artillery. The advantage of the formation was that our army, in case of a strong attack from cavalry and infantry on the left or rear, could assume the form of a hollow square with the baggage in the centre.

Our line of march was in contact with the French left, under Prince Napoleon, it being understood that Sir de Lacy Evans's division on the extreme right should act in concert with that of the Prince, which was furthest from the sea. At the distance of two miles we halted to obtain a little time to gather up our rear, and then the troops steadily advanced in grand lines, like the waves of the ocean. The bright scarlet and red, with the white slashings of the breast of the coat and the cross belts, though rendering a man conspicuous enough, give him an appearance of size which other uniforms do not produce. The dark French columns on our right looked very small compared to our battalions, though we knew they were quite as strong; but the marching of our allies, laden as they were with all their packs, etc., was wonderful – the pace at which they went was really 'killing'. It was observable, too, that our staff was showy and more numerous than that of the French. Nothing in the shape of head-dress strikes the eye so much as a cocked hat and bunch of white cock's feathers, and several of our best officers very wisely doffed the latter adornment, thinking that they were quite conspicuous enough by their advanced positions on horseback and by the number of their staff around them. At this time I was riding in front, and when the regiments halted I went through the Light Division, part of the 2nd Division, the Guards and the Highlanders. I found all my friends, save one or two, in high spirits. Some had received letters from wives and children by the mail, which made them look grave and think seriously on the struggle to come. Others were joking and laughing in the best possible spirits. Many a laugh did I hear from lips which in two hours more were closed for ever. The officers and men made the most of this delay and ate whatever they had with them; but there was a great want of water, and the salt pork made them so thirsty that in the subsequent passage of the Alma, under the heaviest fire, the men stopped to drink and to fill their water canteens.

The plan of attack has been already described, as well as the circumstances of our early march. As we advanced, we could see the enemy very distinctly – their great-coated masses resembling patches of wood on the hill sides. The line of the river below the heights they occupied was indicated by patches of the richest verdure and by belts of fine fruit trees and vineyards. The Alma is a tortuous little stream, deepening its course as it proceeds seawards, at times too deep to be forded, though it can generally be crossed by waders who do not fear to wet their knees. The high banks vary from the right side to the left, according to the course of the stream. The drop from the edge to the water varies also from two to six or eight feet. Along the right or north bank there is a number of Tartar houses, at times numerous enough to form a cluster deserving the name of a hamlet. The bridge over which the post road passes from Bouljanak to Sebastopol runs close to one of these hamlets – a village, in fact, of some fifty houses. At the left or south side of the Alma the ground assumes a very different character – it rises at once from the water in steep banks up to plateaux at the top of varying height and extent. The general surface is pierced here and there by the course of the winter's torrents, which have formed small ravines, commanded by the heights above.

On the slope of the rising ground to their right of the bridge the Russians had erected two earthwork epaulements, mounted with 16-pounder brass guns, supported by numerous field-pieces and howitzers. On the right of this battery and further in the rear, the enemy had thrown up another breastwork to defend the gunners who were to work nine guns which played on their right of the bridge and swept the glacis leading up to it. To the left, on a low ridge in front of the village, they had placed two and a half field batteries, the first constructed on the side of a gentle hill about 300 yards distant from the river, the second turned more towards their right, and behind it again were three or four guns very near the top of the high ground in the rear. Such was the position, as far as we could see it, but we were at the time ignorant of the formation of the artillery, or of the site of the terrible batteries opposed to us. As I had slept at the headquarters camp, I joined the general staff and for some time rode with them. There was at the time very little to be seen and there were so many officers with Lord Raglan that it was difficult to see in front at all; so, observing Sir de Lacy Evans on higher ground about a quarter of a mile away, I turned my horse to join him. An instant afterwards a round shot rushed over the heads of the staff, being fired at the Rifles in advance of them. By the time I had reached Sir de Lacy the round shot were rolling through the columns, and the men halted and lay down by order of Lord Raglan. Sir de Lacy said, 'Well, if you want to see a great battle, you're in a fair way of having your wish gratified.' At this moment the whole of the village in our front burst into flames – the hayricks and wooden sheds about it causing the fire to run rapidly, fanned by a gentle breeze, which carried the smoke and sparks towards our line. Sir de Lacy rode towards the left to get rid of this annoyance, and to get to his men, and as he did so, the round shot came bounding among the men lying down just before us. From the groans and stifled cries, it was too plain they left dead and dying in their course.

The Rifles in advance of our left were sharply engaged with the enemy in the vineyard, and, anxious to see what was going on, I rode over in that direction, and arrived at the place where were stationed the staff of the Light Division. Sir George Brown was just at the time

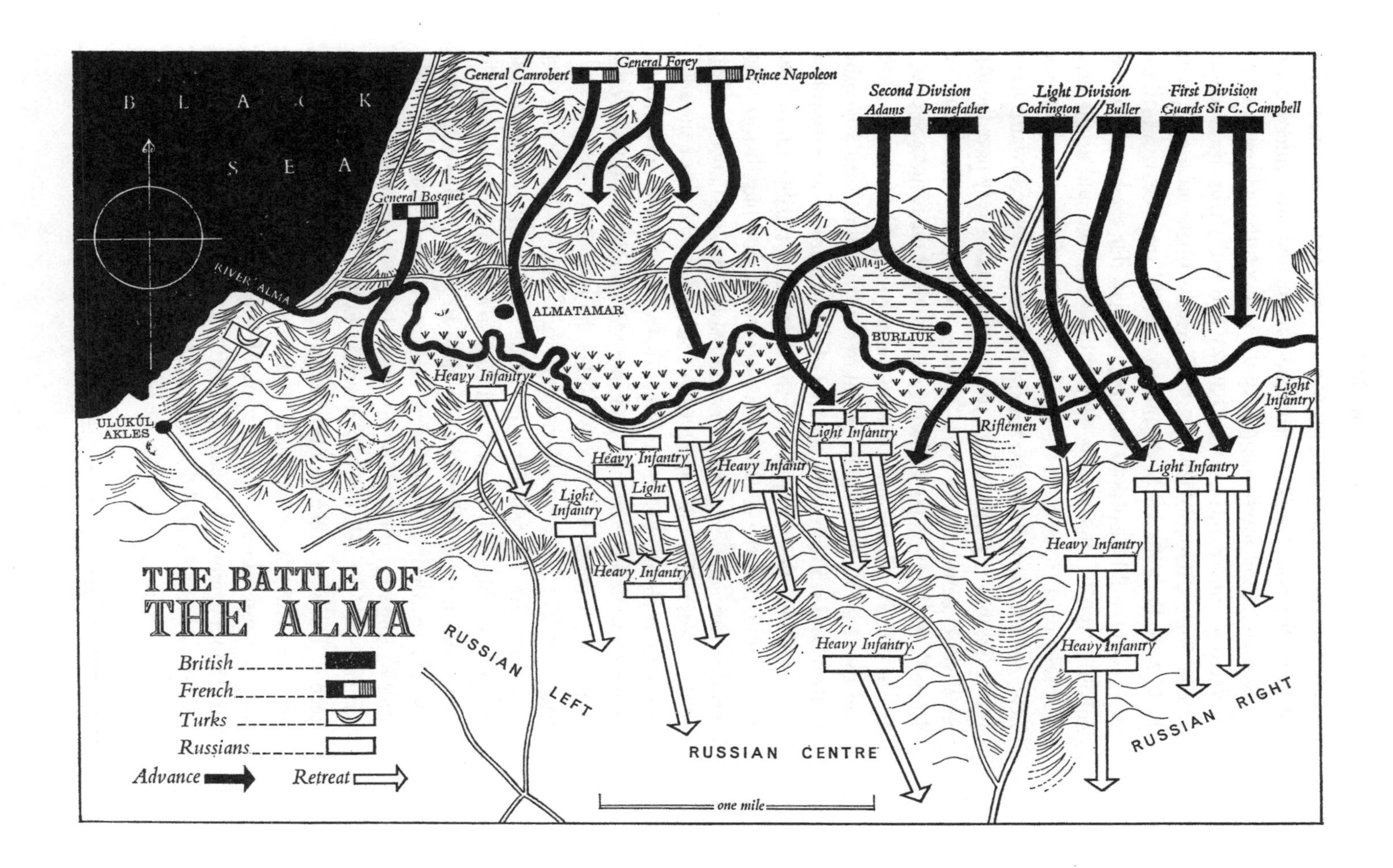
THE BATTLE OF
THE ALMA
British
French
Turks
Russians
Advance
Retreat
BLACK SEA
RIVER ALMA
ULÚKÚL AKLES
ALMATAMAR
BURLIUK
General Bosquet
General Canrobert
General Forey
Prince Napoleon
Second Division
Adams
Pennefather
Light Division
Codrington
Buller
First Division
Guards
Sir C. Campbell
Heavy Infantry
Light Infantry
Light
Riflemen
RUSSIAN LEFT
RUSSIAN CENTRE
RUSSIAN RIGHT
one mile

giving some orders to one of his Aides relative to the 'Russian cavalry on our left front'. I looked across the stream, and saw, indeed, some cavalry and guns slowly moving down towards the stream from the elevated ground over its banks; but my eye at the same time caught a most formidable-looking mass of burnished helmets, tipped with brass, just above the top of the hill on our left, at the other side of the river. One could see plainly through the glass that they were Russian infantry, but I believe the gallant old General thought at the time that they were cavalry. Sir George looked full of fight, clean-shaven, neat and compact; I could not help thinking, however, there was a little pleasant malice in his salutation to me. As he rode past, he said, in a very jaunty, Hyde Park manner, 'It's a very fine day, Mr Russell'. At this moment the whole of our right was almost obscured by the clouds of black smoke from the burning village on our right, and the front of the Russian line above us had burst into a volcano of flame and white smoke – the roar of the artillery became terrible – we could hear the heavy rush of the shot, those terrible dumps into the ground, and the crash of the trees, through which it tore with resistless fury and force; splinters and masses of stone flew out of the walls. It was rather provoking to be told so coolly it was a very fine day amid such circumstances; but at that very moment the men near us were ordered to advance, and they did so in quick time in open line towards the walls which bounded the vineyards before us. As I had no desire to lead my old friends of the Light Division into action, I rode towards the right to rejoin Sir de Lacy Evans, if possible; and as I got on the road, I saw Lord Raglan's staff riding towards the river, and the shot came flinging close to me, one, indeed, killing one of two bandsmen who were carrying a litter close to my side, after passing over the head of my horse. It knocked away the side of his face, and he fell dead – a horrible sight. The batteries of the Second Division were unlimbered in front, and were firing with great steadiness on the Russians; and now and then a rocket, with a fiery tail and a huge waving mane of white smoke, rushed with a shrill shout against the enemy's massive batteries. Before me all was smoke – our men were lying down still; but the Rifles, led by Major Norcott, conspicuous on a black horse, were driving back the enemy's sharp-shooters with signal gallantry, and clearing the orchards and vineyards in our front by a searching fire.

My position was becoming awkward. Far away in the rear was the baggage, from which one could see nothing; but where I was placed was very much exposed. A shell burst over my head, and one of the fragments tore past my face with an angry whir-r-r, and knocked up the earth at my poor pony's feet. Close at hand, and before me, was a tolerably good stone-house, one storey high, with a large court-yard, in which were several stacks of hay that had not as yet caught fire. I rode into this yard, fastened up my pony to the rope binding one of the ricks, and entered the house, which was filled with fragments of furniture, torn paper, and books, and feathers, and cushion linings, and established myself at the window, from which I could see the Russian artillerymen serving their guns, their figures, now distinctly revealed against the hill side, and again lost in a spurting whirl of smoke. I was thinking what a terrible sort of field-day this was, and combating an uneasy longing to get to the front, when a tremendous crash, as though a thunderclap had burst over my head, took place right above me, and in the same instant I was struck and covered with pieces of broken tiles, mortar and stones, the window out of which I was looking flew into pieces, parts of the roof fell down, and the room was filled with smoke.

There was no mistaking this warning to quit. A shell had burst in the ceiling. As I ran out into the yard I found my pony had broken loose, but I easily caught him, and scarcely had I mounted when I heard a tremendous roll of musketry on my left front, and looking in the direction, I saw the lines of our red jackets in the stream, and swarming over the wooden bridge. A mass of Russians were at the other side of the stream, firing down on them from the high banks, but the advance of the men across the bridge forced these battalions to retire; and I saw, with feelings which I cannot express, the Light Division, scrambling, rushing, foaming like a bloody surge up the ascent, and in a storm of fire, bright steel, and whirling smoke, charge towards the deadly epaulement, from which came roar and flash incessantly. I could distinctly see Sir George Brown and the several mounted officers above the heads of the men, and could detect the dark uniforms of the Rifles scattered here and there in front of the waving mass. The rush of shot was appalling and I recollect that I was particularly annoyed by the birds, which were flying about distractedly in the smoke, as I thought they were fragments of shell. Already the wounded were passing by me. One man limped along with his foot dangling from the ankle, supporting himself on his firelock. 'Thank you kindly, sir,' said he, as I gave him a little brandy, the only drop I had left. 'Glory be to God, I killed and wounded some of the Russians before they crippled me. anyway.' He halted off towards the rear. In another moment two officers approached – one leaning on the other – and both wounded, as I feared, severely. They went into the enclosure I had left, and having assured them I would bring them help, I rode off towards the rear and returned with the surgeon of the Cavalry Division, who examined their wounds.

All this time the roar of the battle was increasing. I went back to my old spot; in doing so I had to ride gently, for wounded men came along in all directions. One was cut in two by a round shot as he approached. Many of them lay down under the shelter of a wall, which was, however, enfiladed by the enemy. Just at this moment I saw the Guards advancing in the most majestic and stately order up the hill, while through the intervals and at their flanks poured the broken masses of the Light Division, which their officers were busy in re-forming. The Highlanders who were beyond them I could not see; but I never will forget the awful fury, the powerful detonation of the tremendous volleys which Guards and Highlanders poured in upon the Russian battalions, which in vain tried to defend their batteries and to check the onward march of that tide of victory. All of a sudden the round shot ceased to fly along the lane; then there was a sharp roll of musketry and a heavy fire of artillery which lasted for some moments. Then one, two, three round shot pitched into the line, ricochetting away to the rear. As I looked round to see what mischief they did, I saw a British regiment rapidly advancing towards the river. I at once rode towards them. 'Colonel,' said I, 'the cannon shot come right down this way, and you'll suffer frightfully if you go on.' As I spoke, a shell knocked up the dust about twenty yards to our right, and the Colonel who was burning to take a part in the honours of the day, pushing on the left, led his men across the river.

The approach of the Light Division – why should I not dwell fondly on every act of that gallant body, the first 'put at' everything throughout the campaign? – was in double columns of brigades. Their course was marked by killed and wounded, for the Russians poured down a heavy vertical fire on our straggling lines. They were straggling, but not weak; the whole Brigade, at a word from their officers, made a simultaneous rush up the bank and as they crowned it, met their enemies with a furious and close fire of their deadly rifles. The dense battalions were smitten deeply and as the Light Division advanced to meet them, they rapidly fell back to the left, leaving many dead and wounded men close to the river's banks. After a momentary delay, these gallant regiments, led by Brigadier Codrington and Sir George Brown, advanced up the slope which was swept by the guns of the entrenched battery.

Grape, canister, round and shell tore through their ranks, and the infantry on the flanks of the battery advancing at an angle to it, poured in a steady fire upon them from point-blank distance. It must be confessed that this advance was very disorderly – the men had not only got into confusion in the river from stopping to drink, but had disordered their ranks by attacks on the grapes in the vineyards on their way. Every foot they advanced was marked by lines of slain or wounded men. The 7th Fusileers, smitten by a storm of grape, reeling to and fro like some brave ship battling with a tempest, but which still holds on its desperate way, within a few seconds lost a third of its men. It still went on – a colour lost for the time, their officers down, their files falling fast – they closed up, and still with eye which never left the foe, pressed on to meet him. The 23rd Regiment was, however, exposed more, if that were possible, to that lethal hail. In less than two minutes from the time they crowned the bank till they neared the battery, the storm had smitten down twelve of their officers, of whom eight never rose again. The 19th marched right up towards the mouths of the roaring cannon which swept down their ranks; the 33rd, which had moved up with the greatest audacity over broken ground towards the flank of the epaulement, was for the moment checked by the pitiless pelting of this iron rain. Their general seemed to have but one idea—to lead them slap at the battery, into the very teeth of its hot and fiery jaws. As he rode in front, cheering on his men, his horse fell, and down he went in a cloud of dust. He was soon up, and called out, 'I'm all right. Twenty-third, be sure I'll remember this day.' When Sir George Brown went down, a rifleman assisted him on his horse again, and with the greatest coolness, as they stood under a murderous fire, saluted the General as he got once more into his seat, and said, 'Are your stirrups the right length, sir?'

And so the battle went on until well into the afternoon, when the Russians, in spite of their huge superiority in numbers, were forced to begin withdrawing their artillery.

But the enemy had not yet abandoned their position. An enormous division of infantry, consisting of several battalions, came in sight from the rear of the hill, and marched straight upon the Brigade of Guards, which it exceeded in numbers by three to one. The Guards advanced to meet them in perfect order. Some round shot struck the rear of the Russian columns, and immediately they began to melt away from the rear, and wavered for an instant; still they came on slowly, and began file-firing from their fronts instead of charging, as their officers evidently intended them to do. The distance between them was rapidly diminishing, when suddenly the whole Brigade poured in on their dense masses a fire so destructive that it annihilated the whole of their front ranks in an instant, and left a ridge of killed and wounded men on the ground. The enemy, after a vain attempt to shake off the panic and disorder occasioned by that rain of death, renewed their fire very feebly for a few seconds, and then without waiting for a repetition of our reply, turned as our men advanced with bayonets at the charge, retreated over the brow of the hill, and marched off to join the mass of the Russian army, who were retreating with all possible speed. Our cavalry rode up to the crest of the hill and looked after the enemy. They even took a few prisoners, but they were ordered to let them go again. Lord Raglan had expressed his intention of keeping his cavalry 'in a bandbox', and he was apprehensive of getting into any serious difficulty with the enemy at the close of such a day. It was near five o'clock; the Battle of the Alma was won. The men halted on the battlefield, and as the Commander-in-Chief, the Duke of Cambridge, Sir de Lacy Evans, and the other popular generals rode in front of the line, the soldiers shouted, and when Lord Raglan was in front of the Guards, the whole army burst into a tremendous cheer, which made one's heart leap – the effect of that cheer can never be forgotten by those who heard it.

This summary of the fighting by French and British troops is followed in Russell's original account by a detailed description of the engagement based on Russian reports. He then continues:

The Russian dead were all buried together in pits, and were carried down to their graves as they lay. Our parties buried 1,200 men. The British soldiers who fell were buried in pits in the same way. Their firelocks and the useful portions of their military equipment were alone preserved. It was a sad sight to see the litters borne in from all quarters hour after hour – to watch the working parties as they wandered about the plain turning down the blankets which had been stretched over the wounded, to behold if they were yet alive, or were food for the worms, and then adding many a habitant to the yawning pits which lay with insatiable mouths gaping on the hill side – or covering up the poor sufferers destined to pass another night of indescribable agony. The thirst of the wounded seemed intolerable, and our men – all honour to the noble fellows – went about relieving the wants of the miserable creatures as far as they could.

The quantity of firelocks, of greatcoats, of bearskin caps, of shakos, of Russian helmets and flat forage caps, of knapsacks, of cross and sling belts, bayonets, cartouch-boxes, cartridges, swords, lying all over the hills, exceeded all computation; and round shot, fragments of shell smeared with blood and hair, grape-shot, Minié balls and bullets, were under the foot and eye at every step. Our men broke all the enemies' firelocks and rifles which lay on the ground. As many of them were loaded, the concussion set them off and balls were singing through the air in all directions, so that dropping shot never ceased for about forty hours. The men were also busy cleaning out the firelocks which got choked or would not go off during the fight and kept up a constant discharge all over the country. The Russian musket was a good weapon to look at, but must be rather a bad one to use. The barrel, which was longer than ours, and was kept polished, was made of iron and was secured to the stock by brass straps, like the French. The lock was, however, tolerably good. The stock was of the old narrow Oriental pattern, and the wood of which it was made – white-grained and something like sycamore, broke easily. From the form of the heel of the stock, the 'kick' of the musket must have been sharp with a good charge. The bayonets were soft and bent easily. Some good swords belonging to officers were picked up, and very effective weapons, probably belonging to drummers or bandsmen, exactly like the old Roman sword, very sharp and heavy, were also left on the field. No ensign, eagle, standard, or colour of any kind was displayed by the enemy or found on the field. Our regiments marched with their colours, as a matter of course, and the enemy made the latter a special mark for the rifles. Thus it was so many ensigns, lieutenants and sergeants fell.

The sad duty of burying the dead was completed on the 22nd. The wounded were collected and sent on board ship in arabas and litters, and the surgeons with humane barbarity were employed night and day in saving life.

There was more than an acre of Russian wounded when they were brought and disposed on the ground. Our men were sent to the sea three miles distant on jolting arabas or tedious litters. The French had well-appointed covered hospital vans to hold ten or twelve men, drawn by mules, and their wounded were sent in much greater comfort than our poor fellows. Not only the wounded but the sick were sent on board the fleet, the Russian officers who were wounded, and all prisoners of rank likewise. We had 1,000 sick on board, in addition to our wounded. The French return of 1,400 killed and wounded was understood to include those who died of cholera during the passage from Varna and the march to the Alma.

Many men died of cholera in the night. My sleep was disturbed by the groans of the dying, and on getting up in the morning I found the corpse of a Russian outside the tent in which I had been permitted to rest. He was not there when we retired, so that the wretched creature, who had probably been wandering about without food upon the hills ever since the battle, must have crawled down towards our fires and there expired in the attempt to reach them: several men died in a similar way close to the tent.

Late at night on the 22nd, orders were sent round the divisions to be prepared for marching after daybreak, and early on the 23rd, we left the bloodstained heights of the Alma – a name that will be ever memorable in history.

7

The Flank March

SOON AFTER DAWN THE FRENCH ASSEMBLED ALL THEIR drums and trumpets on the top of the highest of the hills they carried, and a wild flourish and roll, repeated again and again, and broken by peals of rejoicing from the bugles of the infantry, celebrated their victory ere they departed in search of the enemy. It was spirit-stirring and thrilling music and its effect as it swelled through the darkness of early morning down over the valley can never be forgotten.

Our watch-fires were still burning languidly as the sleepers roused themselves, all wet with dew, and prepared to leave the scene of their triumphs. The fogs of the night crept slowly up the hillsides and hung in uncertain folds around their summits, revealing here and there the gathering columns of our regiments in dark patches on the declivities, or showing the deep black-looking squares of the French battalions, already in motion towards the south. Dimly seen in the distance, the fleet was moving along slowly by the line of the coast, the long lines of smoke trailing back on their wake. But what was that grey mass on the plain, which seemed settled down upon it almost without life or motion? Now and then, indeed, an arm might be seen waved aloft, or a man raised himself for a moment, looked around, and then fell down again. Alas! that plain was covered with wounded Russians. Nearly sixty long hours they passed in agony upon the ground, and with but little hope of help or succour; we were compelled to leave them. Seven hundred and fifty wounded men, and we could do nothing for them. Their wounds had been bound and dressed, we had done all we could do for them, and were obliged to depart.

Ere our troops marched, however, General Estcourt[1], by order of Lord Raglan, sent into the Tartar village up the valley, into which the inhabitants were just returning, and having procured the attendance of the head men, he proceeded to explain to them that the wounded Russians would be confided to their charge, and that they were to feed and maintain them, and when they were well they were to be let go their ways. In order to look after their wounds, an English surgeon was left behind with these seven hundred and fifty men. This most painful and desolate duty devolved on Dr Thomson, of the 44th regiment. He was told his mission would be his protection in case the Cossacks came, and that he was to hoist a flag of truce should the enemy appear in sight, and then, provided with some rum, biscuit and salt meat, he was left alone with his charge, attended only by a single servant. Ere the army went, however, one of the Russian officers addressed the wounded, and explained the position in which they were placed, and they promised to obey Dr Thomson's orders, to protect him as far as they could, and to acquaint any Russian force which might arrive with the peculiar circumstances under which he was among them.

It was nearly eight o'clock ere the tents of headquarters were struck, and the march began. As we moved along, the unfinished stone building around which some of the most violent fighting had occurred between the French and the Russians, intended for a telegraph station, came into view. The French had cut upon the entablature the simple inscription – *La Bataille d'Alma, 20 Septembre, 1854*.

The country through which we marched was hilly and barren. Amidst steep hillocks covered with thistles, and separated from each other at times by small patches of steppe, wound the road to Sebastopol – a mere beaten track marked with cart-wheels, hoofs, and gun-carriage wheels. We advanced uninterruptedly at an average rate of two and a quarter miles an hour, halting occasionally to rest the troops and allow the baggage-waggons to come up.

[1] Adjutant-General of the Army.

At three o'clock the beautiful valley of the Katcha came in sight, its opposite side formed by a ridge of hills clad with verdure and small forests of shrubs, through which here and there shone the white walls of villas and snug cottages. The country over which we marched slid down, as it were, gradually to the level of the river, whose course was marked all along the base of the hills to the stream by lines of trees, and by the most luxuriant vegetation, forming a strong contrast to the barren and bleak-looking tract on which our troops advanced. Lord Raglan and his staff rode on considerably in advance of the troops, to the great astonishment and indignation of a Prussian officer who loudly declared such conduct was quite opposed to the rules of war. Fluellen himself could not have been more angry at such disregard of martial etiquette than the gallant gentleman in question, and certainly we did show marked contempt for the enemy, till Captain Chetwode and his troop of the 8th Hussars pushed on in the front to reconnoitre. However, there was not a trace of the enemy, except that which we found soon afterwards in the houses.

The Katcha is a small and rapid rivulet with banks like those of the Alma. We found its whole course was marked by neat white cottages, and that it watered the most delicious vineyards and gardens, amid which habitations were placed, but no inhabitants were visible. Wheeling over the bridge, we turned eastward towards the little village of Eskel, on the left-bank. The first building on the road was the Imperial Post-house, with its sign-post of the double-headed eagle, and an illegible inscription. The usual wooden direction-post, with a black and red riband painted round it diagonally on a white ground, informed us we were on our way to Sebastopol, distant about ten miles. The place was abandoned, and the house destitute of the smallest particle of furniture. The road now assumed the character of an English by-way in Devonshire or Hampshire. Low walls at either side were surmounted by fruit trees laden with apples, pears, peaches and apricots, all ripe and fit for use, and at their foot clustered grapes of the most delicate flavour.

The first villa we came to was the residence of a physician or country surgeon. It had been ruthlessly destroyed by the Cossacks.

A verandah laden with clematis, roses and honeysuckle in front, was filled with broken music-stools, work-tables and lounging chairs. All the glasses of the windows were smashed. Everything around betokened the hasty flight of the inmates. Two or three side-saddles were lying on the grass outside the hall-door; a parasol lay near them, close to a Tartar saddle and a huge whip. The wine casks were broken and the contents spilt; the barley and corn of the granary were thrown about all over the ground; broken china and glass of fine manufacture were scattered over the pavement outside the kitchen – and amid all the desolation and ruin of the place, a cat sat blandly at the threshold, winking her eyes in the sunshine at the new comers.

No pen can describe the scene within. Mirrors in fragments were lying on the floor; the beds had been ripped open and the feathers littered the rooms a foot deep; chairs, sofas, fauteuils, bedsteads, book-cases, picture-frames, images of saints, women's needlework, chests of drawers, shoes, boots, books, bottles, physic jars, all smashed or torn in pieces, lay in heaps in every room. Even the walls and doors were hacked with swords. The physician's account-book lay open on a broken table: he had been stopped in the very act of debiting a dose to some neighbour, and his entry remained unfinished. Beside his account-book lay a volume of *Madame de Sévigné's Lettres* in French, and a pharmacopoeia in Russian. A little bottle of prussic acid lay so invitingly near a box of bon-bons that I knew it would be irresistible to the first hungry private who had a taste for almonds, and I accordingly poured out the contents to prevent the possible catastrophe. Our men and horses were soon revelling in grapes and corn; and we pushed on to Eskel and established ourselves in a house which had belonged to a Russian officer of rank – at least, many traces of the presence of one were visible.

Every house and villa in the place was a similar scene. The better the class of the residence, the more complete and pitiable the destruction. Grand pianos and handsome pieces of furniture covered with silk and damasked velvet rent to pieces with brutal violence, were found in more than one house; but one of the instruments retained enough of its vital organs to breathe out 'God save the Queen' from its lacerated brass ribs, and it was made to do so accordingly – ay, under the very eye of a rigid portrait of his Imperial Majesty the Czar, which hung on the wall above! These portraits of the autocrat were not uncommon in the houses – nearly as common as pictures of saints with gilt and silver glories around their heads. The houses, large and small, consisted of one story only and magnitude was gained by lateral extension. Each house stood apart, with a large patch of vineyard around it, and a garden of fruit trees, and was fenced in from the road by a stone wall and a line of poplars or elms. A porch, covered with vines, protected the entrance. The rooms were clean and scrupulously white-washed.

On our march a deserter came in and was taken before Lord Raglan. He was, however, only a Tartar, but he gave such information respecting the feelings of the inhabitants towards us that steps were at once taken to inform those who were hiding that if they returned to their homes their lives and property would be protected. Some hour or so after we had arrived at Eskel, a number of bullet-headed personages, with sheepskin caps and loose long coats and trousers made their appearance, stealthily creeping into the houses and eyeing the new occupants with shy curiosity. From the people who thus returned, we heard that the Russians had arrived at the Katscha in rather a fatigued and dispirited condition, the night of the battle of Alma, and had taken up their position in the villages and in the neighbouring houses. At twelve o'clock the same night they continued their march. A part of the army went towards Bakschiserai. They were said to consist of about 20,000, and to be under the command of Menschikoff in person. The rest proceeded direct to Sebastopol, and entered the city in some disorder. The evidences of their march were found along the road, in cartridges, shakos, caps, and articles of worn-out clothing. In the house which we occupied were abundant traces of the recent visit of a military man of rank: books on strategy, in Russian, lay on the floor, and a pair of handsome epaulets were found in the passage.

Throughout the night of September 23rd the allied armies remained encamped on the Katscha. Reinforcements having been landed at the mouth of the river during the night, the march was resumed shortly before noon the next day. Reconnaissance had shown that strong enemy batteries had been posted north-west of Sebastopol harbour.

It occurred to Sir John Burgoyne that, by a flank movement performed with energy and decision on Balaklava, we should turn and neutralize the effect of these batteries, secure a new base of operations (of which we were in want, having abandoned that of the Katscha) and completely distract the enemy, who would find the weakest part of Sebastopol exposed to the fire of our batteries and our attacks directed against a point where they had least reason to expect it. The whole army accordingly marched towards the south-east, on the Black [Tchernaya] River, and as they were obliged to pass through thickly-wooded country, intersected by narrow lanes winding up and down the hills, the troops were necessarily in some disorder, and had the enemy possessed the smallest enterprise they might have inflicted severe loss upon us and caused great annoyance by a spirited attack on our flank whilst we were rounding the head of the harbour.

On the day of our march from the Katscha I was struck down by fever, fell from my pony into the stream where he was drinking, and was placed by one of the staff surgeons in a jolting araba carrying a part of the baggage of the Light Division. I saw but little that day except the march of men and the fine country around us. The armies marched close together; the sun was exceedingly powerful, and when from the top of a wooded hill we saw the delicious valley of the Belbek studded with little snow-white cottages, with stately villas, with cosy snug-looking hamlets buried in trees, and fringed with a continuous line of the most gloriously green vineyards and the noblest orchards of fruit-trees, there was an exclamation, a murmur of delight throughout the whole army, which, precipitating itself like a torrent down the steep slopes of the hill-sides, soon swarmed in every garden, and clustered in destructive swarms around every bush. Their halt was, however, a short one.

The word was given to push over the stream, and its bright waters were soon defiled by the tramp of many feet. Just as the araba in which I lay was passing by a beautiful little chateau, said to belong to a Russian general, I saw a stream of soldiers issue from it, laden with the most incongruous, but at the same time the richest, spoils which a man of taste and wealth could abandon to an enemy: others were engaged inside in smashing the house to atoms, breaking the glasses, throwing mirrors, pictures and furniture out of the open frames. Shocked by such wanton outrage I inquired the cause and learned from an officer who was standing by that the soldiers had not done the smallest mischief till they saw an English staff officer of rank take a bronze statuette out of the house and ride away with it, whereupon the cry arose, 'Let us plunder too, if our officer sets the example'. I could not help thinking what would have been the fate of that officer if he had served under our great Duke.

At the other side of the narrow valley of the Belbek, the hill-sides are exceedingly steep and covered with dwarf wood and undergrowth. It was with difficulty the men crept up to the summit, and the waggons were urged up the rugged and narrow paths. Lord Raglan occupied one of the plundered villas, near the only bridge the Russians had left across the stream. Marshal St Arnaud encamped on the top of the southern ridge. There was very great confusion in getting the men into their places on this wooded and steep ridge of hills intersected with ravines and it was long after sunset ere the men finally settled down at their bivouac fires.

After a night disturbed by an outbreak of abortive firing by the enemy, and in which more men were seized with cholera, the armies were ready to move early next morning. At seven o'clock Lord Raglan and his staff conferred with Marshal St Arnaud. It was noticeable that the Marshal was very unwell, but he insisted on carrying on.

At the conferences, the French proposed to force the Inkerman bridge across the Tchernaya and to make a push at the town. Sir John Burgoyne proposed that we should cross the stream by the bridge, at a place called Traktir, near Tchorgun, and by his representations carried the majority of those present with him, as he adduced strong reasons for seizing Balaklava, Kamiesch, and Kazatch, which were as much appreciated by our allies as by the English.

It was therefore decided that the armies should continue their march on the ridge between the Belbek and the Tchernaya.

Our march was continuous, but by different routes, the artillery proceeding by a difficult road, which allowed only one horseman to ride by the side of each gun. The Duke of Cambridge's baggage was actually within gunshot of Sebastopol for a quarter of an hour. As Lord Raglan was riding on in front of his staff he found himself, on emerging from a wooded road on the open space in front, in the immediate presence of a body of Russian infantry, which turned out to be the baggage guard of a large detachment of the Russian army marching from Sebastopol to Bakschiserai. They were not more than a few hundred yards distant. Lord Raglan simply turned his horse, and accelerating his pace, he and his staff quietly cantered back to the rear of the first division of Artillery. The cavalry were quickly got in front – the guns were unlimbered and opened on the retreating mass of Russians; the 2nd battalion of Rifles in skirmishing order threw in a volley of Minié balls, the cavalry executed a charge, and the result was that after a few rounds the Russians broke and fled along the road in great haste, leaving behind them an enormous quantity of baggage of every description for two miles strewed over the ground in the direction of their flight.

This was fair and legitimate plunder and the troops were halted and allowed to take what they liked. They broke open all the carts and tumbled out the contents on the road, but the pillage was conducted with regularity and the officers presided over it to see that there was no squabbling and that no man took more than his share. Immense quantities of wearing apparel, of boots, shirts, coats, dressing cases, valuable ornaments and some jewellery were found in the baggage carts, as well as a military chest containing some money (there are people who say it held £3,000). A Russian artillery officer was found in one of the carriages in a very jovial mood and had evidently been making rather free with the bottle. Plenty of champagne was discovered among the baggage and served to cheer the captors during their cold bivouac that night. A great number of very handsome hussar jackets richly laced with silver and made of fine light-blue cloth, which had never yet been worn, were also taken and sold by the soldiers for sums varying from 20s. to 30s. a-piece. Fine large winter cloaks of cloth lined with rich furs were found in abundance. The enemy were pursued two or three miles on the road to Bakschiserai, but they fled so precipitately the cavalry could not come up with them.

This plunder put the soldiers in great good humour, and they marched on the whole day in excellent spirits, leaving Sebastopol on their right, till they arrived at the little hamlet of Traktir, on the Tchernaya river, just before sunset and halted for the night. As the baggage was separated from the bulk of the army by the distance of some miles, Lord Raglan was fain to put up in a miserable little lodge for the night, while the bulk of his staff slept on the ground in a ditch outside it. Not the smallest attempt was made by the enemy to interrupt or annoy us during this very remarkable march, which could at any time have been greatly harassed by the least activity on the part of the Russians. Our march was through woods, along bad and often precipitous roads, and a few trees felled at intervals would have sufficed to stop the army for hours. Continuing our advance early next morning, we crossed the Tchernaya, and proceeded across the plains to Balaklava.

8

Digging in

I NEVER WAS MORE ASTONISHED IN MY LIFE THAN WHEN on the morning of Tuesday September 26th I halted on the top of one of the numerous hills of which this portion of the Crimea is composed, and looking down saw under my feet a little pond, closely compressed by the sides of high rocky mountains; on it floated some six or seven English ships, for which exit seemed quite hopeless. The bay is like a highland tarn, some half mile in length from the sea, and varies from 250 to 120 yards in breadth. The shores are so steep and precipitous that they shut out as it were the expanse of the harbour, and made it appear much smaller than it really is. Towards the sea the cliffs close up and completely overlap the narrow channel which leads to the haven, so that it is quite invisible. On the south-east of the poor village, which struggles for existence between the base of the rocky hills and the margin of the sea, are the extensive ruins of a Genoese fort, built some 200 feet above the level of the sea. It must have once been a large and important position, and its curtains, bastions, towers, and walls, all destroyed and crumbling in decay though they are, evince the spirit and enterprise of the hardy seamen who penetrated these classic recesses so long ago.

The staff advanced first on the town, and were proceeding to enter it, when, to their surprise, from the old forts above came four spirts of smoke in rapid succession, and down came four shells into the ground close to them. The dose of shell was repeated, but by this time the 'Agamemnon', outside the rocks, was heard busily sending her shot against the fort. The Rifles and some of the Light Division opened fire, and the fort hung out a flag of truce. The colonel or commandant had only sixty men under him and they were all made prisoners. On being asked why he fired from a position which he must have known to be untenable he replied that he did so in order that he might be summoned, and that he felt bound to fire till required to surrender.

Lord Raglan entered about twelve o'clock in the day. As he approached the principal street the inhabitants came out to meet him, bearing trays laden with fruit and flowers. Some of them bore loaves of bread cut up in pieces and placed on dishes covered with salt, in token of good will and submission. The fleet and army were thus once more united, and Lord Raglan had secured his base of operations. Towards evening the 'Agamemnon' glided in between the rocks in the narrow harbour, and anchored opposite the house of the General, whom Sir E. Lyons speedily visited.

Our cavalry in the afternoon took Mr Upton, son of the English engineer who constructed so many useful works at Sebastopol. He was captured on his farm, and was taken before Lord Raglan, but at first he refused in the most decisive way to give any information respecting the Russians, as he said he could not reconcile it to his notions of honour to injure a Government in whose military service he had been, and it was only on the representations made to him of the penalties incurred by an English subject in refusing to aid his countrymen in war that he was induced to give some particulars respecting the town, it being also understood that he would receive compensation for any losses he might incur at the hands of the enemy.

The town is a poor fishing village, inhabited by a Greek colony. There were, however, at the period of our arrival, one or two good houses of the usual character in the neighbourhood, and we found very seasonable stores of hay in the farmyards. All the hills around were barren rock; towards the land they became more fertile, and for a mile towards Sebastopol and Simpheropol were studded with pleasant-looking white villas and farm-houses, principally inhabited by Russian officials from Sebastopol. The city was quite visible below us. Across the north of the harbour, near the most easterly of the creeks, was placed a two-decker, painted so as to look like a three-decker, with her broadside turned towards our position. On the northern side a large circular work, with three tiers of guns – Fort Constantine – was visible, and more inland there was another large fortification, called the Star Fort. On the near side was a very large fortification, with curtains, running inland, a semi-circular bastion, and some rudimentary earthworks – all outside, the town. Lord Raglan and staff rode out and made a reconnaissance.

As frequent references are made hereafter to the various strong-points in Sebastopol's land defence system, it may be as well to give an outline of the arrangement of the system. The perimeter of the defence area, which was shaped something like a blunt and irregular arrow-head, extended for about five miles. Along the greater part of its length – that is to say, where it was not protected by the natural formation of the land – there was a chain of forts joined together by ramparts or 'curtains'. These forts were situated at various points on the perimeter and in between were a number of lesser fortifications and gun batteries. At the north-east extremity of the chain, overlooking the entrance to Sebastopol harbour, was the Artillery Fort. Next came the Quarantine Bastion, then the Central Bastion, and at the tip of the arrow-head, as it were, the Flagstaff Bastion, or Bastion du Mât (Russell sometimes calls it by one name, sometimes by the other). Further eastward was the Redan, and then the most powerful fort of all, the Malakoff; about 300 yards south-east of the Malakoff, outside the perimeter, was a small fortified hill known as the Mamelon. The next fort beyond the Malakoff was the Little Redan, and at the north-east end of the perimeter was the Battery of the Point.

The Allies were disposed round the perimeter in a vast semi-circle some seven or eight miles in extent, the western sector being occupied by the French, with their left flank and rear resting on the Black Sea, the eastern sector by the British, whose right flank and rear were protected by a range of rugged hills. In the rear and at the eastern end of the French position the Turks occupied a high irregular ridge, about a mile long. Part of the western sector and most of the eastern sector was traversed by deep, tortuous ravines which added considerably to the Allies' operational difficulties.

Within three days of the army's arrival at Balaklava the siege-train, which had been brought round from Eupatoria by boat, had been landed and all the heavy guns were in position. The French had landed their guns at Kamiesch and Khagatel on the north-west coast of the peninsula.

On September 29th, Marshal St Arnaud, who had been obliged to resign his command to General Canrobert on the march, was carried from his quarters in Balaklava on board the 'Berthollet' in a dying state, and expired at sea ere she reached the Bosphorus.

On October 1st there was a general rest throughout the army. The enemy the whole of that day amused themselves firing shot and shell over the heads of our artillery, and General Cathcart was obliged to move his quarters, as the Russians found out his range and made beautiful practice at them. However, he left his flagstaff, which seemed of much attraction to them, in the same place, and they continued to hammer away at it as usual.

We heard strange things from the deserters who now began to join us. They said that thirty Russian ladies went out of Sebastopol to see the battle of the Alma, as though they were going to a play or a picnic. They were quite assured of the success of the Russian troops and great was their alarm and dismay when they found themselves obliged to leave the telegraph house on the hill, and to fly for their lives in their carriages. There is no doubt but that our enemies were perfectly confident of victory.

During the first three weeks of our stay in the Crimea we lost as many of cholera as perished on the Alma. The town was in a filthy, revolting state. Lord Raglan ordered it to be cleansed, but there was no one to obey the order, and consequently no one attended to it.

Lord Raglan and staff moved from the town and established headquarters in a snug farm-house, surrounded by vineyards and extensive out-offices, about four and a half miles from Balaklava, on October 5th. From the rising ground, about a mile and a half distant from headquarters, in front, the town of Sebastopol was plainly visible. The Russians were occupied throwing up works and fortifying the exposed portions of the town with the greatest energy.

The investment of the place on the south side was, as far as possible, during the night of the 7th, completed. Our lines were to be pushed

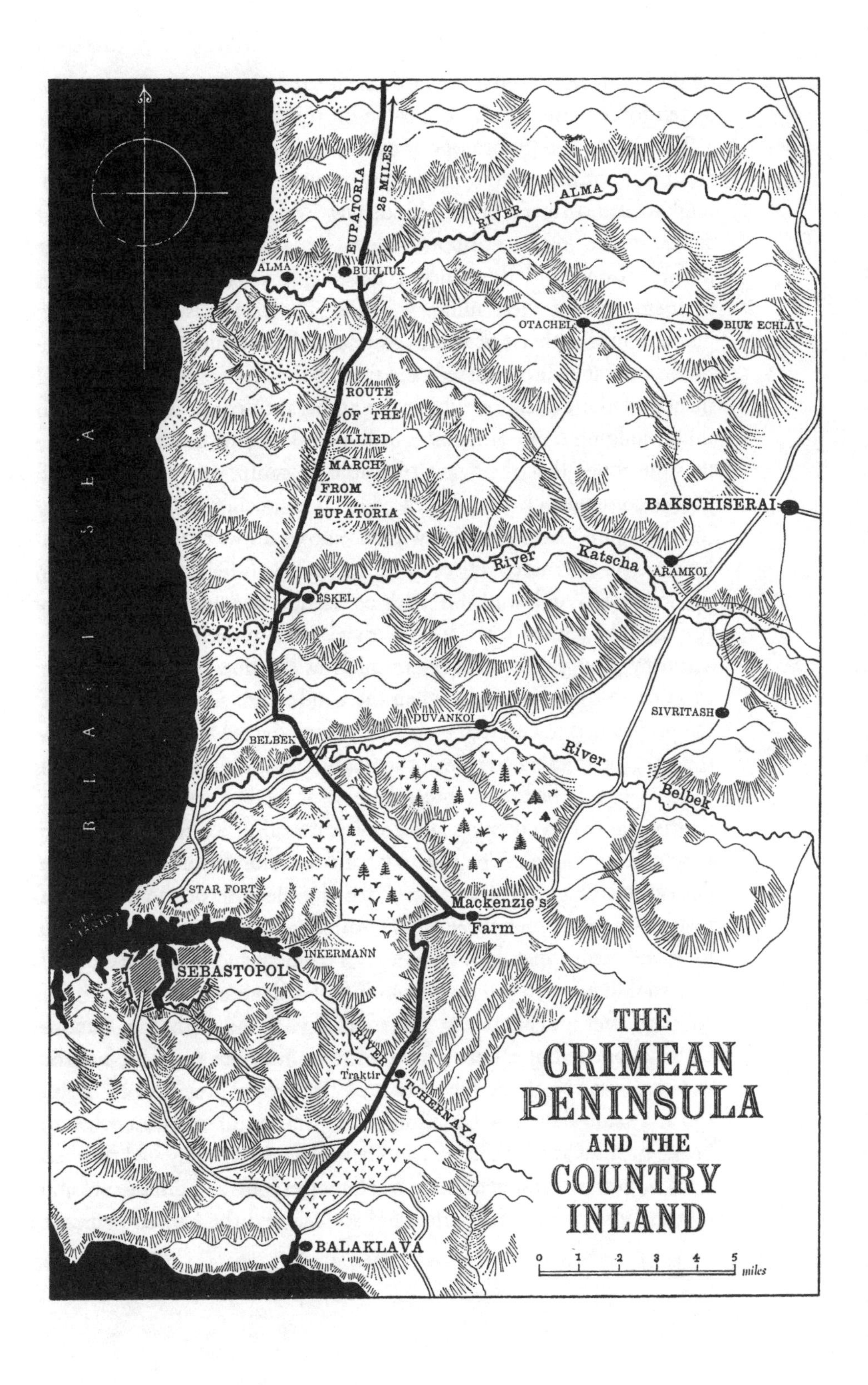
THE
CRIMEAN
PENINSULA
AND THE
COUNTRY
INLAND
BLACK SEA
EUPATORIA
25 MILES
RIVER ALMA
ALMA
BURLIUK
OTACHEL
BIUK ECHLAV
ROUTE
OF THE
ALLIED
MARCH
FROM
EUPATORIA
BAKSCHISERAI
River Katscha
ARAMKOI
ESKEL
SIVRITASH
DUVANKOI
BELBEK
River
Belbek
STAR FORT
Mackenzie's
Farm
INKERMANN
SEBASTOPOL
RIVER
Traktir
TCHERNAYA
BALAKLAVA
0 1 2 3 4 5
miles

on the right and closed in towards the north, so as to prevent supplies or reinforcements passing out or in on this side of the Black River.

The silence and gloom of our camp, as compared with the activity and bustle of that of the French, were very striking. No drum, no bugle-call, no music of any kind, was ever heard within our precincts, while our neighbours close by kept up incessant rolls, fanfaronnades, and flourishes, relieved every evening by the fine performances of their military bands. The fact was many of our instruments had been placed in store and the regimental bands were broken up and disorganized, the men being devoted to the performance of the duties for which the ambulance corps was formed. I think, judging from one's own feelings, and from the expressions of those around, that the want of music in camp was productive of graver consequences than appeared likely to occur at first blush from such a cause. Every military man knows how regiments, when fatigued on the march, cheer up at the strains of their band, and dress up, keep step and walk on with animation and vigour when it is playing. At camp, I always observed with pleasure the attentive auditory who gathered every evening at the first taps of the drum to listen to the music, and when the bands were silenced because of the prevalence of cholera, out of a humane regard for the feelings of the sick, the soldiers were wont to get up singing parties in their tents in lieu of their ordinary entertainment. It seemed to be an error to deprive them of a cheering and wholesome influence at the very time they needed it most. The military band was not meant alone for the delectation of garrison towns, or for the pleasure of the officers in quarters, and the men were fairly entitled to its inspiration during the long and weary march in the enemy's country and in the monotony of a standing camp ere the beginning of a siege.

Soon after daybreak on the morning of the 10th the Russian batteries opened up a heavy fire on the right of our position, but the distance was too great for accuracy of range or precision of flight. On the same day four battalions of French numbering 2,400 men, broke ground at nine o'clock, and before daybreak they had finished a ditch, parapet, and banquette 1,200 metres long at a distance of 900 metres from the enemy's line; and so little did the Russians suspect the operation that they never fired a gun to disturb them. Each man worked and kept guard at one of the covering parties in turn till daybreak, and by that time each man had finished his half metre of work, so that the 1,200 metres were completed. From this position a considerable portion of the enemy's defences on their right was quite under control and the French could command the heaviest fort on that side. From the top of the ditch seventy-six guns could be counted in the embrasures of this work, which was called the Bastion du Mât. The French had got forty-six guns ready to mount when the embrasures should be made and faced with gabions and fascines, and the platforms were ready. Their present line was from 200 to 300 yards nearer to the enemy's lines than ours; but the superior weight of our siege guns more than compensated for the difference of distance.

On the night of October 10th, soon after dark, 800 men were marched out silently on our left front and commenced making the first British trenches before Sebastopol. About 1,200 yards of trench were made, though the greatest difficulty was experienced in working owing to the rocky nature of the ground. The cover was tolerably good. The Russians, who usually ceased firing at sunset, were on the alert all night and continued their fire against the whole line of our approaches almost uninterruptedly. Every instant the darkness was broken by a flash which had all the effect of summer lightning – then came darkness again, and in a few seconds a fainter flash denoted the bursting of a shell. Our amusement was to sit with stop-watches and count till the report came bursting upon us, followed by the roaring sound of the shot, the peculiar noise which the Scotch would call the 'soughing' of the shell, and the explosion of the bomb, and then to estimate the distance of the gun and the range of the ball.

Lord Raglan, accompanied by our active Quartermaster-General, General Airey, and several officers of his staff, started at ten o'clock, and rode along the lines, minutely inspecting the state and position of the regiments and works. They returned at half-past one o'clock in the morning. The only casualties we had during this heavy fire on the night of the 10th were, one man died of wounds; one man killed by cannon-shot; another man, arm shot off; Lieutenant

Rotherham, 20th, slightly wounded in the leg by a stone, which had been 'started' by a cannon-shot.

The following night another force was sent out, under the protection of strong covering parties, to construct trenches on the British right flank, for conversion into batteries. The party successfully completed 363 yards of trench.

It was intended that a party of similar strength should be employed on the left and centre, but owing to one of those accidents which unavoidably occur in night work, the sappers and miners missed their way and got in advance towards the lines of the enemy. They were perceived by an advanced post, which opened fire on them at short distance and, wonderful to relate, missed them all. The flashes, however, showed our men that strong battalions of Russian infantry were moving silently towards our works and the alarm was given to the division in the rear. At twenty-five minutes past one a furious cannonade was opened by the enemy on our lines, as they had then ascertained that we had discovered their approach. The Second and Light Divisions turned out, and our field guns attached to them opened fire on the enemy, who were advancing under the fire of their batteries. Owing to some misunderstanding, the covering parties received orders to retire and fell back on their lines – all but one company of riflemen who maintained the ground with tenacity and fired into the columns of the enemy with effect. The Russians pushed on field-pieces to support their assault. The batteries behind them were livid with incessant flashes, and the roar of shot and shell filled the air, mingled with the constant 'ping-pinging' of rifle and musket-balls. All the camps 'roused out'. The French on our left got under arms and the rattle of drums and the shrill blast of trumpets were heard amid the roar of cannon and small arms. For nearly half-an-hour this din lasted, till all of a sudden a ringing cheer was audible on our right, rising through the turmoil. It was the cheer of the 88th, as they were ordered to charge down the hill on their unseen enemy. It had its effect, for the Russians, already pounded by our guns and shaken by the fire of our infantry, as well as by the aspect of the whole hill-side lined with our battalions, turned and fled under the shelter of their guns. Their loss was not known, ours was very trifling. The sortie was completely foiled and not an inch of our lines was injured.

At the distance of about 700 sagenes (a sagene is seven feet) from the south extremity of the Careening Bay was placed a round tower, around which the Russians had thrown up extensive entrenchments, armed with heavy guns, which, equally with those in the earthworks below, threw shot and shell right over our advanced posts and working parties, and sometimes pitched them over the hills in our front into the camps below. At the distance of 1,200 yards from this round tower, in a direction nearly due south south-east, our first batteries were to be formed and the earthworks had been thrown up there, inclining with the slope of the hill towards the end of the Dockyard Creek. The guns of this work were intended to command the Dockyard Creek, the ships placed in it, and the part of the town and its defences on the west and south of the creek.

Our left attack extended up towards the slope of the ravine which divided the French from the British and which ran south-east from the end of the Dockyard Creek up to our headquarters at Khutor. Dominating both of these entrenchments for most of their course was a heavy battery of eight Lancaster and ten-inch naval guns. The extreme of the French right was about two and a half miles from the extreme of the British left.

The front of both armies united, and the line of offensive operations covered by them, extended from the sea to the Tchernaya for seven and a half or eight miles. From our extreme right front to Balaklava our lines extended for about the same distance, and the position of the army had been made so strong on the eastern [and] southern-eastern flanks and rear as to set all the efforts of the Russians to drive us from it utterly at defiance. In the first place, the road from Kadikoi to Kamara, and the western passes of the mountains had been scarped in three places so effectually that it would have been difficult for infantry, and therefore impossible for artillery, to get along it to attack us. A heavy gun had, however, been placed in position on the heights to command this road, and to sweep the three scarps effectually. From Kadikoi towards Traktir the ground was mountainous, or rather it was exceedingly hilly, the heights having a tumular appearance and the ridges being intersected by wide valleys, through a series of which passed on one side Prince Voronzoff's road, the road to Inkerman, and thence to Sebastopol, by a long *detour* over the Bakschiserai road, and that to Traktir.

On five of these tumular ridges overlooking the road to Balaklava, a party of 2,000 Turks were busily engaged casting up earthworks for redoubts. These poor fellows worked most willingly and indefatigably, though they had been exposed to the greatest privations. For some mysterious reason the Turkish government sent a body of soldiers of only two years' service, the latest levies of the Porte, many belonging to the non-belligerent class of barbers, tailors, and small shopkeepers. Still they were patient, hardy, and strong – how patient I am ashamed to say. I was told, on the best authority, that these men were landed without the smallest care for their sustenance, except that some Marseilles biscuits were sent on shore for their use. These were soon exhausted – the men had nothing else. From the Alma up to October 10th, the whole force had only two biscuits each! The rest of their food they had to get by the roadside as best they might, and in an inhospitable and desolated country they could not get their only solace, tobacco; still they marched and worked day after day, picking up their subsistence by the way as best they might, and these proud Osmanli were actually seen walking about our camps looking for fragments of rejected biscuit. But their sorrows were turned to joy, for the British people fed them, and such diet they never had before since Mahomet enrolled his first army of the faithful. They delighted in their coffee, sugar, rice, and biscuits, but many of the True Believers were much perturbed in spirit by the aspect of our salt beef, which they believed might be pork in disguise, and they subjected it to strange tests ere it was incorporated with Ottoman flesh and blood.

9

The First Bombardment

EIGHTEEN DAYS HAD ELAPSED SINCE OUR ARMY BY A brilliant and daring forced march on Balaklava obtained its magnificent position on the heights which envelop Sebastopol on the south side from the sea to the Tchernaya; the delay was probably unavoidable. Any officer who has been present at great operations of this nature will understand what it is for an army to land in narrow and widely separated creeks all its munitions of war – its shells, its cannon shot, its heavy guns, mortars, its powder, its gun carriages, its platforms, its fascines, gabions, sandbags, its trenching tools, and all the various *matériel* requisite for the siege of extensive and formidable lines of fortifications and batteries. But few ships could come in at a time to Balaklava or Kamiesch; in the former there was only one small ordnance wharf, and yet it was there that every British cannon had to be landed. The nature of our descent on the Crimea rendered it quite impossible for us to carry our siege train along with us, as is the wont of armies invading a neighbouring country only separated from their own by some imaginary line. We had to send all our *matériel* round by sea, and then land it as best we could. But when once it was landed the difficulties of getting it up to places where it was required seemed really to commence. All these enormous masses of metal had to be dragged by men, aided by such inadequate horse-power as was at our disposal, over a steep and hilly country on wretched broken roads to a distance of eight miles, and one must have witnessed the toil and labour of hauling up a Lancaster or ten-inch gun under such circumstances to form a notion of the length of time requisite to bring it to its station. It will, however, serve to give some idea of the severity of this work to state one fact – that on the 10th October no less than thirty-three ammunition horses were found dead, or in such a condition as to render it necessary to kill them after the duty of the day before. It follows from all these considerations that a great siege operation cannot be commenced in a few days when an army is compelled to bring up its guns.

Again, the nature of the ground around Sebastopol offered great impediments to the performance of the necessary work of trenching, throwing up parapets, and forming earthworks. The surface of the soil was stony and hard, and after it had been removed the labourer came to strata of rock and petrous masses of volcanic formation which defied the best tools to make any impression on them, and our tools were far from being the best. The result was that the earth for gabions and for sand-bags had to be carried from a distance in baskets, and in some instances enough of it could not be scraped together for the most trifling parapets. This impediment was experienced to a greater extent by the British than by the French. The latter had better ground to work upon and they found fine beds of clay beneath the first coating of stones and earth, which were essential service to them in forming their works.

On the night of October 16th it was determined that our fire should be opened on the Russian lines the following morning, as it was evident the enemy was intrenching himself with much activity and greatly strengthening his position. In spite of the efforts of our engineers, our works were not quite completed and most of the mortars could not be mounted in the batteries. Our siege-train was divided into two 'attacks' – the 'right' and the 'left' attack. Our left attack consisted of four batteries and 36 guns; our right attack, of 20 guns, in battery. There were also two Lancaster batteries and a four-gun battery of 68-pounders on our right. The French had about 46 guns. In all we were supposed to have 117 guns to silence about 130 guns of the Russians. The night was one of great anxiety, and early in the morning we all turned out to see the firing.

From 6.30 a.m. until dusk there were furious and prolonged exchanges in which the French batteries took a severe hammering and by half-past ten they were virtually out of action. The guns of the allied fleets joined in the assault and poured their fire on to the Russian positions from the north-west. Orders had been given to spare the town itself as far as possible and to concentrate on military objectives.

The fire was resumed on the morning of the 18th, soon after daybreak. At 10 a.m. the alarm was given that the Russians were marching to attack our rear on the Balaklava road. Lord Raglan and staff, with large bodies of French troops, at once moved there and found the Russian cavalry and two battalions of infantry with one gun endeavouring to creep up in a fog to the outposts. The Turks opened a fire from the redoubts and the Russians retired.

The enemy scarcely fired a shot during the night of the 18th. Our batteries were equally silent. The French on their side opened a few guns on their right attack, at which they worked all night to get them into position; but they did not succeed in firing many rounds before the preponderance of the enemy's metal made itself felt, and their works were damaged seriously; in fact, their lines, though nearer to the enemy's batteries than our own in some instances, were not sufficiently close for the light brass guns with which they were armed.

At daybreak on the 19th the firing continued as usual from both sides. The Russians, having spent the night in repairing the batteries, were nearly in the same position as ourselves, and, unaided or at least unassisted to the full extent we had reason to expect by the French, we were just able to hold our own during the day. Some smart affairs of skirmishers and sharp-shooters took place in front. Our riflemen annoyed the Russian gunners greatly and prevented the *tirailleurs* from showing near our batteries. On one occasion the Russian riflemen and our own men came close upon each other in a quarry before the town. Our men had exhausted all their ammunition; but as soon as they saw the Russians, they seized the blocks of stone which were lying about and opened a vigorous volley on the enemy. The latter either had empty pouches or were so much surprised that they forgot to load, for they resorted to the same missiles. A short fight ensued, which ended in our favour, and the Russians retreated, pelted vigorously as long as the men could pursue them. The coolness of a young artillery officer, named Maxwell, who took some ammunition to the batteries through a tremendous fire along a road so exposed to the enemy's fire that it has been called 'The Valley of Death',[1] was highly spoken of on all sides. The blue-jackets were delighted with Captain Peel,[2] who animated the men by the exhibition of the best qualities of an officer, though his courage was sometimes marked by an excess that bordered on rashness. When the Union Jack in the sailors' battery was shot away, he seized the broken staff, and leaping up on the earthworks, waved the old bit of bunting again and again amid a storm of shot, which fortunately left him untouched.

The French fire slackened very much towards one o'clock, the enemy pitching shells right into their lines and enfilading part of their new works. Hour after hour one continuous boom of cannon was alone audible and the smoke screened all else from view. As it was very desirable to destroy the ships anchored in the harbour below us, and to fire the dockyard buildings, our rockets were brought into play and, though rather erratic in their flight, they did some mischief, but not so much as was expected. Wherever they fell the people could be seen flying up the streets when the smoke cleared. At three o'clock p.m. the town was on fire; but after the smoke had excited our hopes for some time, it thinned away and went out altogether. They kept smartly at work from three guns in the Round Tower [Malakoff] works, and from some four or five in the Redan, on our batteries.

Two 68-pounders were mounted during the night of the 19th in our batteries and the firing, which nearly ceased after dark, was renewed by daybreak. We were all getting tired of this continual 'pound-pounding', which made a great deal of noise, wasted much powder and did very little damage. Rome was not built in a day, nor could Sebastopol be taken in a week. In fact, we had run away with

[1] It was apparently a coincidence that Lord Tennyson chose to describe the scene of the charge of the Light Brigade as 'the valley of death'. The charge, in fact, occurred not in a valley, but on the plain above Balaklava.

[2] Third son of Sir Robert Peel. Captain Peel was later awarded the Victoria Cross for an act of bravery during the campaign.

the notion that it was a kind of pasteboard city which would tumble down at the sound of our cannon as the walls of Jericho fell at the blast of Joshua's trumpet. The news that Sebastopol had fallen, which we received via England, excited great indignation and ludicrous astonishment. The whole army was enraged about it, as they felt the verity, whenever it might be realized, must fall short of the effect of that splendid figment. They thought, too, that the laurels of the Alma would be withered in the blaze of popular delight at the imaginary capture. In fact, people at home must have known very little about us or our position. I was much amused at seeing in a journal a letter from an 'Old Indian', on the manufacture of campaign bread, in which he advised us to use salt! milk! and butter! in the preparation of what must be most delicious food. Salt was a luxury which was rarely to be had, except in conjunction with porky fibre, and as to milk and butter, the very taste of them was forgotten. Lord Raglan was very glad to get a little cold pig and ration rum and water the night before we entered Balaklava. However, the hardest lot of all was reserved for our poor horses. All hay rations for baggagers were rigidly refused; they only received a few pounds of indifferent barley. There was not a blade of grass to be had – the whole of these *plateaux* and hills were covered with thistles only, and where the other covering of the earth went I know not. The hay ration for a charger was restricted to 6 lb. daily. Under these circumstances horseflesh was cheap, and friendly presents were being continually offered by one man to another of 'a deuced good pony', which were seldom accepted.

On the 18th, early in the morning, a vedette was seen 'circling left' most energetically – and here, in a parenthesis, I must explain that when a vedette 'circles left', the proceeding signifies that the enemy's infantry are approaching, while to 'circle right' is indicative of the approach of cavalry. On this signal was immediately heard the roll-call to 'boot and saddle'; the Scots Greys and a troop of Horse Artillery assembled with the remaining cavalry on the plain, the 93rd got under arms, and the batteries on the heights were immediately manned. The distant pickets were seen to advance, and a dragoon dashed over the plain with the intelligence that the enemy was advancing quickly. Then cavalry and infantry moved upon the plain, remaining in rear of the eminences from which the movements of the vedettes had been observed. This state of things continued for an hour, when, from the hills, about 3,000 yards in front, the Turks opened fire from their advanced entrenchments. The Moskows then halted in their onward course and in the evening lighted their watch-fires about 2,000 yards in front of our vedettes, the blaze showing bright and high in the darkness. Of course, we were on the alert all night, and before the day broke were particularly attentive to our front. If the Russians had intended to attack us at that time they could not have had a more favourable morning, a low dense white fog covering the whole of the plain. The sun rose, and the mist disappeared, when it was found the Russians had vanished also.

The next day, the 19th, we naturally expected would be a quiet one and that we should not be annoyed by having to remain at our arms for our final work. Not a bit of it; we had just laden ourselves with haversacks to forage among the merchant shipping in the harbour, when a vedette was seen to 'circle right' most industriously. 'Boot and saddle' again resounded through the cavalry camps, and another day passed like its predecessor, the enemy finally once more retiring, this time without advancing near enough for a shot from the Turks.

The next day, the 20th, I had a foraging expedition, and returned with a goose, butter, preserved milk, etc. – a very successful foray and a full haversack. We were just beginning our meal of commissariat beef and pork, tempered with the contents of the aforesaid haversack, when away went the vedette again, first circling right and then reversing as suddenly to the left. Again sounded trumpet, bugle and drum through the plain, and masses again moved into position. So we remained till dark, a night attack on the Turkish position in our front being anticipated, and so we again stood all ready for some hours, during which the only amusement was in the hands of the Turks, who fired a round or two; darkness found us similarly occupied.

The Russians opened a very heavy cannonade on us in the morning of the 22nd; they always did so on Sundays. Divine Service was performed with a continued bass of cannon rolling through the responses and liturgy. The Russians made a stealthy sortie during the night, and advanced close to the French pickets. When challenged, they replied, 'Inglis, Inglis', which passed muster with our allies as *bona fide* English; and before they knew where they were, the Russians had got into their batteries and spiked five mortars. They were speedily repulsed; but this misadventure mortified our brave allies exceedingly.

Lord Dunkellin, Captain Coldstream Guards, was taken prisoner on the 22nd. He was out with a working party of his regiment which had got a little out of their way, when a number of men were observed through the dawning light in front of them. 'There are the Russians,' exclaimed one of the men. 'Nonsense,' they're our fellows,' said his lordship, and off he went towards them, asking in a high tone as he got near, 'Who is in command of this party?' His men saw him no more, but he was afterwards exchanged for the Russian Artillery officer.

The return of killed and wounded for the 22nd of October, during the greater part of which a heavy fire was directed upon our trenches, and battery attacks right and left, showed the excellent cover of our works and their great solidity. But sickness continued, and the diminution of our numbers every day was enough to cause serious anxiety. Out of 35,600 men borne on the strength of the army, there were not at this period more than 16,500 rank and file fit for service. In a fortnight upwards of 700 men were sent as invalids to Balaklava. There was a steady drain of some forty or fifty men a day going out from us, which was not dried up by the numbers of the returned invalids. Even the twenty or thirty a day wounded and disabled, when multiplied by the number of the days we had been here, became a serious item in the aggregate. We were badly off for spare gun carriages and wheels, for ammunition and forage. Whilst our siege works were languishing and the hour of assault appeared more distant, the enemy were concentrating on our flank and rear and preparing for a great attempt to raise the siege. The position we occupied in reference to Balaklava was supposed by most people to be very strong – even impregnable. Our lines were formed by natural mountain slopes in the rear, along which the French had made very formidable entrenchments. Below these entrenchments, and very nearly in a right line across the valley beneath, were four conical hillocks, one rising above the other as they receded from our lines; the furthest; which joined the chain of mountains opposite to our ridges being named Canrobert's Hill, from the meeting there of that general with Lord Raglan after the march to Balaklava. On the top of each of these hills the Turks had thrown up earthen redoubts, each being defended by 250 men armed with two or three heavy ship guns – lent by us to them, with one artilleryman in each redoubt to look after them.

At the distance of two or two and a half miles across the valley was an abrupt rocky mountain range of most irregular and picturesque formation, covered with scanty brushwood here and there, or rising into barren pinnacles and *plateaux* of rock. In outline and appearance this portion of the landscape was wonderfully like the Trossachs. A patch of blue sea was caught in between the overhanging cliffs of Balaklava as they closed in the entrance to the harbour on the right. On the left the hills and rocky mountain ranges gradually closed in towards the course of the Tchernaya, till, at three or four miles' distance from Balaklava, the valley was swallowed up in a mountain gorge and deep ravines. It was very easy for an enemy at the Belbek, or in command of the road to Mackenzie's farm, Inkerman, Simpheropol, or Bakschiserai, to debouch through these gorges at any time upon this plain from the neck of the valley, or to march from Sebastopol by the Tchernaya and to advance along it towards Balaklava, till checked by the Turkish redoubts on the southern side or by the fire from the French works on the northern – i.e. the side which, in relation to the valley at Balaklava, formed the rear of our position. It was evident enough that Menschikoff and Gortschakoff had been feeling their way along this route for several days past, and very probably at night the Cossacks had crept up close to our pickets, which were not always as watchful as might be desired, and had observed the weakness of a position far too extended for our army to defend and occupied by their despised enemy, the Turks.

10

Balaklava

AT HALF-PAST SEVEN O'CLOCK ON THE MORNING OF THE 25th, an orderly came galloping in to the headquarters camp with the news that at dawn a strong corps of Russian horse, supported by guns and battalions of infantry, had marched into the valley and had nearly dispossessed the Turks of the redoubt No. 1 (that on Canrobert's Hill, which was farthest from our lines), and had opened fire on the redoubts Nos. 2, 3 and 4. Lord Lucan, who was in one of the redoubts when they were discovered, had brought up his guns and some of his heavy cavalry, but they were obliged to retire owing to the superior weight of the enemy's metal.

Orders were despatched to Sir George Cathcart and to H.R.H. the Duke of Cambridge, to put their respective divisions, the Fourth and the First, in motion for the scene of action; and intelligence of the advance of the Russians was also furnished to General Canrobert. Immediately on receipt of the news, the General commanded General Bosquet to get the Third Division under arms, and sent a strong body of artillery and some 200 Chasseurs d'Afrique to assist us in holding the valley. Sir Colin Campbell, who was in command of Balaklava, had drawn up the 93rd Highlanders a little in front of the road to the town, at the first news of the advance of the enemy. The marines on the heights got under arms; the seamen's batteries and marines' batteries on the heights close to the town were manned, and the French artillerymen and the Zouaves prepared for action along their lines. Lord Lucan's little camp was the scene of great excitement. The men had not had time to water their horses; they had not broken their fast from the evening of the day before and had barely saddled at the first blast of the trumpet when they were drawn up on the slope behind the redoubts in front of their camp to operate on the enemy's squadrons.

It was soon evident that no reliance was to be placed on the Turkish infantry or artillerymen. All the stories we had heard about their bravery behind stone walls and earthworks proved how differently the same or similar people fight under different circumstances. When the Russians advanced, the Turks fired a few rounds at them, got frightened at the distance of their supports in the rear, looked round, received a few shots and shell, then 'bolted' with an agility quite at variance with the common-place notions of Oriental deportment on the battle-field.

Soon after eight o'clock, Lord Raglan and his staff turned out and cantered towards the rear of our position. The booming of artillery, the spattering roll of musketry, were heard rising from the valley, drowning the roar of the siege guns before Sebastopol. As I rode in the direction of the firing, over the thistles and large stones which cover the undulating plain that stretches away towards Balaklava, I observed a French light infantry regiment advancing from our right towards the ridge near the telegraph-house, which was already lined by companies of French infantry, while mounted officers scampered along its broken outline in every direction.

General Bosquet, a stout soldierlike-looking man, who reminds one of the old *genre* of French generals, as depicted at Versailles, followed with his staff and a small escort of Hussars at a gallop. Faint white clouds rose here and there above the hill from the cannonade below. The fleecy vapours still hung around the mountain tops, and mingled with the ascending volumes of smoke; the patch of sea sparkled freshly in the rays of the morning sun, but its light was eclipsed by the flashes which gleamed from the masses of armed men below.

Looking to the left towards the gorge, we beheld six compact masses of Russian infantry, which had just debouched from the mountain passes near the Tchernaya, and were slowly advancing with solemn stateliness up the valley. Immediately in their front was a regular line of artillery at least twenty pieces strong. Two batteries of light guns were already a mile in advance of them and were playing with energy on the redoubts, from which feeble puffs of smoke came at long intervals. Behind these guns, in front of the infantry, were enormous bodies of cavalry. They were in six compact squares, three on each flank, moving down *en echelon* towards us, and the valley was lit up with the blaze of their sabres and lance points and gay accoutrements. In their front, and extending along the intervals between each battery of guns, were clouds of mounted skirmishers, wheeling and whirling in the front of their march, like autumn leaves tossed by the wind. The Zouaves close to us were lying like tigers at the spring, with ready rifles in hand, hidden chin deep by the earthworks which ran along the line of these ridges on our rear; but the quick-eyed Russians were manœuvring on the other side of the valley, and did not expose their columns to attack. Below the Zouaves we could see the Turkish gunners in the redoubts, all in confusion as the shells burst over them. Just as I came up, the Russians had carried No. 1 redoubt, the farthest and most elevated of all, and their horsemen were chasing the Turks across the interval which lay between it and redoubt No. 2.

At that moment the cavalry, under Lord Lucan, were formed in glittering masses – the Light Brigade, under Lord Cardigan, in advance; the Heavy Brigade, under Brigadier-General Scarlett, in reserve. They were drawn up just in front of their encampment, and were concealed from the view of the enemy by a slight 'wave' in the plain. Considerably to the rear of their right the 93rd Highlanders were drawn up in line, in front of the approach to Balaklava. Above and behind them, on the heights, the marines were visible through the glass, drawn up under arms, and the gunners could be seen ready in the earthworks, in which were placed the ships' heavy guns. The 93rd had originally been advanced somewhat more into the plain, but the instant the Russians got possession of the first redoubt they opened fire on them from our own guns, which inflicted some injury, and Sir Colin Campbell 'retired' his men to a better position.

Meantime the enemy advanced his cavalry rapidly. To our inexpressible disgust, we saw the Turks in redoubt No. 2 fly at their approach. They ran in scattered groups across towards redoubt

No. 3 and towards Balaklava; but the horse-hoof of the Cossack was too quick for them, and sword and lance were busily plied among the retreating herd. The yells of the pursuers and pursued were plainly audible. As the Lancers and Light Cavalry of the Russians advanced they gathered up their skirmishers with great speed and in excellent order – the shifting trails of men, which played all over the valley like moonlight on the water, contracted, gathered up, and the little *peloton* in a few moments became a solid column. Then up came their guns, in rushed their gunners to the abandoned redoubt, and the guns of No. 2 redoubt soon played with deadly effect upon the dispirited defenders of No. 3. Two or three shots in return and all was silent. The Turks swarmed over the earthworks, and ran in confusion towards the town, firing their muskets at the enemy as they ran. Again the solid column of cavalry opened like a fan and resolved itself into a 'long spray' of skirmishers. It lapped the flying Turks, steel flashed in the air, and down went the poor Moslem, quivering on the plain, split through fez and musket-guard to the chin and breast-belt. It was evident the Russians had been too quick for us. The Turks had been too quick also, for they had not held their redoubts long enough to enable us to bring them help. In vain the naval guns on the heights fired on the Russian cavalry; the distance was too great for shot or shell to reach. In vain the Turkish gunners in the earthen batteries which were placed along the French entrenchments endeavoured to protect their flying countrymen; their shot flew wide and short of the swarming masses.

The Turks betook themselves towards the Highlanders, where they checked their flight and formed into companies on the flanks of the Highlanders. As the Russian cavalry on the left of their line crowned the hill across the valley, they perceived the Highlanders drawn up at the distance of some half mile, calmly waiting their approach. They halted, and squadron after squadron came up from the rear, till they had a body of some 3,500 men along the ridge – Lancers, and Dragoons, and Hussars. Then they moved *en echelon*, in two bodies, with another in reserve. The cavalry who had been pursuing the Turks on the right were coming up to the ridge beneath us, which concealed our cavalry from view. The Heavy

Brigade in advance was drawn up in two lines. The first line consisted of the Scots Greys, and of their old companions in glory, the Enniskillens; the second, of the 4th Royal Irish, of the 5th Dragoon Guards, and of the 1st Royal Dragoons. The Light Cavalry Brigade was on their left, in two lines also.

The silence was oppressive; between the cannon bursts one could hear the champing of bits and the clink of sabres in the valley below. The Russians on their left drew breath for a moment, and then in one grand line charged in towards Balaklava. The ground flew beneath their horses' feet; gathering speed at every stride, they dashed on towards that thin red streak[1] tipped with a line of steel. The Turks fired a volley at eight hundred yards and ran. As the Russians came within six hundred yards, down went that line of steel in front, and out rang a rolling volley of Minié musketry. The distance was too great; the Russians were not checked, but still swept onwards through the smoke, with the whole force of horse and man, here and there knocked over by the shot of our batteries above. With breathless suspense every one awaited the bursting of the wave upon the line of Gaelic rock; but ere they came within two hundred and fifty yards, another deadly volley flashed from the levelled rifle and carried terror among the Russians. They wheeled about, opened files right and left and fled faster than they came. 'Bravo, Highlanders! well done!' shouted the excited spectators. But events thickened; the Highlanders and their splendid front were soon forgotten – men scarcely had a moment to think of this fact, that the 93rd never altered their formation to receive that tide of horsemen. 'No,' said Sir Colin Campbell, 'I did not think it worth while to form them even four deep!' The ordinary British line, two deep, was quite sufficient to repel the attack of these Muscovite cavaliers.

Lord Raglan perceived that the intention of the Russians was to attack Balaklava, and sent orders to Lord Lucan to move down his heavy horse to cover the approaches, and they were just moving from their position near the vineyard and orchard, when his lordship, seeing that a large body of the enemy's cavalry were coming after

[1] This description of the 93rd Highlanders' stand, later misquoted as a 'thin red line', provided the origin of that famous phrase.

him over the ridge, rode after them, wheeled them round, and advanced to meet them. We saw Brigadier-General Scarlett ride along in front of his massive squadrons. The Russians – evidently *corps d'élite* – their light blue jackets embroidered with silver lace, were advancing on their left at an easy gallop towards the brow of the hill. A forest of lances glistened in their rear and several squadrons of grey-coated dragoons moved up quickly to support them as they reached the summit. The instant they came in sight, the trumpets of our cavalry gave out the warning blast which told us all that in another moment we should see the shock of battle beneath our very eyes. Lord Raglan, all his staff and escort, and groups of officers, the Zouaves, French generals and officers, and bodies of French infantry on the height, were spectators of the scene as though they were looking on the stage from the boxes of a theatre. Nearly every one dismounted and sat down, and not a word was said. The Russians advanced down the hill at a slow canter, which they changed into a trot, and at last nearly halted. Their first line was at least double the length of ours – it was three times as deep. Behind them was a similar line, equally strong and compact.

The trumpets rang out again through the valley, and the Greys and Enniskilleners went right at the centre of the Russian cavalry. The space between them was only a few hundred yards; it was scarce enough to let the horses 'gather way', nor had the men quite space sufficient for the full play of their sword arms. The Russian line brought forward each wing as our cavalry advanced, and threatened to annihilate them as they passed on. Turning a little to their left, so as to meet the Russian right, the Greys rushed on with a cheer that thrilled to every heart – the wild shout of the Enniskilleners rose through the air at the same instant. As lightning flashed through cloud, the Greys and Enniskilleners pierced through the dark masses of Russians. The shock was but for a moment. There was a clash of steel and a light play of sword-blades in the air, and then the Greys and the redcoats disappeared in the midst of the shaken and quivering columns. In another moment we saw them emerging with diminished numbers and in broken order, charging against the second line. It was a terrible moment. The first line of Russians, which had been utterly smashed by our charge, and had fled off at one flank and towards the centre, were coming back to swallow up our handful of men. By sheer steel and sheer courage Enniskillener and Scot were winning their desperate way right through the enemy's squadrons, and already grey horses and red coats had appeared right at the rear of the second mass, when, with irresistible force, like one bolt from a bow, the 4th Dragoon Guards, riding straight at the right flank of the Russians, and the 5th Dragoon Guards, following close after the Enniskilleners, rushed at the remnants of the first line of the enemy, went through it as though it were made of pasteboard and put them to utter rout.

The Russian Horse in less than five minutes after it met our dragoons was flying with all its speed before a force certainly not half its strength. A cheer burst from every lip – in the enthusiasm, officers and men took off their caps and shouted with delight; and thus keeping up the scenic character of their position they clapped their hands again and again. Lord Raglan at once despatched Lieutenant Curzon, aide-de-camp, to convey his congratulations to Brigadier-General Scarlett, and to say 'Well done!' The gallant old officer's face beamed with pleasure when he received the message. 'I beg to thank his lordship very sincerely,' was his reply.

The cavalry did not long pursue their enemy. Their loss was very slight, about thirty-five killed and wounded in both affairs. Our most material loss was from the cannon playing on our Heavy Dragoons afterwards, when covering the retreat of our Light Cavalry.

Following this repulse of the enemy, the British forces were re-deployed in the expectation of another attack. This re-deployment left the Light Cavalry Brigade, 636 strong, under Lord Cardigan, on the left flank, where it stood awaiting further orders. Directly in front of the brigade, a mile and a half away, about thirty Russian guns had been placed to protect the gorge leading to the Tchernaya. On the heights to the left of and above this position there were more guns, and others in the three redoubts that had been captured by the Russians. Behind the battery of thirty guns stood six battalions of Russian infantry and more were massed on the hills behind the redoubts. The reason for what now occurred can never be fully explained because there is no conclusive evidence of what took place.

Soon after, it appeared that the Quartermaster-General, Brigadier Airey, thinking that the Light Cavalry had not gone far enough in front when the enemy's horse had fled, gave an order in writing to Captain Nolan, 15th Hussars, to take to Lord Lucan, directing his Lordship 'to advance' his cavalry nearer to the enemy. A braver soldier than Captain Nolan the army did not possess. A matchless horseman and a first-rate swordsman, God forbid I should cast a shade on the brightness of his honour, but I am bound to state what I am told occurred.

When Lord Lucan received the order from Captain Nolan, and had read it, he asked, we are told, 'Where are we to advance to?' Captain Nolan pointed with his finger to the line of the Russians, and said, 'There are the enemy, and there are the guns,' or words to that effect, according to the statements made after his death.

Precisely what was meant by the order remains obscure: its actual wording was: Lord Raglan wishes the cavalry to advance rapidly to the front, follow the enemy, and try to prevent the enemy carrying away the guns; troops of Horse Artillery may accompany. French cavalry is on your left. Immediate. *The ambiguity of these instructions – what exactly was to be the role of the Horse Artillery, and of the French cavalry? – did not seem to occur to Brigadier Airey, or if it did, he still did not question the propriety of the message. Captain Nolan's interpretation of it was his own, as was Lord Lucan's. The result of the confusion caused by Lord Raglan's lack of precision can hardly have been what he intended.*

Lord Lucan, with reluctance, gave the order to Lord Cardigan to advance upon the guns, conceiving that his orders compelled him to do so. The noble Earl, though he did not shrink, also saw the fearful odds against him. It is a maxim of war, that 'cavalry never act without a support', that 'infantry should be close at hand when cavalry carry guns, as the effect is only instantaneous', and that it is necessary to have on the flank of a line of cavalry some squadrons in column, the attack on the flank being most dangerous. The only support our light cavalry had was the reserve of heavy cavalry at a great distance behind them, the infantry and guns being far in the rear. There were no squadrons in column at all, and there was a plain to charge over before the enemy's guns could be reached, of a mile and a half in length.

At ten minutes past eleven, our Light Cavalry Brigade advanced. As they rushed towards the front, the Russians opened on them from the guns in the redoubt on the right with volleys of musketry and rifles. They swept proudly past, glittering in the morning sun in all the pride and splendour of war. We could scarcely believe the evidence of our senses. Surely that handful of men were not going to charge an army in position? Alas! it was but too true – their desperate valour knew no bounds, and far indeed was it removed from its so-called better part – discretion. They advanced in two lines, quickening their pace as they closed towards the enemy. A more fearful spectacle was never witnessed than by those who, without the power to aid, beheld their heroic countrymen rushing to the arms of death. At the distance of 1,200 yards the whole line of the enemy belched forth, from thirty iron mouths, a flood of smoke and flame, through which hissed the deadly balls. Their flight was marked by instant gaps in our ranks, by dead men and horses, by steeds flying wounded or riderless across the plain. The first line was broken – it was joined by the second, they never halted or checked their speed an instant. With diminished ranks, thinned by those thirty guns, which the Russians had laid with the most deadly accuracy, with a halo of flashing steel above their heads, and with a cheer which was many a noble fellow's death-cry, they flew into the smoke of the batteries; but ere they were lost from view, the plain was strewed with their bodies and with the carcasses of horses. They were exposed to an oblique fire from the batteries on the hills on both sides, as well as to a direct fire of musketry.

Through the clouds of smoke we could see their sabres flashing as they rode up to the guns and dashed between them, cutting down the gunners as they stood. To our delight we saw them returning, after breaking through a column of Russian infantry and scattering them like chaff, when the flank fire of the battery on the hill swept them down, scattered and broken as they were. At the very moment when they were about to retreat a regiment of Lancers was hurled upon their flank. Colonel Shewell, of the 8th Hussars, saw the danger, and rode his few men straight at them, cutting his way through with fearful loss. The other regiments turned and engaged in a desperate encounter. With courage too great almost for credence they were breaking their way through the columns which enveloped them, when there took place an act of atrocity without parallel in the modern warfare of civilized nations. The Russian gunners, when the storm of cavalry passed, returned to their guns, and poured murderous volleys of grape and canister on the mass of struggling men and horses. It was as much as our Heavy Cavalry Brigade could do to cover the retreat of the miserable remnants of that band of heroes as they returned to the place they had so lately quitted in all the pride of life. At thirty-five minutes past eleven not a British soldier, except the dead and dying, was left in front of these bloody Muscovite guns.

Captain Nolan, as he rode in advance of the first line, cheering them on, was killed by the first shot fired. Lord Lucan was slightly wounded. Lord Cardigan received a lance thrust through his clothes.

While our affair was going on, the French cavalry made a most brilliant charge at the battery on our left, which was firing on our men, and cut down the gunners; but they could not get off the guns without support and had to retreat. The ground was left covered with our men and with hundreds of Russians, and we could see the Cossacks busy searching the dead. Our infantry made a forward movement towards the redoubts after the cavalry came in, and the Russian infantry in advance slowly retired towards the gorge; at the same time the French cavalry pushed forward on their right, and held them in check, pushing out a line of skirmishers, and forcing them to withdraw their guns. The Russians, feeling alarmed at our steady advance and at the symptoms of our intention to turn or cut off their right, retired from No. 1 redoubt, which was taken possession of by the allies. At fifteen minutes past eleven, they abandoned redoubt No. 2, blowing up the magazine; and, as we still continued to advance, they blew up and abandoned No. 3, but to our great regret, we were not in time nor in force to prevent their taking off seven out of nine guns in these earthworks.

Lord Raglan continued on the hill-side all day, watching the enemy. It was dark ere he returned to his quarters. With the last gleam of day we could see the sheen of the enemy's lances in their old position in the valley; and their infantry gradually crowned the heights on their left.

On the night of the 25th, when our guns were taken into Sebastopol there was joy throughout the city, and it was announced that the Russians had gained a great victory. A salvo of artillery was fired, and at nine o'clock p.m., a tremendous cannonade was opened against all our lines by the enemy. It did no injury.

11

Inkerman

The next day, November 26th, an attack on the British right flank was made by 4,000 Russians, but was decisively beaten off by the Second Division under Sir de Lacy Evans. For nine days thereafter the opposing armies continued to harass each other with artillery fire by day and by night. Patrolling and reconnaissance went on as usual, but neither side attempted anything in the nature of a full-scale attack. Instead, they concentrated their energies on strengthening their respective positions and making preparations for the winter. In doing so, however, whether from 'indolence or a false sense of security and an overweening confidence', the British lagged considerably behind the Russians. In spite of the attack on their flank on November 26th and in defiance of repeated warnings by Sir de Lacy Evans about the dangerously exposed position of the Second Division, nothing was done to safeguard the situation beyond the throwing up of a single sandbag battery on the hill overlooking Inkerman. Seldom in the history of warfare can an army have paid so fearful a price for the indolence and neglect of its leaders, for on November 5th the situation took a very different turn.

It had rained almost incessantly the night before, and the early morning gave no promise of any cessation of the heavy showers which had fallen for the previous four-and-twenty hours. The fog and vapours of drifting rain became so thick as morning broke that one could scarcely see two yards before one.

It was a little after five o'clock when Brigadier-General Codrington, in accordance with his usual habit, visited the outlying pickets of his own brigade of the Light Division. It was reported to him that 'all was well', and the General turned his pony round and retraced his steps through the brushwood towards his lines. He had only proceeded a few paces when a sharp rattle of musketry was heard down the hill and on the left of the pickets of the Light Division. It was here that the pickets of the Second Division were stationed. General Codrington at once turned his horse's head in the direction of the firing, and in a few moments galloped back to turn out his division. The Russians were advancing in force. Their grey great-coats rendered them almost invisible even when close at hand. The pickets of the Second Division had scarcely made out the advancing lines of infantry, who were clambering up the steep sides of the hill through a drizzling shower of rain, when they were forced to retreat by a close sharp volley of musketry, and were driven up towards the brow of the hill, contesting every step, and firing as long as they had a round of ammunition on the Russian advance.

The pickets of the Light Division were assailed soon afterwards and were also obliged to retreat and fall back on their main body, and it was evident that a very strong sortie had been made upon the right of the position of the allied armies with the object of forcing them to raise the siege and, if possible, of driving them into the sea. About the same time, a demonstration was made by cavalry, artillery and a few infantry in the valley against Balaklava to divert the attention of the French on the heights above and to occupy the Highland Brigade and Marines, but only an interchange of a few harmless rounds of cannon and musketry took place, and the enemy contented themselves with drawing up their cavalry in order of battle, supported by field artillery, at the neck of the valley, in readiness to sweep over the heights and cut our retreating troops to pieces should the assault on our right be successful.

Everything that could be done to bind victory to their eagles – if they have any – was done by the Russian Generals. The presence of the Grand Dukes Nicholas and Michael, who told them that the Czar had issued orders that every Frenchman and Englishman was to be driven into the sea ere the year closed, cheered the common soldiers, who regard the son of the Emperor as an emanation of the Divine Presence. They had abundance of a coarser and more material stimulant, which was found in their canteens and flasks; and, above all, the priests of the Greek Catholic Church 'blessed' them ere they went forth upon their mission, and assured them of the aid and protection of the Most High.

The men in our camps had just begun a struggle with the rain in endeavouring to light their fires for breakfast when the alarm was given.

At once Brigadier-General Pennefather (replacing Sir de Lacy Evans, who had met with an accident) got the troops of the 2nd Division under arms, and such of the 4th as were not in the trenches were immediately assembled by Sir George Cathcart. Meanwhile, the Light Division, under Sir George Brown, was brought up speedily to the scene of the fighting.

While all the army was thus in motion, the Duke of Cambridge was not behindhand in bringing up the Guards. These splendid troops with the greatest rapidity and ardour advanced to the front on the right of the Second Division and gained the summit of the hill overlooking the valley of the Tchernaya and the ruins and plains of Inkerman. Between their extreme left and the right of the Second Division, there was a deep ravine which lost itself on the plateau of their camp close to the road that led by the top of the ravine to the city of Sebastopol. On arriving at the edge of the plateau the Duke of Cambridge, riding forward to get a glimpse of the enemy, saw two columns of them in front, charging up the steep ground covered with brushwood which descends almost precipitously to the valley. His Royal Highness at once led the Guards to the charge and drove them out of the work.

Then commenced the bloodiest struggle ever witnessed since war cursed the earth. The bayonet was often the only weapon employed in conflicts of the most obstinate and deadly character. We had been prone to believe that no foe could withstand the British soldier wielding his favourite weapon, but at Inkerman not only did we charge in vain – not only were desperate encounters between masses of men maintained with the bayonet alone – but we were obliged to resist bayonet to bayonet again and again, as they charged us with incredible fury and determination.

The battle of Inkerman admits of no description. It was a series of dreadful deeds of daring, of sanguinary hand-to-hand fights, of despairing rallies, of desperate assaults – in glens and valleys, in brushwood glades and remote dells, and from which the conquerors, Russian or British, issued only to engage fresh foes, till our old supremacy, so rudely assailed, was triumphantly asserted, and the battalions of the Czar gave way before our steady courage and the chivalrous fire of France. No one, however placed, could have witnessed even a small portion of the doings of this eventful day, for the vapours, fog, and drizzling mist obscured the ground where the struggle took place to such an extent as to render it impossible to see what was going on at the distance of a few yards. Besides this, the irregular nature of the ground, the rapid fall of the hill towards Inkerman, where the deadliest fight took place, would have prevented anyone under the most favourable circumstances from seeing more than a very insignificant and detailed piece of the terrible work below.

It was six o'clock when all the Headquarter camp was roused by roll after roll of musketry on the right, and by the sharp report of field guns. Lord Raglan was informed that the enemy were advancing in force, and soon after seven he rode towards the scene of action, followed by his staff and accompanied by several aides-de-camp. As they approached, the volume of sound, the steady, unceasing thunder of gun, and rifle and musket told that the engagement was at its height. The shells of the Russians, thrown with great precision, burst so thickly among the troops that the noise resembled continuous discharges of cannon, and the massive fragments inflicted death on every side. One of the first things the Russians did, when a break in the fog enabled them to see the camp of the Second Division, was to open fire on the tents with round shot and large shell, and tent after tent was blown down, torn to pieces, or sent into the air, while the men engaged in camp duties, and the unhappy horses tethered up in the lines, were killed or mutilated.

Our generals could not see where to go. They could not tell where the enemy were – from what side they were coming, nor where they were coming to. In darkness, gloom, and rain they had to lead our lines through thick scrubby bushes and thorny brakes, which broke our ranks and irritated the men, while every pace was marked by a corpse or man wounded by an enemy whose position was only indicated by the rattle of musketry and the rush of ball and shell.

Sir George Cathcart, advancing in haste from the centre of our position, came to the hill where the Guards were engaged, and after a word with the Duke, led the 63rd Regiment, which had just arrived, down on the right of the Guards into a ravine, filled with brushwood, which descended towards the valley of the Tchernaya. He perceived, just as he did so, that the Russians had actually gained possession of a portion of the hill in rear of the right flank of his men, but his stout heart never failed him for a moment. He rode at their head encouraging them, and when a cry arose that the ammunition was failing, he said, coolly, 'Have you not got your bayonets?' As he led on his men, it was observed that another body of the enemy had gained the top of the hill behind them on the right. A deadly volley was poured into our scattered companies. Sir George cheered them and led them back up the hill, but a flight of bullets passed where he rode, and he fell from his horse close to the Russian columns. Poor, kindly, gallant Colonel Seymour, who was wounded, got down from his horse to aid his chief, but the enemy rushed in on them and when our men had driven them back, both lay dead side by side. The men had to fight their way through a host of enemies and suffered fearfully. They were surrounded and bayoneted on all sides and won their desperate way up the hill with diminished ranks and the loss of nearly 500 men. Sir George Cathcart's body was afterwards recovered, with a bullet wound in the head and three bayonet wounds in the body.

The fight had not long commenced before it was evident that the Russians had received orders to fire at all mounted officers. Sir George Brown was hit by a shot, which went through his arm and struck his side. I saw with regret his pale and sternly composed face, as his body was borne by me on a litter early in the day, his white hair flickering in the breeze, for I knew we had lost the services of a good soldier that day. Further to the right, a contest the like of which, perhaps, never took place before, occurred between the Guards and dense columns of Russian infantry of five times their number. The Guards for a second time had charged them and driven them back, when they perceived that the Russians had out-flanked them. They were out of ammunition too. They were uncertain whether there were friends or foes in the rear. They had no support, no reserve, and they were fighting with the bayonet against an enemy who stoutly contested every inch of ground, when the corps of another Russian column appeared on their right far in their rear. Then a fearful *mitraille* was poured into them, and volleys of rifle and musketry. They had lost fourteen officers; they had left one-half of their number on the ground, and at last they retired along the lower road of the valley. They were, however, soon reinforced and speedily avenged their fallen comrades by a desperate charge, in which they drove the Russians before them like sheep.

Meanwhile the Second Division, in the centre of the line, was exposed to a terrible fire. In fact, the whole division numbered only 300 [out of 2,956] men when assembled in rear of their camp after the fight was over. The regiments did not take their colours into the battle, but the officers, nevertheless, were picked off wherever they went, and it did not require the colour-staff to indicate their presence. Our ambulances were soon filled, and ere nine o'clock they were busily engaged in carrying loads of men, all covered with blood, and groaning, to the rear of the line.

About half-past nine o'clock, Lord Raglan and his staff were assembled on a knoll, in the vain hope of getting a glimpse of the battle which was raging below them. A shell came right among the staff – it exploded in Captain Somerset's horse, ripping him open; it then struck down Captain Gordon's horse and killed him at once, and then blew away General Strangway's leg, so that it hung by a shred of flesh and bit of cloth from the skin. The poor old General never moved a muscle of his face. He said merely, in a gentle voice, 'Will anyone be kind enough to lift me off my horse?' He was taken down and laid on the ground, while his life-blood ebbed fast, and at last he was carried to the rear.

The fight about the battery was most sanguinary. The Russians advanced mass after mass of infantry. As fast as one column was broken and repulsed, another took its place. For three long hours about 8,500 British infantry contended against at least four times their number. No wonder that at times they were compelled to retire. But they came to the charge again. The admirable devotion of the officers, who knew they were special objects of attack, can never be too highly praised. At one time the Russians succeeded in getting up close to the guns in the gloom of the morning. Uncertain whether they were friends or foes, our artillerymen hesitated to fire. The Russians charged them suddenly, bore all resistance down before them, drove away or bayoneted the gunners, and succeeded in spiking four of the guns.

The rolling of musketry, the crash of steel, the pounding of the guns were deafening, and the Russians as they charged up the heights yelled like demons. They advanced, halted, advanced again, received and returned a close and deadly fire. This disproportion of numbers was, however, too great – our men were exhausted with slaying – but at last came help. About ten o'clock a body of French infantry appeared on our right – a joyful sight to our struggling regiments.

The Zouaves came on at the *pas de charge*. Three battalions of the Chasseurs d'Orleans rushed by, the light of battle on their faces. They were accompanied by a battalion of Chasseurs Indigènes – the Arab Sepoys of Algiers. Their trumpets sounded above the din of battle, and when we watched their eager advance right on the flank of the enemy we knew the day was won. Assailed in front by our men – broken by the impetuosity of our charge, renewed again and again – attacked by the French infantry, sometimes led on by English officers, on the right, and by artillery all along the line – the Russians began to retire, and at twelve o'clock they were driven pell-mell down the hill towards the valley, where pursuit would have been madness, as the roads were all covered by their artillery. They left mounds of dead behind them.

At twelve o'clock the battle of Inkerman seemed to have been won, but the day, which had cleared up about eleven, so as to enable us to see the enemy, again became obscured. Rain and fog set in, and as we could not pursue the Russians, who were retiring under the shelter of their artillery, we formed in front of our lines, and the enemy, covering his retreat by bodies of horse on the slopes, near the Careening Bay, and, by a tremendous fire of artillery, fell back upon the works and retreated, in immense confusion, across the Inkerman Bridge.

Two days later Russell made a tour of the battle-field.[1]

The British and the French, many of whom had been murdered by the Russians as they lay wounded, wore terrible frowns on their faces, with which the agonies of death had clad them. Some in their last throes had torn up the earth in their hands, and held the grass between their fingers up towards heaven. All the men who exhibited such signs of pain had been bayoneted; the dead men who lay with an eternal smile on their lips had been shot. But the wounded – for two days they had lain where the hand and the ball had felled them. There were very few, it is true, but it was towards noon on the 7th ere the last of our soldiers had been found in his lair and carried to the hospital.

The Russians, groaning and palpitating as they lay around, were far more numerous. Some were placed together in heaps, that they might be the more readily removed. Others glared upon you from the bushes with the ferocity of wild beasts, as they hugged their wounds. Some implored, in an unknown tongue, but in accents not to be mistaken, water, or succour; holding out their mutilated and shattered limbs, or pointing to the track of the lacerating ball. The sullen, angry scowl of some of these men was fearful. Fanaticism and immortal hate spake through their angry eyeballs, and he who gazed on them with pity and compassion could at last (unwillingly) understand how these men would in their savage passion kill the wounded, and fire on the conqueror who, in his generous humanity, had aided them as he passed. It was a relief to see that their arms were broken – that their cartridges were lying opened in heaps on the ground. Litter-bearers, French and English, dotted the hillside, toiling painfully up with a heavy burden for the grave, or with some subject

[1] November 6 is the date given by Russell, but it seems obvious from his account of what he said that in fact his tour must have been made on November 7.

for the doctor's care, hunting through the bushes for the dead or dying. Our men had acquired a shocking facility in their diagnosis. A body was before you; there was a shout, 'Come here, boys, I see a Russian!' (or 'a Frenchman', or 'one of our fellows!') One of the party advanced, raised the eyelid if it was closed, peered into the eye, shrugged his shoulders, saying quietly, 'He's dead, he'll wait,' and moved back to the litter; others pulled the feet, and arrived at equally correct conclusions by that process. The dead were generally stripped of all but their coats. The camp followers and blackguards from Balaklava, and seamen from the ships, anxious for trophies, carried off all they could take from the field.

At particular spots men were seen busy at work. Groups were digging away all along the hillside, forty or fifty yards apart. On going over, you found them around a yawning trench, thirty feet in length by twenty feet in breadth and six feet in depth, at the bottom of which, in every conceivable attitude, lay packed together with exceeding art some thirty or forty corpses. The grave-diggers stood chatting on the mounds by the sides, waiting for the arrival of some bearers to complete the number of the dead. They speculated on the appearance of the body which was being borne towards them. 'It's Corporal ——, of the —th, I think,' says one. 'No! it's my rear rank man, I can see his red hair plain enough,' and so on. At last the number in the trench was completed. The bodies were packed as closely as possible. Some of them had upraised arms, in the attitude of taking aim; their legs stick up through the mould as it was thrown upon them; others were bent and twisted into shapes like fantoccini. Inch after inch the earth rose upon them.

For about one mile and a half in length by half a mile in depth, the hillside offered such sights as these. Upwards of 2,000 Russians had been buried by these men. The carnage at the Alma did not present anything like the scene round the Sandbag Battery, which was placed on a steep descent towards the Tchernaya. The piles of dead here were frightful. Upwards of 1,200 dead and dying Russians laid [*sic*] behind and around and in front of it, and many a bearskin cap and tall English Grenadier were mixed with frequent corpses of French Chasseur and infantry soldiers. At one time, while the Duke was rallying his men, a body of Russians began to single him out, and to take shots at him in the most deliberate manner. A surgeon, Mr Wilson, 7th Hussars, who was attached to the brigade, perceived the danger of his Royal Highness, and, with the greatest gallantry and coolness, assembled a few men of the Guards, led them to the charge, and utterly routed and dispersed the Russians. The Duke's horse was killed in the course of the fight. At the close of the day he called Mr Wilson in front of the regiment, and publicly thanked him for having in all probability saved his life.

The conduct of the Russians towards the wounded Guards' officers was brutal in the extreme. Russian officers were seen passing their swords through the bodies of our men, and pointing to their troops to bayonet them as they passed.

The revolvers carried by our officers saved their lives on several occasions this day. Our men were very short of ammunition; the Guards in particular expended all theirs very soon.

From a prisoner whom we examined I gleaned some interesting particulars respecting the formation of the Russian army. The man was not very 'bright', but he told the truth according to the light that was in him, and I believe the statements he made were tolerably correct. It had long been a puzzle to ignorant people like ourselves why the Russian soldiers had numbers on their shoulder-straps different from those on their buttons or on their caps. It will appear that these numbers referred not to regiments, but to divisions. So let our Pole – he was a deserter – one of the few who came in soon after Inkerman, speak for himself through an interpreter:

'What does the number on the strap on your shoulder indicate?'

'It is No. 16. It shows that I belong to the 16th Division of the army.'

'Who commands it?'

'I don't know – a General.'

'What does the number 31 on your buttons mean?'

'It means that I belong to Regt. 31, of the 16th Division.'

'What does the number 7 on your cap, with P after it, mean?'

'It indicates that I belong to the 7th rota of the polk.'

'What does a rota mean?'

'It means a company of 250 men.'

'How many rotas are in a polk?'

'There are sixteen rotas in each polk.'

'And how many polks are in a division?'

'There are four polks in a division?'

'If that is so, why have you 31 on your buttons?' (A pause, a stupid look.) 'I don't know.'

Finding our friend was getting into that helpless state of confusion into which the first glimpses of decimal fractions are wont to plunge the youthful arithmetician, we left him. Now let us combine our information, and see what, according to this Polish authority, a Russian division consists of. It stands thus:

1 Rota =		250 men.		
16 Rotas =	1 Polk =	4,000	,,	
4 Polks =	1 Division =	16,000	,,	2nd Division of Infantry

The men resembled those we met at the Alma, and were clad and armed in the same way. We saw no infantry with helmets, however, and our soldiers were disappointed to find the Russians had, in most cases, come out without their knapsacks. Their persons were very cleanly, and the whiteness of their faces and of their feet were remarkable. Few of them had socks on, and the marauders, who ever prowl over a battlefield, had removed their boots whenever they were worth taking. Our soldiers and sailors, as well as the French, looked out with avidity for a good pair of Russian boots and were quite adepts in fitting themselves to a nicety by their simple mode of measurement – viz., placing their feet against those of the dead men. Officers and men wore the same long grey coats, the former being alone distinguishable by the stripe of gold lace on the shoulder. Their uniform coatees, of dark green with white facings and red and yellow trimmings, were put on underneath the greatcoat.

A considerable number of Liège double-grooved rifles were found on the field. The bayonets were long, but not well steeled. They bent if rudely handled or struck with force against the ground. The long and polished gun-barrels were made of soft, but tough iron. They could be bent to an acute angle without splitting.

It was again asserted – and I sincerely believe with truth – that the dying and wounded Russians killed many of our men as they passed on towards the front against the retreating enemy. For this reason our soldiers smashed the stock and bent the barrel of nearly every firelock they came across. Some, however, carried bundles of them off the field, as well as heaps of Liège rifles, and of a heavy, thick sword with a saw-back, borne by the Grenadiers or Artillerymen, which they sold to the captains and soldiers of merchantmen, or to those who are anxious for mementoes of the fight. Medals, ribands, the small brass crucifixes, and pictures of saints, and charms found upon the dead, were also in great request. The field was visited by shoals of people from Balaklava every day.

If it is considered that the soldiers who met these furious columns of the Czar were the remnants of three British divisions, which scarcely numbered 8,500 men; that they were hungry and wet, and half-famished; that they were men belonging to a force which was generally 'out of bed' four nights out of seven; which had been enfeebled by sickness, by severe toil, sometimes for twenty-four hours at a time without relief of any kind; that among them were men who had within a short time previously lain out for forty-eight hours in the trenches at a stretch – it will be readily admitted that never was a more extraordinary contest maintained by our army since it acquired a reputation in the world's history.

12

The Hurricane

THE OLDEST SOLDIERS NEVER WITNESSED NOR HEARD OF a campaign in which general officers were obliged to live out in tents on the open field, for the want of a roof to cover them, and generals who passed their youth in the Peninsular war, and who had witnessed a good deal of fighting since that time in various parts of the world, were unanimous in declaring that they never knew or read of a war in which the officers were exposed to such hardships. They landed without anything but what they could carry, and they marched beside their men, slept by them, fought by them, and died by them, undistinguished from them in any respect, except by the deadly epaulet and swordbelt, which have cost so many lives. The survivors were often unable to get their things from on board ship. They laid down at night in the clothes which they wore during the day; many delicately-nurtured youths never changed shirt or shoes for weeks together, and they were deprived of the use of water for ablution, except to a very limited extent.

'Rank and fashion', under such circumstances, fell a prey to parasitical invasion – an evil to which the other incidents of roughing it are of little moment. The officers were in rags. Guardsmen, who were 'the best style of men' in the Parks, turned out in coats and trousers and boots all seams and patches, torn in all directions, and mended with more vigour than neatness, and our smartest cavalry and line men were models of ingenious sewing and stitching. The men could not grumble at old coats, boots, or shoes when they saw their officers no better off than themselves.

On the 14th of November came a new calamity – the camp was visited by a hurricane. It commenced shortly after six o'clock a.m., and was preceded by rain and squalls.

For about an hour I had been in a listless state between waking and sleeping, listening to the pelting of the rain against the fluttering canvas of the tent, or dodging the streams of water which flowed underneath it, saturating our blankets and collecting on the mackintosh sheets in pools. The sound of the rain, its heavy beating on the earth, had become gradually swallowed up by the noise of the rushing of the wind over the common, and by the flapping of the tents as they rocked more violently beneath its force. Gradually the sides of the canvas, which were tucked in under big stones to secure them, began to rise and flutter, permitting the wind to enter playfully and drive before it sheets of rain right into one's face; the pegs began to indicate painful indecision and want of firmness of purpose. The glimpses afforded of the state of affairs outside, by the lifting of the tent walls, were little calculated to produce a spirit of resignation to the fate which threatened our frail shelter. The ground had lost its character of solidity, and pools of mud marked the horse and cattle-trucks in front of the tents. Mud – and nothing but mud – flying before the wind and drifting as though it were rain, covered the face of the earth as far as it was visible.

At every fresh blast the pole of the tent played and bent like a salmon-rod; the canvas tugged at the ropes to pull them up, and the pegs yielded gently. A startling crack! I looked at my companions, who seemed determined to shut out all sound and sense by piling as many clothes as they could collect over their heads. A roar of wind, and the pole bent till the fatal 'crack' was heard again. 'Get up, Doctor! up with you, the tent is coming down!' The Doctor rose from beneath his *tumulus* of clothes. Now, if there was anything in which the Doctor put confidence more than another, it was his tent-pole. There was a decided bend in the middle of it, but he used to argue, on sound anatomical, mathematical, and physical principles, that the bend was an improvement. He looked on the pole blandly, as he looked at all things, put his hand out, and shook it. 'Why, man,' said he, reproachfully, 'it's all right – that pole would stand for ever,' and then he crouched down and burrowed under his bed-clothes.

Scarcely had he given the last convulsive heave of the blankets which indicates perfect comfort and satisfaction, when a harsh screaming sound, increasing in vehemence as it approached, struck us with horror As it passed along we heard the snapping of tent-poles and the sharp crack of timber and canvas. On it came, 'a mighty and a strong wind'; the pole broke off short in the middle, as if it were glass, and in an instant we were pressed down and half stifled by the heavy folds of the wet canvas, which beat us about the head with the greatest fury. Half breathless and blind, I struggled for the door. Such a sight met the eye! The whole headquarters' camp was beaten flat to the earth, and the unhappy occupants were rushing through the mud in all directions in chase of their effects and clothes, as they strove to make their way to the roofless and windowless barns and stables for shelter.

Next to our tent was the marquee of Captain de Morel. It laid fluttering on the ground and as I looked, the canvas seemed animated by some great internal convulsion – a mimic volcano appeared to be opening beneath it, and its folds assumed the most fantastic shapes, tossing wildly about in the storm. The phenomenon was speedily accounted for by the apparition of the gallant owner fighting his way out desperately against the wind, which was bent on tearing his very scanty covering from his person; and at last he succeeded in making a bolt of it and squattered through the mud to the huts.

Captain Chetwode was tearing through the rain and dirt like a maniac after a cap which he fancied was his own and which he found, after a desperate run, to be his sergeant's.

The air was filled with blankets, hats, greatcoats, little coats, and even tables and chairs. Mackintoshes, quilts, india-rubber tubs, bed-clothes, sheets of tent-canvas went whirling like leaves in the gale towards Sebastopol. The shingle roofs of the outhouses were torn away and scattered over the camp, and a portion of the roof of Lord Raglan's house was carried off to join them. The barns and commissariat-sheds were laid bare at once, large arabas, or wagons, which stood close to us, were overturned; men and horses were

Sir William Howard Russell

Lord Raglan

Marshal St Arnaud

The Battle of the Alma

General Sir George Brown

Major-General the Earl of Cardigan

The charge of the Heavy Brigade at Balaklava

Lieutenant-General Sir de Lacy Evans

General Canrobert

The charge of the Guards at Inkerman

His Excellency Omar Pasha

The Redan from an advanced parallel

The interior of the Mamelon, 9 June 1855

General Sir William Simpson

Marshal Pelissier

The capture of Malakoff

knocked down and rolled over and over; the ambulance wagons were turned topsy-turvy.

Looking over towards the hill occupied by the Second Division, we could see that the blast had there been of equal violence. The ridges, the plains, and undulating tracts between the ravines, so lately smiling in the autumn sun, with row after row of neat white tents, was bare and desolate, the surface turned into sticky mud as black as ink, and the discoloured canvas rolled up in heaps all over it. The face of the country was covered with horses which had torn away from the pickets. Nearly one-half of our cavalry horses broke loose. The French, flying for shelter, swarmed across the plains in all directions, seeking for the lee of old walls or banks for protection from the blast. Our men, more sullen and resolute, stood in front of their levelled tents while wind and rain tore over them, or collected in groups before their late camps.

On turning towards the ridge on which the large and imposing wooden structures built by the French for hospitals and storehouses were erected, a few scattered planks alone met the eye. The wounded of the 5th November, who to the number of several hundred were in these buildings, had to bear the inclemency of the weather as well as they could. In every direction, fresh scenes of wretchedness met the eye. The guard tents were down, the late occupants huddled together under the side of a barn, their arms covered with mud, lying where they had been thrown from the 'pile' by the wind. The officers of the guard had fled to the commissariat stores and there found partial shelter. Inside the commissariat yard, overturned carts, dead horses, and groups of shivering men were seen – not a tent was left standing.

Our generals' marquees were as incapable of resisting the hurricane as the bell-tents of the common soldiers. Lord Lucan was seen for hours sitting up to his knees in sludge amid the wreck of his establishment, meditative as Marius amid the ruins of Carthage. Lord Cardigan was sick on board his yacht in the harbour of Balaklava. Sir George Brown was lying wounded on board the 'Agamemnon'; Sir de Lacy Evans, sick and shaken, was on board the 'Sanspareil', in Balaklava; General Bentinck, wounded, was on board the

'Caradoc', on his way to England. The Duke of Cambridge, sick and depressed, was passing an anxious time of it in the 'Retribution', off Balaklava, in all the horrors of that dreadful scene at sea – in fact all the generals and colonels and officers in the field were just as badly off as the meanest private.

Towards ten o'clock matters were looking more hopeless and cheerless than ever, when a welcome invitation came through the storm for us to go over to the shelter of a well protected tent. Our first duty was to aid the owner in securing the pole with 'a fish' of stout spars. Then we aided in passing out a stay from the top of the pole to the wall in front, and in a short time afterwards a cup of warm tea was set before each of us, provided by some inscrutable chemistry, and with excellent ration biscuit and some butter, a delicious meal, as much needed as it was quite unexpected, was made by my friends and myself, embittered only by the ever-recurring reflection, 'God help us, what will become of the poor fellows in the trenches and on the hill?' And there we sat, thinking and talking of the soldiers, and of the fleet, hour after hour, while the wind and rain blew and fell, gradually awakening us to the full sense of the calamity with which Providence was pleased to visit us.

Towards twelve o'clock the wind, which had been blowing from the south-west, chopped round more to the west, and became much colder. Sleet fell first, and then came a snow-storm, which clothed the desolate landscape in white, till the tramp of men seamed it with trails of black mud.

The day was going by, and there was no prospect of any abatement of the storm. At two o'clock, however, the wind went down a little, and the intervals between the blasts of the gale became more frequent and longer. We took advantage of one of these halcyon moments to trudge away to the wreck of the tent, and, having borrowed another pole, with the aid of a few men we got it up all muddy and filthy, and secured it as far as possible for the night; but it was evident that no dependence could be placed upon its protection, and the floor was a mass of dirt and puddle, and the bed and clothes dripping wet. Towards evening there were many tents re-pitched along the lines of our camps, though they were but sorry resting-places. They flapped about so much and admitted such quantities of snow, rain, and filth from outside that it was quite out of the question to sleep in them. What was to be done? Suddenly it occurred to us that there might be room in the barn used as a stable for the horses of Lord Raglan's escort of the 8th Hussars, and we at once waded across the sea of nastiness which lay between us and it, tacked against several gusts, fouled one or two soldiers in a different course, grappled with walls and angles of outhouses, nearly foundered in big horse holes, bore sharply up round a corner, and anchored at once in the stable.

What a scene it was! The officers of the escort were crouching over some embers of a wood fire; along the walls were packed some thirty or forty horses and ponies, shivering with cold, and kicking and biting with spite and bad humour. The Hussars, in their long cloaks, stood looking gloomily on the flakes of snow, which drifted in at the doorway or through the extensive apertures in the shingle roof. Soldiers of different regiments crowded about the warm corners, and Frenchmen of all arms, and a few Turks, joined in the brotherhood of misery, lighted their pipes at the scanty fire, and sat close for mutual comfort. The wind blew savagely through the roof, and through chinks in the mud walls and window-holes. The building was a mere shell, as dark as pitch, and smelt as it ought to do – an honest, unmistakeable stable – improved by a dense pack of moist and mouldy soldiers.

A staff officer, dripping with rain, came in to see if he could get any shelter for draughts of the 33rd and 41st Regiments, which had just been landed at Kamiesch, but he soon ascertained the hopelessness of his mission so far as our quarters were concerned. The men were packed into another shed, 'like herrings in a barrel'. Having told us, 'There is terrible news from Balaklava – seven vessels lost, and a number on shore at the Katscha,' and thus made us more gloomy than ever, the officer went on his way, as well as he could, to look after his draughts.

The storm, from half-past six o'clock till late in the day, passed over the camp with the fury of Azrael, vexing and buffeting every living thing and tearing to pieces all things inanimate. We sat in the dark till night set in – not a soul could stir out. Nothing could be heard but the howling of the wind, the yelping of wild dogs driven into the enclosures, and the shrill neighings of terrified horses. At length a candle-end was stuck into a horn lantern, to keep it from the wind – a bit of ration pork and some rashers of ham, done over the wood fire, furnished an excellent dinner, which was followed by a glass or horn of hot water and rum, then a pipe, and as it was cold and comfortless, we got to bed – a heap of hay on the stable floor, covered with our clothes, and thrown close to the heels of a playful grey mare, who had strong antipathies to her neighbours, a mule and an Arab horse, and spent the night in attempting to kick in their ribs. Amid smells, and with incidents impossible to describe or to allude to more nearly, we went to sleep.

Throughout the day there had been very little firing from the Russian batteries. In the middle of the night, however, we were all awoke by one of the most tremendous cannonades we had ever heard, and, after a time, the report of a rolling fire of musketry was borne upon the wind. Looking eagerly in the direction of the sound, we saw the flashes of the cannon through the chinks in the roof, each flash distinct by itself, just as a flash of lightning is seen in all its length and breadth through a crevice in a window shutter. It was evident there was a sortie on the French lines. The cannonade lasted for half-an-hour, and gradually waxed fainter. In the morning we heard that the Russians had sallied out from their comfortable warm barracks on the French in the trenches, but that they had been received with an energy which quickly made them fly back again to the cover of their guns.

With the morning of the 15th of November came a bright cold sky, and our men, though ankle deep in mud wherever they went, cheered up when they beheld the sun once more. The peaks of the hills and mountain sides were covered with snow. As rumours of great disasters reached us from Balaklava, I rode into town, after breakfasting in my stable, and made my way there as well as I could. The roads were mere quagmires. Dead horses and cattle were scattered all over the country, and here and there a sad little procession, charged with the burden of some inanimate body, might be seen wending its way slowly towards the hospital marquees, which had been again pitched.

On approaching the town, signs of the tempest increased at every step. At the narrow neck of the harbour two or three large boats were lying, driven inland several yards from the water; the shores were lined with trusses of hay which had floated out of the wrecks outside the harbour, and masts and spars of all sizes were stranded on the beach or floated about among the shipping.

The condition of Balaklava at that time is utterly indescribable. The narrow main street was a channel of mud, through which horses, wagons, camels, mules, and soldiers and sailors, and men of all nations – English, French, Turks, Arabs, Egyptians, Italians, Maltese, Tartars, Greeks, Bulgarians, and Spaniards – scrambled, and plunged, and jostled, and squattered along; while 'strange oaths', yells, and unearthly cries of warning or expostulation, filled the air, combined with the noise of the busy crowds around the sutlers' stores, and with the clamorous invitations of the vendors to their customers. Many of the houses were unroofed, several had been destroyed altogether, and it was quite impossible to find quarters in the place, the preference having been apparently given to the sutlers and store-keepers, who swarmed on shore from every ship, and who were generally Levantines, with the most enlarged notions of the theory and practice of buying in the cheapest and selling in the dearest market.

13

In the Grip of Winter

DURING THIS WINTER NEWSPAPER CORRESPONDENTS IN the Crimea were placed in a rather difficult position. In common with generals and chiefs, and men-at-arms, they wrote home accounts of all we were doing to take Sebastopol, and they joined in the prophetic cries of the leaders of the host, that the fall of the city of the Czar – the centre and navel of his power in those remote regions – would not be deferred for many hours after our batteries had opened upon its defences. They believed, in common with the leaders, whose inspiration and whose faith were breathed through the ranks of our soldiers, that the allied forces were to reduce Sebastopol long ere the lines they penned could meet the expectant gaze of our fellow-countrymen at home; and they stated, under that faith and in accordance with those inspirations, that the operations of war undertaken by our armies were undertaken with reference to certain points of position and with certain hope of results, the knowledge of which could not have proved of the smallest service to the enemy once beaten out of their stronghold.

It mattered little, therefore, if we pointed out the losses of our men, the number and position of our guns, the site of our quarters, the position of our magazines, or the range of the Russian cannon. How much knowledge of this sort the enemy gleaned through their spies, or by actual observation, it is not needful to inquire; but it may be inferred that much of the information conveyed to them, or said to have been conveyed to them, by the English press, could have been ascertained through those very ordinary channels of communication, the eye and ear, long ere our letters had been forwarded to Sebastopol, and translated.

Although it might be dangerous to communicate facts likely to be of service to the Russians, it was certainly hazardous to conceal the truth from the English people. They must have known, sooner or later, that the siege towards the end of November had been for many days practically suspended, that our batteries were used up and silent, and that our army were much exhausted by the effects of excessive labour and watching, and by the wet and storm to which they have been so incessantly exposed. The Russians knew this soon enough, for a silent battery speaks for itself. The relaxation of our fire was self-evident, but our army, though weakened by sickness, were still equal to hold their position, and to inflict the most signal chastisement upon any assailants who might venture to attack them. In fact, I believe nothing would have so animated our men, deprived as they were of the cheering words and of the cheering personal presence and exhortations of their generals, and destitute of all stimulating influences beyond those of their undaunted spirit and glorious courage, as the prospect of meeting the Russians outside their entrenchments, and deciding the campaign by the point of the bayonet. Rain kept pouring down – the skies were black as ink – the wind howled over the staggering tents – the trenches were turned into dikes – in the tents the water was sometimes a foot deep – our men had neither warm nor waterproof clothing – they were out for twelve hours at a time in the trenches – they were plunged into the inevitable miseries of a winter campaign – and not a soul seemed to care for their comfort, or even for their lives. These were hard truths, which sooner or later must have come to the ears of the people of England. It was right they should know that the wretched beggar who wandered about the streets of London in the rain led the life of a prince compared with the British soldiers who were fighting for their country, and who, we were complacently assured by the home authorities, were the best appointed army in Europe. They were well fed, indeed, but they had no shelter, no rest, and no defence against the weather. The tents, so long exposed to the blaze of a Bulgarian sun, and continually drenched by torrents of rain, let the wet through like sieves, and were perfectly useless as protections against the weather.

As the year waned and winter began to close in upon us, the army suffered greatly; worn out by night-work, by vigil in rain and storm, by hard labour in the trenches, they found themselves suddenly reduced to short allowance, and the excellent and ample rations they had been in the habit of receiving were cut off or miserably reduced. For nine days, with very few exceptions, no issue of tea, coffee, or sugar, to the troops took place. These, however, are luxuries – not the necessaries of military life.

The direct cause of this scarcity was the condition of the country, which, saturated by heavy rains, had become quite unfit for the passage of carts and arabas; but there was also a deficiency of supplies, which might be attributed to the gales at sea. There was, therefore, a difficulty in getting food up to the army from Balaklava, and there was besides, a want of supplies in the commissariat magazines in the latter place. But though there was a cause, there was no excuse for the privations to which the men were exposed. We were all told that when the bad weather set in, the country roads would be impassable. Still the fine weather was allowed to go by, and the roads were left as the Tartar carts had made them, though the whole face of the country was covered thickly with small stones which seem expressly intended for road metal. As I understood, it was suggested by the officers of the Commissariat Department that they should be allowed to form depots of food, corn, and forage, as a kind of reserve at the headquarters at the different divisions; but instead of being permitted to carry out this excellent idea, their carts, arabas, wagons, and horses were, after a few days' work in forming those depots, taken for the use of the siege operations, and were employed in carrying shot, shell, ammunition, etc., to the trenches. Consequently, the magazines at headquarters were small, and were speedily exhausted when the daily supplies from Balaklava could no longer be procured. The food, and corn, and hay, provided by the commissariat, were stowed in sailing vessels, which were ordered to lie outside the harbour, though they had to ride in thirty or forty fathoms of water on a rocky bottom, with a terrible coast of cliff of 1,200 feet in perpendicular height stretching around the bay, and though it was notorious that the place was subject at that season to violent storms of wind. A hurricane arose – one of unusual and unknown violence – these ships were lost, and with them went to the bottom provender and food for fully twenty days of all the horses in the army, and of many of the men.

It happened that we had a forewarning of what might be expected. On Friday, the 10th of November, just four days ere the fatal catastrophe which caused such disasters, I was on board the 'Jason', which happened to be lying outside, and as it came on to blow I could not return to the shore or get to the camp that evening. The ship was a noble steamer, well manned and ably commanded, but ere midnight I would have given a good deal to have been on land; for the gale, setting right into the bay, raised a high wild sea, which rushed up the precipices in masses of water and foam, astonishing by their force and fury; and the strain on the cable was so great that the captain had to ease it off by steaming gently a-head against the wind. The luckless 'Prince', which had lost two anchors and cables on bringing up a day or two before, was riding near the 'Agamemnon', and adopted the same expedient; and, of the numerous vessels outside, and which in so short a time afterwards were dashed into fragments against those cruel rocks, the aspect of which was calculated to thrill the heart of the boldest seaman with horror, there were few which did not drag their anchors and draw towards the iron coast which lowered with death on its brow upon us. Guns of distress boomed through the storm, and flashes of musketry pointed out for a moment a helpless transport which seemed tossing in the very centre of the creaming foam of those stupendous breakers, the like of which I never beheld, except once, when I saw the Atlantic running riot against the cliffs of Moher. But the gale soon moderated – for that once – and wind and sea went down long before morning. However, Sir Edmund Lyons evidently did not like his berth, for the 'Agamemnon' went round to Kamiesch on Sunday morning, and ordered the 'Firebrand', which was lying outside, to go up to the fleet at the Katscha. As to the 'Prince', and the luckless transports, they were allowed, nay, ordered, to stay outside till the hurricane rushed upon them.

The cholera, which broke out on the night of the 28th of November, continued its ravages, and we could not estimate the number of deaths from it and its abettors in the destruction of life lower than sixty per diem.

As to the town itself, words could not describe its filth, its horrors, its hospitals, its burials, its dead and dying Turks, its crowded lanes, its noisome sheds, its beastly purlieus, or its decay. All the pictures ever drawn of plague and pestilence, from the work of the inspired writer who chronicled the woes of infidel Egypt, down to the narratives of Boccacio, Defoe, or Moltke, fall short of individual 'bits' of disease and death, which any one might see in half-a-dozen places during half an hour's walk in Balaklava. In spite of all our efforts, the dying Turks made of every lane and street a *cloaca*, and the forms of human suffering which met the eye at every turn, and once were wont to shock us, made us callous, and ceased even to attract passing attention. By raising up the piece of matting or coarse rug which hung across the doorway of some miserable house, from within which you heard wailings and cries of pain and prayers to the Prophet, you saw in one spot and in one instant a mass of accumulated woes that would serve you with nightmares for a lifetime. The dead, laid out as they died, were lying side by side with the living, and the latter presented a spectacle beyond all imagination. The commonest accessories of a hospital were wanting; there was not the least attention paid to decency or cleanliness – the stench was appalling – the foetid air could barely struggle out to taint the atmosphere, save through the chinks in the walls and roofs, and, for all I could observe, these men died without the least effort to save them. There they laid just as they were let gently down upon the ground by the poor fellows, their comrades, who brought them on their backs from the camp with the greatest tenderness, but who were not allowed to remain with them. The sick appeared to be tended by the sick, and the dying by the dying.

Apart from the attack on the allied redoubts at Balaklava on October 25th and the onslaught that resulted in the battle of Inkerman, the Russians had made no serious attempt to dislodge the Allies from their positions. Sporadic attacks were kept up by both sides, in daylight as well as at night, and occasionally there was a reconnaissance in force. But at the end of December the positions occupied by the opposing forces were virtually the same as when the siege had begun at the end of September. The same could not be said, however, of the conditions in which the British forces were now existing.

At the commencement of 1855 I could not conceal my impression that our army was likely to suffer severely unless instant and most energetic measures were taken to place it in a position to resist the inclemency of the weather. We had no means of getting up the huts – all our army could do was to feed itself. As to 'warm clothing', the very words immediately suggest to us all some extraordinary fatality. Some went down with the ill-fated and ill-treated 'Prince', some of it was lost, and we heard that a ship with clothing for the officers had been burnt off Constantinople; that some of it had been saturated with water; and I had an opportunity of seeing several lighters full of warm greatcoats, etc., for the men, lying a whole day in the harbour of Balaklava beneath a determined fall of rain and snow. There was no one to receive them when they were sent to the shore, or rather no one would receive them without orders. In fact, we were ruined by etiquette, and by 'service' regulations. No one would take 'responsibility' upon himself even to save the lives of hundreds.

We were cursed by a system of 'requisitions', 'orders', and 'memos', which was enough to depress an army of scriveners, and our captains, theoretically, had almost as much work to do with pen and paper as if they had been special correspondents or bankers' clerks; that is, they ought to have had as much to do, but, thanks to the realities of war, they had no book-keeping; their accounts being lost, and the captain who once had forty or fifty pounds' weight of books and papers to carry, had not so much as a penny memorandum book. This fact alone showed the absurdity of our arrangements. In peace, when these accounts were of comparatively little importance, we had plenty and too much of checks and returns, but in time of war the very first thing our army did was to leave all its stationery on board the steamer that carried it to the scene of action.

The cold was developing itself, and I regret to say our efforts to guard against it were attended with mischief. Captain Swinton, of the Royal Artillery, a gallant and excellent officer, was found dead in his tent, suffocated by the fumes of charcoal from a stove which he had placed within it for the purposes of warmth. Great numbers of iron stoves were brought out from Constantinople, and were not used with proper caution, and several officers were half-killed by carbonic acid gas generated in these deadly apparatus. Fatigue parties from the different regiments were employed every day in bringing up biscuit and provisions to headquarters, where they made some sort of attempt to establish a central depot. This duty was very hard on officers and men, and was almost as severe as the labour of carrying up shot and shell. Sometimes the military escorts missed their way or lost their provisions, and the divisions to which they belonged were deprived of their rum and biscuit.

We were obliged to apply to the French to place guards over the line of our march, for the instant a cart with provisions or spirits broke down it was plundered by our active friends the Zouaves, who really seemed to have the gift of ubiquity. Let an araba once stick, or break a wheel or an axle, and the Zouaves sniffed it out just as vultures detect carrion; in a moment barrels and casks were broken open, the bags of bread were ripped up, the contents were distributed, and the commissary officer, who had gone to seek for help and assistance, on his return found only the tires of the wheels and a few splinters of wood left, for our indefatigable foragers completed their work most effectually and carried off the cart, body and boxes, to serve as firewood.

We had rather a rough and dreary Christmas of it, and not a very happy New Year, on these heights before Sebastopol. Where were our presents – our Christmas-boxes – the offerings of our kind country-men and country-women, and the donations from our ducal parks? Where were the fat bucks, the potted meats, which covered the decks and filled the holds of adventurous yachts; and the various worsted devices which had employed the fingers and emptied the crochet-boxes of our fair sympathizers at home? At the close of the year there were 3,500 sick in the British camp before Sebastopol, and it was not too much to say that their illness had, for the most part, been caused by hard work in bad weather and by exposure to wet without any adequate protection. Think of a tent pitched, as it were, at the bottom of a marsh, into which some twelve or fourteen miserable creatures, drenched to the skin, had to creep for shelter after twelve hours of vigil in a trench like a canal, and then reflect what state these poor fellows must have been in at the end of a night and day spent in such *shelter*, huddled together without any change of clothing, and lying packed up as close as they could be stowed in saturated blankets. But why were they in tents? Where were the huts which had been sent out to them? The huts were on board ships in the harbour of Balaklava. Some of these huts, of which we heard so much, were floating about the beach; others had been landed, and now and then I met a wretched pony, knee-deep in mud, struggling on beneath the weight of two thin deal planks, a small portion of one of these huts, which were most probably converted into firewood after lying for some time in the camp, or turned into stabling for officers' horses when enough of *disjecta membra* had been collected. Had central depots been established while the fine weather lasted, much, if not all, of the misery and suffering of the men and of the loss of horses would have been averted.

It may be true that the enemy were suffering still more than our own men, but the calculation of equal losses on the part of England and on the part of Russia in the article of soldiery cannot be regarded as an ingredient in the consideration of our position. It is an actual truth that our force was deprived day by day of the services of about a hundred men in every twenty-four hours. The 63rd Regiment had only seven men fit for duty on the 7th [January]. The 46th had only thirty men fit for duty at the same date. A strong company of the 90th had been reduced by the week's severity to fourteen file in a few days, and that regiment, though considered very healthy, lost fifty men by death in a fortnight. The Scots Fusileer Guards, who had had out from beginning 1,562 men, mustered 210 men on parade. Many other regiments suffered in like proportion. There were at one time between 7,000 and 8,000 men sick, wounded, and convalescent in the hospitals on the Bosphorus. The transport horses were quite beaten, and dropped and died by dozens. The number of, dead horses on the roadside, augmented by every day's work, was very considerable. Each ditch or deep furrow across the path was marked by a heap of decaying horseflesh. The cavalry division lost about sixty horses during one night; and out of one division alone 150 men were taken out of the trenches to the hospital tents, seized with cramp and half-frozen, not so much perhaps from the cold as from the want of proper clothing and inability to move about to circulate the blood.

By the first week in January the scenery of our camping ground and of the adjacent country had assumed a truly wintry aspect. The lofty abrupt peaks and sharp ridges of the mountains which closed up the valley of Balaklava were covered with snow, giving them an appearance of great height and ruggedness; and the valley and plateau were of a blanched white, seamed and marked by lines of men and horses carrying up provisions. The duty of the fatigue parties was, indeed, very trying. The men were provided with a stout pole for each couple, and a cask of rum, biscuits, or beef, was slung from it between them, and then they went off on a tramp of about five miles from the commissariat stores at Balaklava to head-quarters. I saw officers dividing this labour with their men; and as I was coming in from the front one Saturday, I met a lad who could not long have joined in charge of a party of the 38th Regiment. He had taken the place of a tired man, and struggled along under his load, while the man at the other end of the pole exhausted the little breath he had left in appeals to his comrades. 'Boys! boys! won't you come and relieve the young officer?' Horses could not do this work, for they could not keep their legs.

Hundreds of men had to go into the trenches at night with no covering but their greatcoats, and no protection for their feet but their regimental shoes. The trenches were two and three feet deep with mud, snow, and half-frozen slush. Many when they took off their shoes were unable to get their swollen feet into them again, and they might be seen bare-footed, hopping along about the camp, with the thermometer at twenty degrees, and the snow half a foot deep upon the ground. Our fine patent stoves were wretched affairs.

They were made of thin sheet iron. Besides, with charcoal they were mere poison manufactories, and they could not be left alight in the tents at night. They answered well for drying the men's clothes at day.

I don't know how the French got on, but I know this, that our people did not get a fair chance for their lives while wintering in the Crimea – at least, at this time. Providence had been very good to us. With one great exception, which must have done as much mischief to the enemy as to ourselves, we had wonderful weather from the day the expedition landed in the Crimea.

One day as I was passing through the camp of the 5th (French) Regiment of the line, and urging my poor steed through heaps of mud, an officer came out of his tent, and, with the unfailing kindness and courtesy of our allies, invited me to dismount and take a glass of the brandy which had been sent out by the Emperor as a Christmas gift. Although he was living in a tent, the canvas was only a roof for a capacious and warm pit in which there was a bright wood fire sparkling cheerily in a grate of stones. We 'trinqued' together and fraternized as our allies will always do when our officers give them a chance. My host showed me with pride the case of sound Bordeaux, the box of brandy, and the pile of good tobacco sent to him by Napoleon III – '*le premier ami du soldat.*'

A similar present had been sent to every officer of the French army, and a certain quantity of wine, brandy, and tobacco had been forwarded to each company of every regiment in the Crimea. That very day I heard dolorous complaints that the presents sent by the Queen and Prince Albert to our army had miscarried, and that the Guards and Rifles had alone received the royal bounty in the very acceptable shape of a ton of Cavendish [tobacco].

It must not be inferred that the French were all healthy while we were all sickly. They had dysentery, fever, diarrhoea, and scurvy, as well as pulmonary complaints, but not to the same extent as ourselves, or to anything like it in proportion to their numbers.

One of the most melancholy subjects for reflection in the world was the sight of our army. It consisted of officers, men, and regiments almost new to this campaign. The generation of six months before had passed away; generals, brigadiers, colonels, captains, and men, the well-known faces of Gallipoli, of Scutari, of Varna – ay, even of the bivouac of Bouljanak, had changed; and there was scarcely one of the regiments once so familiar to me which I could then recognize save by its well-known number. Excepting Lord Raglan, Lord Lucan, and Sir R. England, not one of our generals remained of those who went out originally; the changes among our brigadiers and colonels were almost as great – all removed from the army by wounds, by sickness, or by death. And so it was with the men themselves.

On the 16th the thermometer was at 14° in the morning and at 10° on the heights over Balaklava. The snow fell all night, and covered the ground to the depth of three feet; but the cold and violent wind drifted it in places to the depth of five or six feet. The wind blew almost a gale, and the native horses refused to face it, but our poor fellows came trudging along in the same dreary string, and there was something mournful in the very aspect of the long lines of black dots moving across the vast expanse of glittering snow between Sebastopol and Balaklava. When these dots came up, you saw they had very red noses and very white faces and very bleared eyes; and as to their clothes, Falstaff would have thought his famous levy a *corps d'élite* if he could have beheld our gallant soldiery. Many of the officers were as ragged and as reckless in dress. It was inexpressibly odd to see Captain Smith, of the —— Foot, with a pair of red Russian leather boots up to his middle, a cap probably made out of the tops of his holsters, and a white skin coat tastefully embroidered all down the back with flowers of many-coloured silk, topped by a head-dress *à la* dustman of London, stalking gravely through the mud of Balaklava, intent on the capture of a pot of jam or marmalade. This would be rather facetious and laughable were not poor Captain Smith a famished wretch, with bad chilblains, approximating to frost-bites, a touch of scurvy, and of severe rheumatism.

Work had begun by this time on 'the Grand Crimean Railway (with branch line to Sebastopol)' which it was planned to run from the harbour to the rear of the British camp at Kadikoi. Even without the hazards of war it would have been a formidable undertaking: the ground, consisting mostly of hard rock, rose over a distance of some three miles to a height of 630 feet. However, by the end of January the railway was progressing, in spite of the uncertain weather.

The great variableness of the Crimean climate was its strongest peculiarity. In the morning, you got up and found the water frozen in your tent, the ground covered with snow, the thermometer at 20°; put on mufflers, greatcoat, and mits, and went out for a walk, and before evening you returned perspiring under the weight of clothing which you carried at the end of your stick, unable to bear it any longer, while the snow was turned into slush, and the thermometer was at 45°. There was a white frost on the night of the 22nd of January, and the next morning the thermometer was at 42°. A large number of sick and, I feared dying men, were sent into Balaklava on the 23rd on French mule litters and a few of our bât [pack] horses. They formed one of the most ghastly processions that ever poet imagined. Many of these men were all but dead. With closed eyes, open mouths, and ghastly attenuated faces, they were borne along two and two, the thin stream of breath visible in the frosty air alone showing they were still alive. One figure was a horror – a corpse, stone dead, strapped upright in its seat, its legs hanging stiffly down, the eyes staring wide open, the teeth set on the protruding tongue, the head and body nodding with frightful mockery of life at each stride of the mule over the broken road. No doubt the man died on his way down to the harbour. Another man I saw with the raw flesh and skin hanging from his fingers, the naked bones of which protruded into the cold air, undressed and uncovered. That was a case of frost-bite, I presume. Possibly the hand had been dressed, but the bandages might have dropped off. All the sick in the mule litters seemed alike on the verge of the grave.

It would have astonished a stranger riding out from Balaklava to the front to have seen the multitudes of dead horses all along the road. In every gully were piles of the remains of these wretched animals, torn to pieces by wild dogs and vultures, and many of the equine survivors of the desperate charge at Balaklava lay rotting away by the side of the cavalry camp. The attitudes of some of the skeletons were curious. Some had dropped down dead and were frozen stiff as they fell; others were struggling, as it were, to rise from their miry graves. Nearly all of the carcasses had been skinned by the Turks and French, who used the hides to cover their huts, and many suspicious-looking gaps, too, suggestive of horse-steak, had been cut out in their flanks. For about six miles the country was dotted all over with these carcasses in every stage of decay.

About mid-day on the 24th, Lord Raglan, attended by Major-General Airey and a few staff officers, rode over to Balaklava. He then went on board the 'Caradoc' and there was a kind of council of war at which several officers were present.

I had a long *reconnaissance* of Sebastopol on the same day, in company with an officer of the Horse Artillery. It was a beautifully clear day and at times it was almost warm. We went up to the mound in advance and on the left of the French picket-house, and for a long time we swept every inch of ground visible under the glass. The aspect of the place itself had changed very little, considering the hundreds of tons' weight of shot and shell thrown into it; but the suburbs of low whitewashed houses, roofed with tiles, and at most two stories high, were in ruins. The enemy had dismantled them as much as we had done. All the streets of such houses were broken down and blocked up with masses of rubbish. The roofs, doors and windows of the houses were all off, but the puffs of smoke from the empty frames showed that the shells were used as covers for the Russian riflemen. People were walking about the streets, and relief parties were coming up from the sea-side towards the front, carrying baskets of provisions. At the other side of the harbour Fort Constantine was shining brightly in the sun, its white walls blackened here and there under the line of embrasures by the smoke of the guns. Behind it, new Russian forts were visible – dark walls of earth rising up through the snow and notched like saws by the lines of embrasures. The waters of the harbour, smooth as glass, were covered with boats, plying from one side to the other.

The weather, thanks to Heaven, continued during the last days of January to be extremely favourable to us. Cold, clear nights, with a bright, unclouded moon, were followed by warm, sunny, genial days. The thermometer generally fell to eighteen or twenty degrees at twelve every night, and rose to forty-four degrees of Fahrenheit at noon the following day. At first the more immediate effect of this change of weather was the facility of communication between Balaklava and the camp. The surface of the country and the roads, or mud tracks, were hardened by the frost for several hours each morning, and remained in a state fit for travelling over, with more or less difficulty, till the influence of the sun had resolved them into cloggy, sticky swamps. Towards dark the frost set in again, and enabled the late return parties to get out to camp with forage and stores.

According to what I heard from a few people in the Crimea who were eccentric enough to purchase a stray number of the obscurer London journals, I was honoured by a good deal of abuse from some of them at home for telling the truth. But I could not tell lies to 'make things pleasant'. There was not a single man in the camp who could put his hand upon his heart and declare he believed that one single casualty had been caused to us by information communicated to the enemy by me or any other newspaper correspondent. The only thing the partisans of misrule could allege was, that I did not 'make things pleasant' to the authorities, and that, amid the filth and starvation, and deadly stagnation of the camp, I did not go about 'babbling of green fields', of present abundance, and of prospects of victory.

On the 31st, a spy walked through some of our trenches, counted the guns, and made whatever observations he pleased, in addition to information acquired from the men with whom he conversed. He was closely shaven, and wore a blue frock-coat buttoned up to the chin, and he stopped for some time to look at Mr Murdoch, of the 'Sanspareil', 'bouching' the guns, or putting new vents into them. Some said he was like a Frenchman, others that he 'looked like a doctor'; no one suspected he was a Russian till he suddenly bolted away down the front of the battery towards the Russian pickets, under a sharp fire of musketry, through which he had the singular good luck to pass unscathed. Strict orders were issued, in consequence of this daring act, to admit no one into the trenches or works without a written permission from the proper authorities, and all persons found loitering about the camp were arrested and sent to divisional headquarters for examination.

As hostilities were relaxed by winter, the allies became on better terms with their enemies. The French were in the habit of sending out working parties through our lines to cut wood for gabions and fuel. They frequently came across Cossack pickets, and as it was our interest not to provoke hostilities with them, a kind of good fellowship had sprung up between our allies and the men of the Russian outposts. One day the French came upon three cavalry horses tied up to a tree, and the officer in command ordered them not to be touched. On the same day a Chasseur had left his belt and accoutrements behind him in the ruined Cossack picket-house, and naturally gave up all hope of recovering them, but on his next visit he found them on the wall untouched. To requite this act of forbearance, a French soldier, who had taken a Cossack's lance and pistol, which he found leaning against a tree, was ordered to return them, and leave them in the place in which he had found them. The next time the French went out, one of the men left a biscuit in a cleft stick, beckoning to the Cossacks to come and eat it. The following day they found a white loaf of excellent bread stuck on a stick in the same place, with a note in Russian, which was translated in Balaklava, to the effect that the Russians had plenty of biscuits, and that, though greatly obliged for that which had been left, they really did not want it; but if the French had bread to spare like the sample left in return, it would be acceptable. The sentries on both sides shouted and yelled to each other, and one day a Russian called out, as the French were retiring for the day, 'Nous nous reverrons, mes amis – Français, Anglais, Russes, nous sommes tous amis.' The cannonade before Sebastopol, the echoes of which reached the remote glades distinctly, must have furnished a strange commentary on the assurance.

14

Adventure in the Snow

THE DRYING WINDS CONTINUED DURING THE MIDDLE OF February, and the plateau to the south of Sebastopol could be traversed easily on horse or foot, even at the bottom of the ravines. The aspect of Balaklava was greatly altered for the better. The wretched hovels in which the Turkish soldiery propagated pestilence and died, were cleaned out or levelled to the earth; the cesspools and collections of utter abomination in the streets were filled up; and quicklime was laid down in the streets and lanes, and around the houses. The railway, which swept right through the main street, very effectually cleared away the crowds of stragglers who used to infest the place. The thunder of cannon from the front boomed through the air; the martial music of the French regiments, interrupted by the creaking of cart-wheels, the cries of camels, the yells of drivers in nearly every language of the east or west – worse than all, by the terrible instruments of the Turkish bands – spoke of war which no Englishman had ever known at home in his day.

On Monday night, 19th February, extensive preparations were made very secretly for a *reconnaissance*, to be conducted by Sir Colin Campbell on our side, and by Generals Bosquet and Vinoy on the part of the French, against the enemy between the Tchernaya and Kamara. The weather, the most important condition of action in a winter campaign, had been unfavourable, but the few fine days from the 15th to the 19th had made the country in tolerable order for the movements of artillery and cavalry. The French were to furnish 11,600 men; Sir Colin Campbell's force was to consist of the 42nd, 79th, 93rd Highlanders, the 14th, 71st, detachments of cavalry, and two batteries. Soon after dark the French on the left of the head-quarters camp began to get in readiness, and the hum of men, and the peculiar dull sound of armed masses on the march, betrayed the movement of our allies. By degrees the rumour spread from one confidant to the other, and by midnight a good number of outriders and amateurs were aware of what was going on, and strict orders were issued for early calls and saddling of horses 'to-morrow morning at dawn'.

Nothing excited such interest as a *reconnaissance*. Our army was deprived of the peculiar attractions of most wars in Europe. There was none of the romance of the Peninsular campaigns about it. We were all shut up in one dirty little angle of land, with Cossacks barring the approaches to the heavenly valley around us. There were no pleasant marches, no halts in town or village, no strange scenes or change of position; nothing but the drudgery of the trenches and of fatigue parties, and the everlasting houses and works of Sebastopol, and the same bleak savage landscape around. The hardest-worked officer was glad, therefore, to get away on a *reconnaissance*, which gave him an excitement and varied the monotony of his life.

Before midnight the French assembled in columns of companies close to headquarters. About the same time the wind changed, and began to blow with some violence, and the stars were overcast by clouds. About one o'clock in the morning the rain began to fall heavily, and continued to descend in irregular torrents for an hour. Then the wind chopped round to the north and became intensely cold, and the rain at once crystallized and fell in the form of hail, and at last the snow drifted all across the camp, while the gale rose higher and higher and increased in severity every moment. It was evident that no good could come of exposing the men, and that the attack would be a failure; it certainly would not have enabled us to form any accurate conception of the numbers or position of the enemy, inasmuch as it was impossible for a man to see a yard before him. Major Foley was therefore despatched by General Canrobert from the French headquarters to inform Sir Colin Campbell that the French would not move, and the regiments under arms were ordered back to their tents, which they found with difficulty.

By this time our men had begun to suffer greatly from the cold, to which they had been exposed for several hours. Their fingers were so cold that they could not 'fix bayonets' when the word was given and could scarcely keep their rifles in their hands. The cavalry horses almost refused to face the snow – frostbites began to occur, and men's ears, noses, and fingers gave symptoms of being attacked. Under these circumstances, it would have been exceedingly unwise to proceed with the *reconnaissance*. Sir Colin very unwillingly gave the order to return, and the men arrived at their quarters about ten o'clock a.m., very much fatigued and exhausted by the cold.

Being anxious to get a letter off by the post ere it started from Kamiesch, and not being aware that the expedition had been countermanded, I started early in the morning for the post-office marquee through a blinding storm of snow. The wind howled fiercely over the plain; it was so laden with snow that it was quite palpable, and had a strange *solid* feel about it as it drifted in endless wreaths of fine small flakes, which penetrated the interstices of the clothing and blinded horse and man. For some time I managed to get on very well, for the track was beaten and familiar. I joined a convoy of artillerymen, but at last the drifts became so thick that it was utterly impossible to see to the right or left for twice a horse's length. As I fancied the artillerymen were going too much to the right, I bore away a little, and soon after met a solitary pedestrian, who wanted to know the way to Balaklava. As he was coming from Lord Raglan's, he confirmed me in the justice of my views concerning the route, and I rode off to warn my friends, the artillerymen, of their mistake. They were not to be found. I had only left them three or four minutes, and yet they had passed away as completely as if the earth had swallowed them up. So I turned on my way, as I thought, and riding right into the wind's eye, made, at the best pace I could force the horse to put forth, for my destination.

It was not above an hour's ride on a bad day, and yet at the end of two hours I had not only not arrived, but I could not make out one of the landmarks which denoted an approach to it. Tents and hill-sides and jutting rocks, all had disappeared, and nothing was visible, above, around, below, but one white sheet drawn, as it were, close around me. This was decidedly unpleasant, but there was no help for it but to ride on and trust to Providence. The sea or the lines would soon bring one up. Still the horse went on snorting out the snow from his nostrils and tossing his head to clear the drift from his eyes and ears; and yet no tent, no man – not a soul to be seen in this peninsula, swarming with myriads of soldiery.

Three hours passed. Where on earth, said I to myself, can I be? Is this enchantment? Has the army here, the lines and trenches, and Sebastopol itself, gone clean off the face of the earth? Is this a horrible dream? The horse stopped at last, and refused to go on against the storm. Every instant the snow fell thicker and thicker. A dark form rushed by with a quick snarling bark – it is a wolf or a wild dog, and the horse rushed on affrighted. The cold pierced one's bones as he faced the gale, and now and then he plunged above the knees into snow-drifts, which were rapidly forming at every hillock and furrow in the ground; a good deep fallow – a well or pit – might have put a speedy termination to one's fears and anxiety at a moment's notice. Minutes became hours, and my eyes were bleared and sore striving to catch a glimpse of tent or man, and to avoid the new dangers in our path. Suddenly I plunged in amongst a quantity of brushwood – sure and certain sign that I had gone far astray indeed, and that I was at some place removed from the camp and the wood-cutters. The notion flashed across me that the wind might have changed, and that in riding against it I might have shaped my course for the Tchernaya and the Russian lines. The idea of becoming the property of a Cossack picket was by no means a pleasant ingredient in one's thoughts at such a moment. Still, what was to be done? My hands and feet were becoming insensible from the cold and my face and eyes were exceedingly painful.

There was no help for it but to push on before night. That would indeed have been a serious evil. At this moment there was a break in the snowdrift for one moment, and I saw to my astonishment a church dome and spire on my right, which vanished again in a moment. My impression was that I must either be close to Kamara or to Sebastopol, and that the church was in either of those widely separated localities. Either way the only thing to do was to bear to the left to regain our lines, though I could not help wondering where on earth the French works were, if it was indeed Sebastopol. I had not ridden very far when, through the ravings of the wind, I could hear a hoarse roar before me, and I could just make out a great black wall as it were rising up through the snowdrift. I was on the very edge of the tremendous precipices which overhang the sea near Cape Fiolente! The position was clear at once. I was close to the Monastery of St George. Dismounting, and carefully leading my horse, I felt my way through the storm, and at last arrived at the monastery. The only Zouave in sight was shooting larks out of a sentry-box, but he at once took my horse to the stable, and showed me the way to the guardhouse, where his comrades were enjoying the comforts of a blazing fire, each waiting for his turn to be shaved by the regimental barber.

Having restored circulation to my blood and got the ice out of my hair, I set out once more, and a smart Zouave undertook to show me the way to headquarters; but he soon got tired of his undertaking, and having first adroitly abstracted my Colt's revolver out of my holster, he deserted me on the edge of a ravine, with some very mysterious instructions as to going on always '*tout droit*', which, seeing that one could not see, would have been very difficult to follow. By the greatest good fortune I managed to strike upon the French tents of the wagon train, and halting at every outburst of the tempest, and pushing on when the storm cleared away a little, I continued to work my way from camp to camp, and at last arrived at headquarters, covered with ice and very nearly 'done up', somewhat before four o'clock in the afternoon. It was some consolation to find that officers had lost themselves in the very vineyard, close to the house, that day, and that aides-de-camp and orderlies had become completely bewildered in their passage from one English divisional camp to another.

Next day the sun came out, the aspect of the camps changed, and our French neighbours filled the air with their many-oathed dialogues and snatches of song. A cold Frenchman is rather a morose and miserable being, but his spirits always rise with sunshine, like the mercury of a thermometer. In company with two officers from the headquarters camp, I had a long inspection of Sebastopol from the ground behind the French position, and I must say the result was by no means gratifying. We went up to the French picket-house first and had a view of the left of the town, looking down towards the end of the ravine which ran down to the Dockyard-creek, the buildings of the Admiralty, the north side of the harbour, and the plateaux towards the Belbek and behind Inkerman. As the day was clear, one could see very well through a good glass, in spite of the dazzling effect of the snow and the bitter wind, which chilled the hands so as to render it impossible to retain the glass very long in one position.

The inner part of the town itself seemed perfectly untouched, the white houses shone brightly and freshly in the sun, and the bells of a Gothic chapel were ringing out lustily in the frosty air. Its tall houses running up the hillsides, its solid look of masonry, gave Sebastopol a resemblance to parts of Bath, or at least put one in mind of that city as seen from the declivity which overhangs the river. There was, however, a remarkable change in the look of the city since I first saw it – there were no idlers and no women visible in the streets, and, indeed, there was scarcely a person to be seen who looked like a civilian. There was, however, abundance of soldiers, and to spare. They could be seen in all directions, sauntering in pairs down desolate-looking streets, chatting at the corners or running across the open space from one battery to another; again, in large parties on fatigue duty, or relieving guards, or drawn up in well-known grey masses in the barrack-squares. Among those who were working on the open space, carrying stores, I thought I could make out two French soldiers. At all events, the men wore long blue coats and red trousers, and as we worked our prisoners and made them useful at Balaklava, where I had seen them aiding in making the railway, I suppose the Muscovite commanders adopted the same plan.

Outside the city, at the verge of the good houses, the eye rested on great walls of earth piled up some ten or twelve feet, and eighteen or twenty feet thick, indented at regular intervals with embrasures, in which the black dots which are throats of cannon might be detected. These works were of tremendous strength. For the most part there was a very deep and broad ditch in front of them, and wherever the ground allowed of it, there were angles and *flèches* which admitted of flanking fires along the front, and of cross fires on centre points of each line of attack or approach. In front of most of the works on both the French and English sides of the town, a suburb of broken-down white-washed cottages, the roofs gone, the doors off, and the windows out, had been left standing in detached masses at a certain distance from the batteries, but gaps had been made in them so that they might not block the fire of the guns.

It was rather an unpleasant reflection, whenever one was discussing the range of a missile, and was perhaps in the act of exclaiming, 'There's a splendid shot,' that it might have carried misery and sorrow into some happy household. The smoke cleared away – the men got up – they gathered round one who moved not, or who was racked with mortal agony; they bore him away, a mere black speck, and a few shovelsfull of mud marked for a little time the resting-place of the poor soldier, whose wife, or mother, or children, or sisters, were left destitute of all solace, save memory and the sympathy of their country. One such little speck I watched that day, and saw quietly deposited on the ground inside the trench. Who would let the inmates of that desolate cottage in Picardy, or Gascony, or Anjou, know of their bereavement?

I was woke up shortly after two o'clock on the morning of the 24th of February by the commencement of one of the most furious cannonades we had then heard since the siege began. The whole line of the Russian batteries from our left opened with inconceivable force and noise, and the Inkerman batteries began playing on our right; the weight of this most terrible fire, which shook the very earth, and lighted up the skies with incessant lightning flashes for an hour and a half, was directed against the French.

The cannonade lasted from a quarter-past two to half-past three a.m. When first I heard it, I thought it was a sortie, and up I started and rode into the moonlight towards the fire; but ere I could get over the ground to Inkerman, the horrid tumult ceased, and it was only next morning that we found out the cause of such a tremendous exhibition of power.

The Russians, perturbed by the gradual extension of French trenches towards the Malakoff, had begun to dig trenches communicating with rifle-pits which they had built on the slopes of the Mamelon, a defensive hill position some 300 yards south-east of the Malakoff. The French, observing these preparations, decided to mount a spoiling attack, but were beaten off with considerable losses.

Sorties by both sides were now a regular feature of the campaign and casualties rose accordingly.

An armistice took place for an hour on the 27th. In the orders of the day, Lord Raglan notified that at the request of General Osten-Sacken an armistice was granted from twelve till one o'clock, to enable the Russians to bury their dead. There was not much firing in the morning previously. At twelve o'clock precisely, white flags were run up on the battery flagstaffs on both sides, and immediately afterwards a body of Russians issued from their new work near the Malakoff, which had been the object of the French attack of the 24th, and proceeded to search for their dead. The French were sent down from Inkerman on a similar errand. A few Russian officers advanced about half-way up towards our lines, where they were met by some of the officers of the allies, and extreme courtesy, the interchange of profound salutations, and enormous bowing, marked the interview. The officers sauntered up and down and shakos were raised and caps doffed politely as each came near an enemy.

The exact object of the armistice it would have been hard to say, for neither French nor Russians seemed to find any bodies un-buried. Shortly before one o'clock, the Russians retired inside their earthwork. At one o'clock the white flags were all hauled down in an instant, and the last fluttering bit of white bunting had scarcely disappeared over the parapet when the flash and roar of a gun from Malakoff announced that the war had begun once more. The French almost simultaneously fired a gun from their batteries also; in a minute afterwards the popping of rifles commenced as usual on both sides.

Such exchanges, on a greater or lesser scale, were by this time an everyday occurrence. Meanwhile, the two sides pressed steadily on with their objectives.

15

Springtime

LORD RAGLAN WENT OUT TO ONE OR OTHER OF THE divisions every day he could spare from his desk. Perhaps there was no clerk in England who had so much writing to get through, *ipsâ manu*, as the Field-Marshal in command of the forces. I believe his lordship was frequently up till two or three o'clock in the morning, looking over papers, signing documents, preparing orders and despatches, and exhausting his energies in secretary's work. Such a life could with most men afford little opportunity for energy or action. The system that necessitated such labours on the part of a Commander-in-Chief must be faulty; it certainly was unsuited for the field or for times of war, and was cumbrous and antiquated.

Five months had passed since Inkerman: five months in which sporadic bombardments and occasional sorties, sometimes in considerable strength, were more or less the order of the day. But these were by no means the only activities.

The silence and calm were but the omens of the struggle which was about to be renewed for the possession of Sebastopol. The Russians were silent because the allies did not impede their works. The allies were silent because they were preparing for the contest, and were using every energy to bring up from Kamiesch and Balaklava the enormous mounds of projectiles and mountains of ammunition which were required for the service of the new batteries, and to extend, complete, and strengthen their offensive and defensive lines and trenches.

The railway had begun to render us some service in saving the hard labour attendant on the transport of shot and shell and enabled us to form a sort of small terminal depot two miles and three-quarters from Balaklava. The navvies, notwithstanding the temptations of the bottle, worked honestly and well, with few exceptions, and the dread of the Provost-Marshal had produced a wholesome influence on the dispositions of the refractory. The Croat labourers astonished all who saw them by the enormous loads they carried, and by their great physical strength and endurance. Broad-chested, flat-backed men, round-shouldered, with long arms, lean flanks, thick muscular thighs, and their calfless legs – feeding simply, and living quietly and temperately – the Croats performed daily an amount of work in conveying heavy articles on their backs which would amaze anyone who had not seen a Constantinople 'hamal'. Their camp, outside the town, was extremely picturesque, and, I am bound to add, dirty. A rich flavour of onions impregnated the air for a considerable distance around, mingled with reminiscences of ancient Parmesan, and the messes which the nasty-handed Phillises dressed for themselves did not look very inviting, but certainly contained plenty of nutriment, and were better, I dare say, than the tough pork and tougher biscuit of our own ration. The men were like Greeks of the Isles in dress, arms, and carriage, but they had an expression of honest ferocity, courage, and manliness in their faces, which at once distinguished them from their Hellenic brethren.

We had had only a few warm days, and yet the soil, wherever a flower had a chance of springing up, poured forth multitudes of snowdrops, crocuses, and hyacinths. The Chersonese [i.e., the Crimean peninsula] was covered with bulbous plants, some of great beauty, and the shrubs contained several rare species. The finches and larks had a Valentine's-day of their own and congregated in flocks. Brilliant goldfinches, large buntings, golden-crested wrens, larks, linnets, titlarks, and three sorts of tomtits, the hedge sparrow, and a pretty species of wagtail, were very common, and it was strange to hear them piping and twittering about the bushes in the intervals of the booming of cannon, just as it was to see the young spring flowers forcing their way through the crevices of piles of shot, and peering out from under shells and heavy ordnance. The insides of our huts were also turned into gardens, and grapes sprouted out of the earth in the window-sills, the floor, and the mud walls.

Cormorants and shags haunted the head of the harbour, which was also resorted to by some rare and curious wildfowl, and many sorts of widgeon and diver. The eagles, vultures, kites, buzzards, and ravens wheeled over the whole plateau in hundreds at a time for two or three days, and all at once disappeared for the same time, when they returned, as before, to feast on the garbage. Probably they divided their attention between the allies and the Russians. The Tchernaya abounded with duck, and some of the officers had little decoys of their own, where they went at night, in spite of the Russians. It was highly exciting sport, for the Russian batteries over Inkerman sent a round shot or shell at the sportsman if he was seen by their sentries; but even that did not deter them. In the daytime they adopted the expedient of taking a few French soldiers down with them, who actually, out of love of the thing, and for the chance of a *bonnemain*, were only too happy to go out and occupy the attention of the Cossacks in front, while their patrons were engaged in looking after mallard.

On the 5th our first spring meeting took place and was numerously attended. The races came off on a little piece of undulating ground and were regarded with much interest by the Cossack pickets at Kamara and on Canrobert's Hill. They evidently thought at first that the assemblage was connected with some military demonstration and galloped about in a state of excitement to and fro, but it is to be hoped they got a clearer notion of the real character of the proceedings ere the sport was over.

The weather was extremely mild and fine. The nights were clear, and the moon shone so brightly that it was not easy, without being observed, to carry on the works which were usually performed during a siege at night-time. Nevertheless, certain important alterations and amendments took place in the construction of our offensive line; our defensive line over Balaklava was greatly strengthened and its outworks and batteries were altered and amended considerably. The wreck of Balaklava was shovelled away, or was in the course of removal, and was shot into the sea to form piers, or beaten down to make roads, and stores and barracks of wood were rising up in its place. The oldest inhabitant would not have known the place on his return. If war is a great destroyer, it is also a great creator. The Czar was indebted to it for a railway in the Crimea, and for new roads between Balaklava, Kamiesch and Sebastopol. The hill-tops were adorned with clean wooden huts, the flats were drained, the watercourses dammed up and deepened, and all this was done in a few days, by the newly awakened energies of labour. The health of the troops was better, mortality and sickness decreased, and the spirits of the men were good. Lord Raglan was out about the camps every day, and Generals Estcourt and Airey were equally active. They visited Balaklava, inspected the lines, rode along the works, and by their presence and directions infused an amount of energy which went far to make up for lost time, if not for lost lives.

The filthy heaps accumulated by the wretched Turks who perished in the foetid lanes of Balaklava were removed and the dead horses were collected and buried beneath lime and earth. The railway extended its lines by night and by day. The harbour, crowded as it was, had assumed a certain appearance of order. Cesspools were cleared out, and the English Hercules at last began to stir about the heels of the oxen of Augaeus.

The whole of the Turks were removed to the hillside. Each day there was a diminution in the average amount of sickness, and a still greater decrease in the rates of mortality. Fresh provisions were becoming abundant, and supplies of vegetables were to be had for the sick and scurvy-stricken. The siege works were in a state of completion and were admirably made. Those on which our troops were engaged proceeded uninterruptedly. A great quantity of mules and ponies, with a staff of drivers from all parts of the world, was collected together and lightened the toils of the troops and of the commissariat department. The public and private stores of warm clothing exceeded the demand. The mortality among the horses ceased, and, though the oxen and sheep sent over to the camps would not have found much favour in Smithfield, they were very grateful to those who had to feed so long on salt junk alone.

The electric telegraph had also been established between headquarters and Kadikoi, and the line was ordered to be speedily carried on to Balaklava. It was rather singular that the French preferred the old-fashioned semaphore. They had a telegraphic communication by semaphore established between the camps and naval stations for some time back. The camps of the allies were rapidly concentrated, as it were, by these means of communicating with each of its parts with rapidity.

The news of the death of the Emperor Nicholas produced an immense sensation, and gave rise to the liveliest discussions as to the effect which such an event was likely to produce upon the contest in which we were engaged, and we were all wrong in our surmises. The enemy fired very briskly all the day the intelligence arrived, as if to show they were not disheartened at the news.

Our siege works were a kind of Penelope's web. They were always approaching completion, and never (or at least very slowly) attaining it. Our engineers now and then saw a certain point to be gained by the erection of a work or battery at a particular place. The plans were made and the working parties were sent down, and after a few casualties the particular work was executed; but, as it generally happened that the enemy were quite alive to our proceedings, we found that the Russians had, by the time the work was finished, thrown up another work to enfilade or to meet our guns. Then it became necessary to do something to destroy the advantageous position of the enemy, and fresh plans were drawn up and more trenches were dug and parapets erected. The same thing took place as before, and the process might have been almost indefinite but for the space of soil. The front of Sebastopol, between English, French, and Russians, looked like a huge graveyard, covered with freshly-made mounds of dark earth in all directions. Every week one heard, 'The Russians have thrown up another battery over Inkerman' – 'Yes, the French are busy making another new battery in front of the redoubt'; and so on, day after day, till all confidence in the power of artillery and batteries was destroyed, and the strenuous assurances that 'Our fire will most positively open about the end of next week' were received with an incredulous smile.

The French constructed two new batteries on the right of the position, and were pushing forward the works on their own left and centre.

Every material for carrying on a siege – guns, carriages, platforms, powder, shot, shell, gabions, fascines, scaling-ladders – we had in abundance. The artillery force was highly efficient, notwithstanding the large proportion of young gunners. Our engineers, if not quite so numerous as they ought to have been, were active and energetic; and our army must have consisted of nearly 20,000 bayonets, owing to the great number of men discharged from the hospitals, and returned fit for duty, and to the draughts which had been received. With the exception of the Guards, who were encamped near Balaklava, quite exhausted and reduced to the strength of a company, nearly every brigade in the army could muster many more men than they could have done a month before.

So far, then, the condition of the army was vastly improved, and what was more, it was beginning to *look* like an army, instead of resembling an armed mob, with sheepskin coats and bread-bag and sand-bag leggings and butchers' fur caps. The weather was too warm for sheepskins and the red coat was seen once more, and the influence of 'uniform' returned.

Again, as regarded food and shelter, our men were better off every day than they were the day before. From hunger, unwholesome food and comparative nakedness, the camp was plunged into a sea of abundance, filled with sheep and sheepskins, wooden huts, furs, comforters, mufflers, flannel shirts, tracts, soups, preserved meats, potted game and spirits; but it was, unfortunately, just in proportion as they did not want them that comforts and even luxuries were showered upon them. In such weather a tent was as good as – some say better than – a hut. Where were the huts when the snow was on the ground, and where was the warm clothing when cold rains and bitter winds racked the joints? Just where our fresh meat and vegetables were when scurvy and scorbutic dysentery were raging in the canvas cantonment before Sebastopol.

About the middle of March we were blessed with all the genial influences of a glorious spring. Vegetation struggled for existence beneath the tramp of armed men and the hoof of the war horse, and faint patches of green herbage dotted the brown expanse in which the allied camps had rested so long. The few fruit-trees which had been left standing near Balaklava were in blossom. The stumps on the hill-sides were throwing out green shoots as outlets for the welling sap; the sun shone brightly and warmly from blue skies streaked with clouds, which were borne rapidly along by the breeze that never ceased to blow from the high lands. Of course, the beneficial effects of this permanent fine weather on the health and spirits of the army were very great and became more striking day after day. The voice of song was heard once more in the tents, and the men commenced tuning up their pipes and chanting their old familiar choruses. The railway pushed its iron feelers up the hillside to the camp. Every day the plains and hillsides were streaked with columns of smoke, which marked the spots where fire was destroying heaps of filth and corrupt animal and vegetable matter as sacrifices on the altar of Health. The sanatorium was working in the most satisfactory manner, and had produced the best results. The waters of little streamlets were caught up in reservoirs to provide against drought.

Provisions were abundant. Vegetables for the sick, and fresh meat several times a week, stopped the ravages of scorbutic disease. Up to this date about 700 of the huts had been sent to camp and erected. The army, animated by the constant inspection of Lord Raglan, and by the supervision of the heads of the great military departments, was nearly restored, in all but numbers, to what it was six months before. Balaklava was fast resolving itself into lines of huts. Bakeries, under the control of Government, were established in the town, and the troops were fed on wholesome bread. The silence and gloom of despondency had passed away with the snows and rains and the deadly lethargy of our last terrible winter.

It must not be forgotten, however, that the energy derived equal advantage from the improvement in the weather. Valley and plain were now as firm as the finest road, and the whole country was open to the march of artillery, cavalry, infantry, and commissariat wagons.

Each day the Russian camps on the north of Sebastopol increased and spread out. Each night new watch-fires attracted the eye. We heard that a formidable army had assembled around Eupatoria, and it was certain that the country between that town and Sebastopol was constantly traversed by parties of horse and foot, who were sometimes seen from the sea in very great numbers. The actual works of the siege made no progress to justify one in prophesying. Actual increase of lines and batteries and armament there was no doubt, but it existed on both sides, and there had been no comparative advantage gained by the allies. The impression which had long existed in the minds of many that Sebastopol could not be taken by assault, considering the position of the north forts, the fleet, and the army outside, gained ground. It was generally thought that the army outside ought to have been attacked and dispersed, or that the investment of the place should have been completed, before we could hope to reduce the city and the citadel.

But coupled with this impression was the far stronger conviction that, had our army marched upon the place on the 25th of September, it would have fallen almost without resistance. A Russian officer, who was taken prisoner some time before, and who knew the state of the city well, declared that he could not account for our 'infatuation' in allowing the Russians to throw up works and regain heart, when we could have walked into the place, unless under the supposition that the hand of the Almighty was in it, and that He had blinded the vision and perverted the judgment of our generals. 'And now,' said he' 'He has saved Sebastopol, and we, with His help, will maintain it inviolate.'

On the 13th [March] General Simpson arrived; he was appointed chief of the Staff; and Lord Raglan, who rode into Balaklava, saw for the first time that day Sir John M'Neill and Colonel Tulloch, the commissioners sent out by Lord Panmure[1] to inquire into the commissariat condition of the army.

For several weeks from the middle of March activity on both sides was limited to the usual sporadic bombardments, reconnaissance expeditions,

[1] Secretary of State for War.

and destructive raids, often involving violent and bloody hand-to-hand fighting, but effecting no change in the position of either side. Possession of Russian rifle-pits below the Malakoff was contested with particular violence by the French, but they remained in the enemy's hands.

These rifle-pits, which cost both armies such a quantity of ammunition, and led to so considerable a sacrifice on the part of our allies, were placed in front and to the right and left of the Tower of Malakoff, about 600 yards from our works. They were simple excavations in the ground, faced round with sandbags, which were loopholed for rifles, and banked round with the earth which had been thrown up from the pit. Each of these pits contained about ten men. They were, in fact, little forts or redoubts for offensive proceedings against the besiegers, armed with rifles instead of cannon. Practice made the men placed in them expert, and it was likely they were picked shots, for their fire was exceedingly good, and if a man showed for a moment above the works in front of these pits he had a small swarm of leaden hornets buzzing round his ears.

They were so well covered and so admirably protected by the nature of the ground that our riflemen could do nothing with them, and the French sharpshooters were equally unsuccessful.

In one Russian attack on the mortar battery directly south of the Malakoff, which the enemy succeeded in capturing for a quarter of an hour, Albanian chiefs were among the men's leaders.

Two who were killed led them on with intrepidity and ferocious courage. One of them, who struggled into the battery in spite of a severe wound, while his life-blood was ebbing fast, rushed at a powder-barrel and fired his pistol into it before he fell. Fortunately the powder did not explode, as the fire did not go through the wood. Another charged with a scimitar in one hand and a formidable curved blade, which he used as a dagger, in the other, right into our ranks twice, and fell dead the second time, perforated with balls and bayonets. They were magnificently dressed, and were supposed to be men of rank.

Following this particularly savage encounter, another burial-truce was arranged.

The instant the flags were hoisted, friend and foe swarmed out of the embrasures. The Riflemen of the allies and of the enemy rose from their lairs in the rifle pits, and sauntered towards each other to behold their grim handiwork. The whole of the space between the Russian lines and our own was filled with groups of unarmed soldiery. Passing down by the Middle Picket Ravine, which was then occupied by the French, and which ran down in front of the Light Division camp, I came out upon the advanced French trench within a few hundred yards of the Mamelon. The sight was strange beyond description. French, English, and Russian officers were walking about saluting each other courteously as they passed, and occasionally entering into conversation, and a constant interchange of little civilities, such as offering and receiving cigar-lights, was going on in each little group. Some of the Russian officers were evidently men of high rank and breeding. Their polished manners contrasted remarkably with their plain and rather coarse clothing. They wore, with few exceptions, the invariable long grey coat over their uniforms. The French officers were all *en grande tenue*, and offered a striking contrast to many of our own officers, who were dressed *à la* Balaklava, and wore uncouth head-dresses, catskin coats, and nondescript paletots. Many of the Russians looked remarkably like English gentlemen in 'style' of face and bearing. One tall, fine-looking old man, with a long grey beard and strangely shaped cap, was pointed out to us as Hetman of the Cossacks in the Crimea, but it did not appear as if there were many men of the very high military rank present. The Russians were rather grave and reserved, but they seemed to fraternize with the French better than with ourselves, and the men certainly got on better with our allies than with the few privates of our own regiments who were down towards the front.

But while all this civility was going on, we were walking among the dead, over blood-stained ground, covered with evidences of recent fight. Broken muskets, bayonets, cartouch-boxes, caps, fragments of clothing, straps and belts, pieces of shell, little pools of clotted blood, shot – round and grape – shattered gabions and sand-bags, were visible around us on every side, and through the midst of the crowd stalked a solemn procession of soldiers bearing their departed comrades to their long home. I counted seventy-seven litters borne past me in fifteen minutes – each filled with a dead enemy. In the midst of all this stern evidence of war, a certain amount of lively conversation began to spring up, in which the Russian officers indulged in a little badinage. Some of them asked our officers 'when we were coming in to take the place', others 'when we thought of going away?' Some congratulated us upon the excellent opportunity we had of getting a good look at Sebastopol, as the chance of a nearer view, except on similar occasions, was not in their opinion very probable. One officer asked a private confidentially in English how many men we sent into the trenches? 'Begorra, only seven thousand a night, and a covering party of ten thousand,' was the ready reply. The officer laughed and turned away.

At one time a Russian with a litter stopped by a dead body and put it into the litter. He looked round for a comrade to help him. A Zouave at once advanced with much grace and lifted it, to the infinite amusement of the bystanders; but the joke was not long-lived, as a Russian brusquely came up and helped to carry off his dead comrade.

General Bosquet and several officers of rank of the allied army visited the trenches during the armistice, and staff officers were present on both sides to see that the men did not go out of bounds. The armistice was over about three o'clock. Scarcely had the white flag disappeared behind the parapet of the Mamelon before a round shot from the sailors' battery went slap through one of the embrasures of the Russian work and dashed up a great pillar of earth inside. The Russians at once replied, and the noise of cannon soon re-echoed through the ravines.

16

A Turkish Reconnaisance

On Easter Monday, April 9, following intensive preparations, the Allies began one of the heaviest and most sustained bombardments that had yet taken place, the object being to effect a substantial reduction in the enemy's fire power. The British armament alone included 36 heavy mortars and 87 guns ranging from 24- to 68-pounders. The Russians, apparently taken by surprise, were unable to reply effectively until the next day. Thereafter heavy firing continued on both sides for more than a week, with only short intervals for rest and repairs. As before, at the end of the affair the disposition of the opposing forces remained unchanged. At a council of war on April 13, Lord Raglan and the British generals had favoured an outright assault on Sebastopol, but they were overruled by the French.

While the bombardment was in progress, Turkish reinforcements arrived from Kamiesch.

They mustered about 15,000 men, and finer young fellows than some of the soldiers of the crack regiments I never saw. Very few of the privates wore decorations or medals, but many of the officers had them, and had evidently seen service against the Muscovite. They had had a long march, and their sandal shoon afforded sorry protection against the stony ground; and yet it was astonishing that so few men fell out of the ranks or straggled behind. One regiment had a good brass band, which almost alarmed the bystanders by striking up a quick step (waltz) as they marched past, playing it in excellent style, but the majority of the regiments were preceded by musicians with drums, fifes, and semicircular thin brass tubes with wide mouths, such as those which may have tumbled the walls of Jericho, or are seen on the sculptured monuments of primaeval kings.

The colonel and his two majors rode at the head of each regiment, richly dressed, on small but spirited horses, covered with rich saddle-cloths, and followed by pipe-bearers and servants. The mules, with the tents, marched on the right – the artillery on the left. The two batteries I saw consisted each of four 24lb brass howitzers, and two 9lb brass field-pieces, and the carriages and horses were in a very serviceable state. Each gun was drawn by six horses. The ammunition boxes were rather coarse and heavy. The baggage animals of the division marched in the rear, and the regiments marched in columns of companies three deep, each company on an average with a front of twenty rank and file. One of the regiments had Minié rifles of English make, the majority, however, were only armed with flint firelocks, but they were very clean and bright. They all displayed rich standards, blazing with cloth of gold, and many-coloured flags with the crescent and star embroidered upon them. All the men carried their blankets, squares of carpet for praying and sitting upon, and cooking utensils, and their packs were of various sizes and substances. As they marched along in the sunlight over the undulating ground they presented a very picturesque and warlike spectacle, the stern reality of which was enhanced by the thunder of the guns at Sebastopol and the smoke-wreaths from shells bursting high in the air.

On April 19 a full-scale reconnaissance was undertaken by twelve battalions of Turkish infantry, under the command of their chief, His Excellency Omar Pasha, and supported by English and French cavalry and artillery.

As the morning was fine and clear, the sight presented by the troops advancing towards Kamara across the plain from the heights was very beautiful. So little was known about the *reconnaissance* that many officers at headquarters were not aware of it till they learnt that Lord Raglan, attended by a few members of the staff, and followed by only six orderlies, had started to overtake the troops. A great number of amateurs, forming clouds of very irregular cavalry, followed and preceded the expedition.

The Turks marched in dense columns, bristling with steel. The sunlight flashing on the polished barrels of their firelocks and on their bayonets, relieved the sombre hue of the mass, for their dark blue uniforms, but little relieved by facings or gay shoulder-straps and cuffs, looked quite black when the men were together. The Chasseurs d'Afrique, clad in light powder-blue jackets, with white cartouch belts, and in bright red pantaloons, mounted on white Arabs, caught the eye like a bed of flowers scattered over the plain. Nor did the rich verdure indeed require any such borrowed beauty, for the soil produced an abundance of wild flowering shrubs and beautiful plants. Dahlias, anemones, sweetbrier, whitethorn, wild parsley, mint, thyme, sage, asparagus, and a hundred other different citizens of the vegetable kingdom dotted the plain, and as the Turkish infantry moved along, their feet crushed the sweet flowers, and the air was filled with delicate odours, which overcame the sweltering atmosphere around the columns. Rectangular patches of long, rank, rich grass, waving high above the more natural green meadow, marked the mounds where the slain of the 25th of October[1] were reposing for ever, and the snorting horses refused to eat the unwholesome shoots that sprang there.

As the force moved on, evidences of that fatal and glorious day became thick and painful. The skeleton of an English dragoon lay extended on the plain, with tattered bits of red cloth hanging to the bones of his arms. All the buttons had been cut off the jacket. The man must have fallen early in the day, when the heavy cavalry were close up to Canrobert's Hill and came under the fire of the Russian artillery. There was also a Russian skeleton close at hand in ghastly companionship. The small bullet-skull, round as a cannon-ball, had been picked bare all save the scalp, which was still covered with grisly red locks. Further on, amid fragments of shells and round shot, the body of another Russian seemed starting out of the grave, which scarcely covered his lower extremities. The half-decayed skeletons of artillery and cavalry horses covered with rotting trappings,

[1] The day on which the charge of the Light Brigade took place.

harness, and saddles, lay as they fell in the agonies of death, or had crumbled away into a *débris* of bone and skin, and leather straps, cloth, and buckles. From the numerous graves, the uncovered bones of the tenants had started up through the soil, as if to appeal against the haste with which they had been buried. With the clash of drums and the shrill strains of the fife, with the champing of bits and ringing of steel, man and horse swept over the remnants of their fellows in all the pride of life.

The force descended into the plain and marched towards Kamara, spreading across the ground in front of Canrobert's Hill from No. 2 Turkish Redoubt up to the slope which leads to the ruined village. A party of Turkish infantry followed the cavalry in skirmishing order. The few Cossacks in the village abandoned it after firing a few straggling shots at the advanced skirmishers. One fellow had been taken so completely by surprise that he left his lance leaning against a wall. An officer of the 71st espied it just as the Cossack was making a bolt to recover it. They both rode their best, but the Cossack retreated with effective pantomime representing rage and despair. The Turks were preceded by a wretched man armed with a bow and arrows, who said he was a Tchergess. In addition to his bow and arrows, he carried a quaint old pistol, and his coat-breast was wadded with cartridges.

I looked into the church, the floor of which had formerly been covered an inch in depth with copper money, thrown there by the inhabitants when the expedition first came to Balaklava. The simple faith of the poor people in the protection of their church had not been violated by us, but the Cossacks appeared to have had no such scruples, for not a copeck was to be seen, and the church was bare and desolate and stripped of every adornment, even to the woodwork. The rest of the place was a heap of ruins, but the Cossacks had burrowed here and there into the stones, and made sleeping places and stables in the walls of the houses. As soon as the Turks on the right had gained the summit of the hill above Kamara, three of the columns advanced and took possession of the ruins, and then drew up on the slope in front of the church.

Meantime the great bulk of the force, leaving three columns halted at Kamara, marched on past Canrobert's Hill, the sides of which were covered with the wigwams of the Russians. They passed by the old Turkish redoubts Nos. 1 and 2, towards a very steep and rocky conical hill covered with loose stones, near the top of which the Russians had thrown up a wall of rubbish. A group of Cossacks and some Russian officers had assembled on the top of this hill to examine our strength and watch our movements. As the Turkish skirmishers advanced, the French rocket troop accompanied them. The Turks ascended the hill with ardour and with great agility, firing their pieces as they advanced, to which the Cossacks replied by a petty fusillade. Suddenly an arch of thick white smoke rose from the ground with a fierce, hissing, rushing noise, throwing itself like a great snake towards the crest of the hill; as it flew onward the smoke disappeared, and the fiery trail was lost, but in a second, a puff of smoke burst out with a slight explosion on the hill top, and the Cossacks and Russians disappeared with precipitation. In fact, the French had begun their rocket practice with great accuracy and success. Nothing could be better for such work as this than their light rocket troops. The apparatus was simple and portable – a few mules, with panniers on each side, carried the whole of the tubes, cases, sticks, fusees, etc., and the effect of rockets, though uncertain, was very great, especially against irregular and ill-disciplined cavalry.

The skirmishers crowned this hill also, and the generals and officers of the staff, and numerous idlers and amateurs, followed them. The Russians rode rapidly down the hillside, and crossed the Tchernaya by the bridge and at one or two fords near Tchorgun. Omar Pasha, Lord Raglan, and the French generals then spent some time in surveying the country, while the troops were halted in the rear, the artillery and cavalry first, supported by four battalions of Egyptians. At two o'clock the *reconnaissance* was over, and the troops slowly retired to the camp, the skirmishers of the French cavalry being followed by the Cossacks at a prudent distance, and exchanging long shots with them from time to time. Altogether, the *reconnaissance* was a most welcome and delightful interlude in the dull, monotonous 'performances' of the siege. Every one felt as if he had beaten the Cossacks and got out of prison at last. It was a fillip to our spirits to get a gallop across the greensward once more, and to escape from the hateful feeling of constraint and confinement which bores us to death in the camp.

On the night of the 19th a very gallant and brilliant little feat of arms, attended by severe loss, was performed by the 77th Regiment in front of our right attack. There was nothing more remarkable in the active operations of this siege than the importance of the part played by the sharp-shooters placed in those rifle pits which had been dug by the enemy, and which were constructed with great skill and daring, and defended with vigour and resolution. The pits were complete little batteries for riflemen, and the fire from one well established within 300 or 400 yards of a battery of ordnance was sufficient to silence the guns and keep the gunners from going near the embrasures. In front of the Redan, opposite our right attack, the Russians had established some capacious pits, from which they annoyed us considerably, particularly from the two nearest to us on the left-hand side. Round shot and shell had several times forced the Russians to bolt across the open ground to their batteries, but at night they repaired damages and were back again as busy as ever in the morning. Our advanced battery would have been greatly harassed by this fire when it opened, and it was resolved to take the two pits, to hold that which was found most tenable, and to destroy the other.

About eight o'clock the party of the 77th with a wing of the 33rd in the rear in support, moved down the traverses towards the rifle pits. The night was dark and windy, but the Russian sentries perceived the approach of our men, and a brisk fire was at once opened upon them, to which our troops scarcely replied, for they rushed upon the enemy with the bayonet, and, after a short struggle, drove them out of the two pits and up the slope behind them. Once in the pits, the engineers, officers, and sappers and miners set to work to strengthen the defences, and with great coolness and courage proceeded to connect the trench of the nearest of the rifle pits with our advanced sap. The enemy opened an exceedingly heavy fire of round, grape, and shell upon them, and the Russian sharpshooters from the parapets of the batteries, and from the broken ground behind the abattis, kept up a very severe fusillade; but the working party continued at their labour in defiance of the storm of shot which tore over them; and our men remained in possession of the larger of the pits under these trying circumstances, without any decided attempt being made to turn them out. The General of the day of the right attack telegraphed to headquarters that our troops had gained the pits, and he received directions in reply to keep them at all hazards. At two o'clock in the morning a strong column of Russians, certainly double the strength of our men, advanced against the pits and the combat was renewed. The enemy were met by courage more determined and by arms more nervous than their own; by the bayonet they were thrust back again and again, and at its point they were driven up to their batteries once more. The rifle pit was left in our hands and a smart fire kept up from it. This was most serviceable, not only against the embrasures of the Redan, but in reducing and disturbing the fire of the Russian rifle pits on its flank. A drummer boy of the 77th engaged in the *melée* with a young bugler of the enemy, took his bugle and made him prisoner – a little piece of juvenile gallantry for which he was well rewarded.

On the next night the Russians sought to re-occupy the pits, when our soldiers speedily repulsed them; but we were exposed to loss from the fire of the guns in the Redan, and the 41st Regiment had fifteen men killed and wounded in the fire which the Russians opened upon us. The pit was levelled, filled in with earth, and the men then retired.

A council of war was held on April 24, *at which it was decided that the long-awaited assault on Sebastopol should be begun at* 1 *p.m. on April* 28. *But the next day General Canrobert sent word to Lord Raglan that he had received the news that* 20,000 *reinforcements were on their way, and also that the Emperor might perhaps be coming out to take command. (With some difficulty the Emperor was eventually persuaded to abandon this whimsical pipe-dream). He, Canrobert, had therefore 'resolved not to make the assault on the* 28*th, as intended, but to wait a little longer.'*

The monotony of the camp was relieved on the 26th by a grand military spectacle. The whole of General Bosquet's army of observation, consisting of forty-five battalions of infantry, of two regiments of heavy dragoons, and of two regiments of Chasseurs d'Afrique, together with a numerous and well-appointed field artillery, numbering sixty pieces, were reviewed by General Canrobert, who was accompanied by a large and very brilliant staff, by several English generals, and by an immense 'field' of our officers. The inspection took place on the ridge which formed the natural defence of the plateau on which the allies were encamped.

At half-past two the black columns of the French infantry formed in front of the whole fields of canvas, or streaked the plain of the plateau with flashing lines of light, as they marched from their various camps, with the rays of the bright sun reflected from their arms and the clash of their bands filling the air with the essence of opera. For the space of four or five miles they could be seen converging and drawing up regiment after regiment on the extended ridge till they formed a solid wall, living, yet motionless, crowning its summit. The ground was too limited to contain such a body of men even in the dense manner in which they were formed, and a double wall was soon created by the arrival of fresh regiments.

The greater part of the little army must have been visible to the Russians on the heights over the Tchernaya, to the Cossacks on the redoubts and on Canrobert's Hill in the valley. The spectacle of the review was magnificent in the extreme. At three o'clock, General Canrobert, attended by his staff, arrived on the ground and was received with presented arms. The bands struck up *Partant pour la Syrie.*[1] The *vivandières* standing by the musicians smiled their best. The golden eagles, with their gorgeous standards, were lowered, and General Canrobert, his hat trimmed with ostrich plumes, his breast covered with orders, mounted on a spirited charger, with a thick stick under his arm, followed by his 'esquire' displaying a tricolor guidon in the air, and attended by a suite of Generals, passed along the lines of men, now galloping to the left and now to the right between the intervals, to inspect the various regiments. Generals

[1] This march superseded the *Marseillaise* as the French national anthem during the reign of Napoleon III. It was at first attributed to Queen Hortense of Holland, but is now believed to have been composed by Philip Drouet, a Dutchman.

Estcourt, England, and Pennefather, a great number of staff officers, as well as a ruck of English officers on foot, and on horse and on pony, in all the varied uniforms and mufti of the army, were present. The troops – each gaudy wave heralded as it rolled in sight over the brow of the hill, crested with sparkling bayonets, by the crash of martial music – rolled on for nearly two hours. Chasseurs à pied, infantry of the line, Zouaves, Voltigeurs, and Arabs passed on column after column. The Chasseurs Indigènes, their swarthy faces contrasting with their white turbans, clad in light blue, with bright yellow facings and slashing, and clean gaiters and greaves, showed like a bed of summer flowers, and the Zouaves rushed by with the buoyant, elastic, springing tread which reminded one of their tiger-rush towards Inkerman; nor was the soldier-like, orderly, and serviceable look of the line regiments less worthy of commendation. Then came the roll of the artillery, and in clouds of dust, rolling and bumping and jolting, a storm of guns and carriages swept over the broken ground for a quarter of an hour, till the sixty guns and their carriages had gone by. The General afterwards rode along the lines of the Chasseurs d'Afrique and of the two regiments of dragoons, which went past at a quick trot. The inspection terminated shortly after six o'clock. Each regiment, as it defiled past the General, followed the example of the Colonel, and cried '*Vive l'Empereur!*'

Up to the 27th there was no material change in the position of the allied armies before Sebastopol, or in the attitude of the enemy within and outside the city. Every night there was the usual expenditure of ammunition. Nothing, indeed, was more difficult to ascertain than the particulars of these nocturnal encounters. After a cannonade and furious firing which would keep a stranger in a state of intense excitement all night, it was common to hear some such dialogue as this the following morning: 'I say, Smith, did you hear the row last night?'

'No, what was it?'

'Oh, blazing away like fury. You don't mean to say you didn't hear it?'

'Not a sound; came up from the trenches last night, and slept like a top.'

'Hallo, Jones (to a distinguished 'cocked hat' on horseback, riding past), 'tell us what all the shindy was about last night.'

'Shindy, was there? By Jove, yes, I think I did hear some firing – the French and the Russians as usual, I suppose.'

'No, it sounded to me as if it was in front of our right attack.'

Another thinks it was on the left, another somewhere else, and so the matter ends. In a day or two after the affair was over, one might hear what really had taken place by taking infinite pains and comparing all kinds of stories. It was, in fact, a process of elimination to discover the facts.

Shortly after General Canrobert's review of the French troops, those of another ally began to arrive.

On the 8th General Della Marmora and 5,000 Sardinians arrived in the Crimea, and were attached to the English army. Two or three steamers arrived every four-and-twenty hours laden with those excellent and soldier-like troops. They landed all ready for the field, with horses, carts, etc. Their transport cars were simple, strongly made, covered vehicles, not unlike a London bread-cart, painted blue, with the words 'Armata Sarda' in black letters, and the name of the regiment to the service of which it belonged. The officers were well mounted, and every one admired the air and carriage of the troops, more especially of the Bersaglieri (Chasseurs), and the eye was attracted by their melodramatic head-dress – a bandit-looking hat, with a large plume of black cock's feathers in the side.

17

The Expedition to Kertch

Up till now it was the French who seemed to have borne the brunt of the Russians' attacks and to have taken the initiative in organising counter-measures. Lord Raglan, 'very anxious not to leave the French the credit for doing everything,' now proposed that an allied expedition be sent to destroy the Russians' base along the coast at Kertch, some 150 miles east of Balaklava. The destruction of the base would enable allied shipping to operate in the Sea of Azov, which would be a serious threat to the enemy's eastern lines of supply and communication. General Canrobert at first agreed to this proposal, but a few hours after the expedition had sailed, he sent a message post haste to Lord Raglan cancelling French participation in the enterprise and thereby putting a stop to it, as without French support the expedition would have stood very little chance of achieving its objectives. The reason for the French withdrawal was that word had been received from the Emperor by telegraph – a new-fangled device that proved almost more useful to the Russians than to the French, as the endless spate of commands and exhortations which it enabled the Emperor to send to General Canrobert almost drove the General out of his mind – word had been received that every available French ship was to be sent down immediately to Constantinople to pick up reserves.

Shortly after the return of the expeditionary forces rumours began to circulate about differences of opinion between Lord Raglan and General Canrobert.

To add to these differences, the Emperor Napoleon had sent out a sketch of operations, to which General Canrobert naturally attached great importance, and from which Lord Raglan dissented. The recall of the Kertch expedition precipitated the result. General Canrobert proposed to Lord Raglan to take the command in chief of the allied armies. His lordship, after some hesitation, accepted, and then proposed some changes in the disposition of the two armies, to which General Canrobert would not accede. Finding himself thus compromised with the English commander, General Canrobert demanded permission from the Emperor to resign the command of the French army, and to take charge of a division. The Emperor acceded to the request, and General Canrobert was succeeded by General Pelissier.

Soon after this another expedition to Kertch was decided upon and early on May 23 an allied force once more set sail. It consisted of nearly 16,000 troops, of whom 7,500 were French, 5,000 Turkish, and close on 3,800 British, supported by a considerable force of warships under the command of Rear-Admiral Sir Edmund Lyons.

By noon the expedition was nearing its destination.

At forty minutes past one a huge pillar of white smoke rushed up towards the skies, opened out like a gigantic balloon, and then a roar like the first burst of a thunderstorm told us that a magazine had blown up. At a quarter-past two another loud explosion took place and a prodigious quantity of earth was thrown into the air. A third magazine was blown up at twenty-five minutes past two. A tremendous explosion, which seemed to shake the sea and air, took place about three o'clock, and at half-past three several columns of smoke blending into one, and as many explosions, the echoes of which roared and thundered away together, announced that the Russians were destroying their magazines.

Opposition from forts and warships defending the naval base was eventually silenced by British gunboats supported by French steamers. The troops then began to go ashore at the small town of Ambalaki.

A row of half a mile brought us to a beautiful shelving beach, which was exposed, however, only for a few yards, as the rich sward grew close to the brink of the tideless sea. The water at the shore, unaffected by the current, was clear and it was evident that it abounded in fish. The land rose abruptly two hundred yards from the beach to a ridge parallel to the line of the sea about a hundred feet in height. The interval between the shore and the ridge was dotted with houses, through which the French were already running riot, breaking in doors, pursuing hens, smashing windows – in fact, plundering, in which they were assisted by all of our men who could get away. Some large houses were in flames and storehouses were blazing fiercely in the last throes of fire. On the ridge above us the figures of the French and English soldiers moving about against the horizon stood sharply out, lighted up by the rays of the setting sun.

The houses were clean outside and in – whitewashed neatly and provided with small well-glazed windows, which were barely adequate, however, to light up the two rooms of which each dwelling consisted, but the heavy sour smell inside was most oppressive and disagreeable; it seemed to proceed from the bags of black bread and vessels of fish oil which were found in every cabin. The furniture was all smashed to pieces; the hens and ducks, captives to the bow and spear of the Gaul, were cackling and quacking piteously as they were carried off in bundles from their homes by Zouaves and Chasseurs. Every house we entered was ransacked and every cupboard had a pair of red breeches sticking out of it and a blue coat inside of it. Vessels of stinking oil, bags of sour bread, casks of flour or ham, wretched clothing, old boots, beds ripped up for treasure, the hideous pictures of saints on panelling or paper which adorned every cottage, with lamps suspended before them, were lying on the floors. Drolls dressed themselves in faded pieces of calico dresses or aged finery lying hid in old drawers, and danced about the gardens. One house, which had been occupied as a guardhouse was a scene of especial confusion. Its inmates had evidently fled in great disorder, for their greatcoats and uniform jackets strewed the floors and bags of the black bread filled every corner, as well as an incredible quantity of old boots.

Notwithstanding the great richness of the land, little had been done by man to avail himself of its productiveness. I never in my life saw such quantities of weeds or productions of such inexorable ferocity towards pantaloons, or such eccentric flowers of huge dimensions, as the ground outside these cottages bore. The inhabitants were evidently graziers rather than agriculturists. Around every house were piles of a substance like peat, which is made, we were informed, from the dung of cattle and is used as fuel. The cattle, however, had been all driven away. None were taken that I saw, though the quantity which fed in the fields around must have been very great. A party of Chasseurs who had taken a huge wild-looking boar were in high delight at their fortune and soon despatched and cut him up into junks with their swords.

The next morning, after an exhausting march, the troops reached Yenikale, a town to the north-east of Kertch which guarded the entrance to the Sea of Azov.

The success of the expedition by land and sea was complete, rapid and glorious. The forts which defended the narrow and difficult Straits of Kertch were forced, the magazines of the enemy were exploded by their own hands, all their guns fell into our possession, together with a prodigious quantity of corn, grain, munitions of war, naval stores, and military equipment. The Sea of Azoff was open to us and our flying squadron of steam gunboats searched it from end to end, burning and destroying the ships and trading vessels of the Russians, crushing their forts, and spreading terror and dismay along the seaboard of their inland lake.

There are not many people who ever heard of Kertch or Yenikale until this war, but these towns represented on a small scale those favoured positions which nature seemed to have intended for the seat of commerce and power, and in some measure resembled Constantinople, which was placed, like them, on a narrow channel between two seas, whose trade it profited by and commanded.

When the Allies landed, the enemy fled to Kertch, spreading dismay and terror, and the troops there, afraid of being attacked in the rear and front, by land and sea, made a hasty retreat towards the interior. Kertch, as seen from the sea, was a picturesque and almost a stately town, and the position and air of the place and of the country behind it resembled Naples on a small scale. The bay is semicircular and the principal buildings situated on the waterside, bounded by a noble quay faced with hewn stone. The houses were pure white, or gaily tinted with various colours over the stonework; many of them attained the dimensions and almost deserved the name of palaces.

Our troops suffered greatly from the heat on the march to Yenikale, which was more than twelve miles from their bivouac. The weather was extremely fine, but the mid-day sun was rather too powerful for English constitutions. Of 864 Marines who landed from the fleet, four-fifths fell out on the march, the men of that gallant corps not being accustomed to such exertions. The Highlanders fell out in great numbers also, and the tailing off was extraordinary.

Immense quantities of caviare, of dried sturgeon, and of a coarse-scaled fish like a bream were found in every village and in Yenikale and were relished by our soldiers, but they had very imperfect means of gratifying the thirst which followed, as the water was brackish, and the stores of country wine (some of it excellent, in spite of the adulteration of oil or essence of roses) were nearly all discovered and drunk up.

On Friday night the work of destroying Russian stores began, and the French hurled over several guns into the sea, tore up the platforms, and exploded the shells found in the magazines. Parties of boats were sent in all directions to secure and burn prizes and to fire the Russian storehouses and huts on the sandbanks; by day the sky was streaked with lines of smoke and by night the air was illuminated by the blaze of forts, houses, magazines and vessels aground on all the flats for miles around us.

As there was nothing doing at Yenikale, I took an opportunity of paying Kertch a visit. As we approached the town, long columns of grey smoke were visible rising from the corn stores, and working parties could be made out on the shore engaged in removing various articles which could be turned to the account of the allies.

There were plenty of Tartars in the streets, dressed in black sheepskin cap, or white turban, with handsome jackets and wide breeches of dark silk or fine stuff and gaudy sashes round their waists. These fellows were of the true Calmuck type – with bullet head, forehead villainously low, dark, piggish, roguish, twinkling eyes, obtuse, obstinate noses, straight lips and globular chin. Unlike most people, they improve in looks as they grow old, for their beards, which only attain amplitude in age, then give a grisly dignity and patriarchal air to their faces. Groups of men in long lank frock-coats, long waist-coats, trousers tucked into their boots or falling down over slipshod feet, sat on the doorsteps, in aspect and attire the very image of a congregation of seedy Puseyites. Most of these men wore caps instead of hats, their clothing was of sober snuffy hues, to match their faces, which were sombre and dirty and sallow. Their looks were dejected and miserable and as an Englishman or a Frenchman came near they made haste to rise and to salute his mightiness with uncovered head and obsequious noddings and gesticulations. These were the remnants of the Russian population, but there were among them Jews, who might have stepped on any stage amid rounds of applause, in garb and face and aspect so truly Shylock-like were they, cringing, wily and spiteful, as though they had just been kicked across the Rialto; and there was also a sprinkling of Armenians and Greeks; they were all lean and unhappy alike, and very sorry specimens of Muscovite *bourgeoisie*.

Tartar women, scantily covered, were washing clothes in the sea, like tamed Hecates – withered, angular, squalid, and ugly in face and form. The Russian fair, not much more tastily clad, might be seen flitting about with an air of awkward coquetry, mingled with apprehension and dislike of the intruders, their heads covered with shawls, and their bodies with bright Manchester patterns.

The houses were well supplied with poultry, nor were pigs, rabbits, cats, dogs, and other domestic animals deficient. Each mansion was complete in itself; they were like those in the older streets of Boulogne, and the interiors were furnished somewhat in the same fashion – plenty of mirrors and hard, inflexible, highly-varnished, unsubstantial furniture, no carpets, lots of windows (doubled, by the bye, to keep out the cold) and doors and long corridors, the windows and doors handsomely mounted with brass work. The Russian stove, as a matter of course, was found in each apartment. Spacious vaults underneath the houses were often used as storehouses for corn, and the piles of empty and broken bottles marked the locality of the wine-cellar. Ice-houses were attached to many residences, and their contents were very welcome to the ships.

The market-place is a large piece of ground of an oval shape, surrounded by a piazza and shops and magazines of an inferior class. Most of them were shut and fastened up, but butchers displayed some good English-looking beef, and the sounds of English revelry were very distinct from the interior of a wine-shop at the end of an arcade, where some sailors were drinking Russian champagne at 3s a bottle and smoking cheap and nasty cigars of native manufacture. Amid the distracting alphabetical mysteries of Cyrillus which were stuck up on most of these doors, where all one's knowledge of other languages led him hopelessly astray, and where P was R, and H was N, there was sometimes an intelligible announcement that Mdlle So-and-so was a *modiste* from Paris, or that M. Brugger was a bootmaker 'of the first force' from Vienna. The greater number of the houses in the streets were entered through a large courtyard, surrounded by the offices and out-buildings, to which admission was gained by a *porte-cochère*. There were baths, libraries, schools, literary associations and academies in Kertch of pretensions beyond its size.

The hospital was a large, well-built, clean and excellently ventilated building. As we entered, some women, who were standing at the gate, retreated, and an old man with a good clear eye and an honest soldierly air, came forward to meet us with the word 'Hospital', which he had learned as a kind of safeguard and protection against intrusion. He led the way into a dark corridor on the ground floor, on the walls of which the regulations of the establishment (in Russian) were suspended. The wards opened on each side of this corridor. The old man invited us to enter the first: it was spacious and airy, but the hospital smell of wounded men was there. Five wounded Russians and one drunken Englishman were the occupants of the chamber. Two of the Russians had been blown up when the magazines exploded. Their hands and heads were covered with linen bandages, through which holes were cut for the eyes and mouth. What could be seen of these poor wretches gave a horrible impression of their injuries and of the pain which they were enduring, but they gave no outward indication of their sufferings. Their scorched eyes rolled heavily upon the visitors with a kind of listless curiosity. The other men had been shot in various parts of the body and had probably been sent there from Sebastopol: in one or two I recognized the old Inkerman type of face and expression. The bed and bedclothes were clean and good, and at the head of each bed black tablets of wood were fixed to receive the record of the patient's name, his disease, etc.

On reaching the street we found the people returning to the town – that is, the Tartars were flocking back from the villages where they had been hiding, with bundles of property, much of which they had probably stolen from the Russian houses. As every wrecked house bore a strong family likeness to its fellow, we entered only one or two, and then wandered through the streets, which were almost deserted by the inhabitants during the heat of the day.

Towards evening a number of wounded Russians were brought down from Yenikale, whither they had been taken by the gunboats from various places along the coast, and were landed on the quay. As each wounded man passed, the women crowded round to look at him, but there was more of curiosity than compassion in their looks; and they took care to inform us they were Jews, and had no sympathy with the Muscovite. Once they stared with wonder at the taste and inborn politeness of a French soldier, who joined the group as a Russian was borne by on a litter. The man's eyes were open, and as he went past he caught sight of the Frenchman and smiled feebly, why or wherefore it is impossible for me to say, but the Frenchman at once removed his cap, made a bow to the 'brave' and stood with uncovered head till the latter had been carried some yards beyond him.

In the evening all the inhabitants remaining in the town flocked out of their houses and conversed at the corners of the streets, or at favourite gossip-posts. They were an unhealthy and by no means well-favoured race, whether Tartars, Greeks, Jews or Muscovites. All the people of rank had fled. Some of the tradespeople, with greater confidence in our integrity than could have been expected, kept their shops open. In a well-fitted *apteka* or apothecary's shop, we got a seidlitzy imitation of soda-water, and some of our party fitted themselves at a bootmakers with very excellent Wellingtons, for which they paid at their discretion, and according to a conqueror's tariff, 15s a pair; the proprietor seemed rather apprehensive that he was not going to receive anything at all. Indeed, it would have been well if the inhabitants had remained to guard their houses, instead of flying from them, and leaving them shut up and locked, the very thing to provoke the plunderer.

While allied troops had been dismantling and destroying batteries and dockyard installations at Kertch and Yenikale, Sir Edmund Lyons had sailed his squadron into the Sea of Azov beyond the Straits of Kertch.

Within four days after the squadron passed the Straits they had destroyed 245 Russian vessels employed in carrying provisions to the Russian army in the Crimea, many of them of large size and fully equipped and laden. Immense magazines of corn, flour, and breadstuffs were destroyed, comprising altogether more than 7,000,000 rations.

The point or bank of Tchechka, opposite Yenikale, is one of the many extraordinary spits of land which abound in this part of the world and which are, as far as I know, without example in any other country. Of all these the Spit of Arabat, which is a bank but a few feet above the water, and is in some places only a furlong in breadth, is the most remarkable. It is nearly seventy miles in length and its average width less than half-a-mile from sea to sea. The bank of Tchechka, which runs for nearly eight miles in a south-westerly direction past Yenikale, only differs from Arabat in size and in the absence of the fresh-water wells. In the interior, or on the body of the bank, there are numerous lagunes – narrow strips of water much more salt than that of the adjacent sea. They are all bounded alike by thick high grass and rushes. Every lagune is covered with mallards and ducks in pairs and the fringes of the spit are the resort of pelicans and cormorants innumerable. The silence, the dreary solitude of the scene is beyond description. Even the birds, mute as they are at the season of my visit, appeared to be preternaturally quiet and voiceless. Multitudes of odd, crustaceous-looking polypous plants sprang up through the reeds; and bright-coloured flycatchers, with orange breasts and black wings, poised over their nests below them.

The first day I went over, we landed upon the beach close to the battery which the Russians placed on the spit at the ferry station. It consisted of a quadrangular work of sandbags, constructed in a very durable manner and evidently not long made. In the centre of the square there was a whitewashed house, which served as a barrack for the garrison. The walls only were left and the smoke rose from the ashes of the roof and rafters inside the shell. Our men had fired it when they landed. A pool of brackish water was enclosed by the battery, which must have been the headquarters of ague and misery. The sailors said the house swarmed with vermin and had a horrible odour. Nothing was found in it but the universal black bread and some salt fish. The garrison, some thirty or forty men probably, had employed themselves in a rude kind of agriculture. Patches of ground were cleared here and there and gave feeble indications that young potatoes were struggling for life beneath. A hundred yards from the battery there was another whitewashed house, or the shell of it, with similar signs of rural life about it and an unhappy-looking cat trod gingerly among the hot embers and mewed piteously in the course of her fruitless search for her old corner. The traces of herds of cattle, which were probably driven down from the mainland to feed on the grass round the salt marshes, were abundant. There was a track beaten into the semblance of a road over the sand and it was covered with proofs of the precipitate flight of the garrison. Pieces of uniform, bags containing pieces of the universal black bread, strings of onions, old rags, empty sacks and bottles, were found along the track, and some of our party came upon a large chest which was full of government papers, stamps, custom-house and quarantine dockets, stamped paper for Imperial petitions and postage, books of tariff and customs in Russian, French, German and English, and tables of port dues, which we took away to any amount. But the sun was intensely hot and trudging through the heavy sand very painful. It seems impossible for men to have lived in this pestiferous place for any length of time, as it must be a hot-bed of fever and malaria. The heat of the sun, the vapours from the salt lakes, the mosquitoes, the vermin and the odour, must have formed a terrible combination of misery in the dog-days and have rendered going out, staying in, lying down and standing up, equally desperate and uncomfortable.

When the expedition was about to return to the Chersonese, the Tartars crowded to the beach and requested us to land them at some Russian port. They were about two hundred in number, and they were sent away on board the 'Caton' and the 'Ripon' to the ports in the Sea of Azov and to Yalta. We left ruin and complete desolation behind us. Sir George Brown, no doubt, was most anxious to prevent pillage; but he had to deal with French and Turks as well as English, and he did not succeed in checking rapine, licence and barbarous excess. Our attempts to prevent outrage and destruction were of the feeblest and most contemptible character. If a sailor was found carrying any articles – books, or pictures, or furniture – they were taken from him at the beach and cast into the sea. The result was that the men, when they got loose in the town, where there was no control over them, broke to pieces everything that they could lay their hands upon. We did not interfere with French or Turks and our measures against our own men were harsh, ridiculous and impotent. The Austrian Consul was found to have a large store of corn, which he concealed in magazines painted and decorated to pass as part of his dwelling-house. It was all destroyed. Amid the necessary destruction private plunderers found facility for their work. The scene presented by the town could only be likened to that presented by Palmyra, fresh from the hands of the destroyer, or some other type of desolation. Along the quay there was a long line of walls, which once were the fronts of storehouses, magazines, mansions, and palaces. They were empty shells, hollow and roofless, with fire burning luridly within them by night and streaks and clouds of parti-coloured smoke arising from them by day. The white walls were barred with black bands where the fire had rushed out of the window-frames. These storehouses belonged to Russians and were full of corn – these magazines were the enemy's – these mansions belonged to their nobles and governors – and these palaces were the residences of their princes and rulers. In the whole lengthened front facing the sea and the wide quay which bordered it there was not an edifice untouched but one. This was a fine mansion with a grand semi-circular front ornamented with rich entablatures and a few Grecian pillars. The windows permitted one to see massive mirrors and the framework of pictures and the glitter of brasswork. The house belonged, *on dit*, to Prince Woronzow[1].

The silence of places which a few days before were full of people was exceedingly painful and distressing. It reigned in every street, almost in every house, except when the noise of gentlemen playing on pianos with their boot-heels or breaking up furniture, was heard within the houses, or the flames crackled within the walls. In some instances the people had hoisted the French or Sardinian flag to protect their houses. That poor device was soon detected and frustrated. It was astonishing to find that the humblest dwellings had not escaped. They must have been invaded for the mere purpose of outrage and from the love of mischief, for the most miserable of men could have but little hope of discovering within them booty worthy of his notice.

[1]Mikhail Semenovich Woronzow, a distinguished soldier and member of a family well known in Russian history.

18

Failure

During the absence of the expeditionary force, preparations had been going on behind the allied lines for the bombardment that was to precede the assault on Sebastopol. For the moment, however, things appeared to be going on much as before.

There were intervals in the day when you might suppose that 'villanous saltpetre' had no more to do with a modern siege than an ancient one. There were times at night when angry and sudden explosions sprang up as if by some unaccountable impulse or conjuration and continued with an impetuosity which seemed as if it intended to finish the whole business in a moment. There were times when the red fusees turned and tumbled in the air like hot coals belched out of a volcano, and danced successive hornpipes upon nothing; then the clatter of small arms broke upon the ear in distant imitation of the heavy artillery, like a little dog yelping in gratuitous rivalry of a big one. The fighting was done by jerks and starts, and the combatants, like Homer's heroes, stood at ease the best part of the time and took it coolly, meaning deadly mischief all the while. The sharpest onset was generally on the side of our allies, about the Flagstaff or the Quarantine Battery, where they were sedulously advancing their endless mileage of trench and parallel, and promising themselves a result before long.

But this prolonged period of alternating between 'wearisome indolence' and sudden violence was about to come to an end.

For the third time our fire was opened along the whole range of positions on the 6th of June. At half-past two o'clock on that day,

157 guns and mortars on our side, and above 300 on that of the French, awoke from silence to tumult.

The two armies – one might say the four armies, but that the Turks and Sardinians were not expected to take a very prominent part in the trench work and assault – were in strength equal to any achievement, and in spirits ever chiding the delay and urging that one touch of the bayonet which made all the world scamper. If the strategic necessity pointed to some more decisive action this time, so, on the other hand, the intention of going beyond a vain cannonade was tolerably plain. Our fire was kept up for the first three hours with excessive rapidity, the Russians answering by no means on an equal scale, though with considerable warmth. On our side the predominance of shells was very manifest, and distinguished this cannonade in some degree even from the last. The superiority of our fire over the enemy became apparent at various points before nightfall, especially in the Redan. After dark the animosity on both sides gave signs of relaxing, but the same relative advantage was maintained by our artillery. It was a sultry day, with the dull mist of extreme heat closing down upon the valleys, and with no air to rend away the curtain of smoke which swayed between the town and our batteries; and at night flashes of lightning in the north-east made a counter-illumination on the rear of our position.

The British, with the French supporting them on either side, were now occupying the centre of the allied position, straddling the ravine through which the Woronzow Road curved southwards from the tip of Sebastopol's Southern Harbour.

At four o'clock on the 7th of June a still and sluggish atmosphere, half mist, half the result of gunpowder, hung about the town, and the sun enfilading, as it were, all the points of view from this low level in the horizon, telescopes were put out of joint for the moment. The Redan, however, which rose up boldly, gave some evidence of having yielded to rough treatment, the jaws of its embrasures gaping, and its fire being irregular and interrupted.

At nine a cool breeze, much stronger than usual, sprang up, and continued throughout the day, blowing the wreaths of smoke out of the batteries and carrying off the solid little round nebulae extemporized by bursting shells, which could only be compared in their expansion to the genie who, in the *Arabian Nights*, comes out of the iron pot sealed with Solomon's seal. The whole range of fire from right to left became visible in a bright sun that for once was not a scorching one. On the extreme left, towards the Quarantine, there was very slight firing from the French. The perpetual hiss and crack of shells was still the chief point of contrast with the bombardment in April. All the early part of the day we had the work very much to ourselves, but, since it has been the habit of the Russians to knock off work in the hotter part of the twenty-four hours, no very important disclosure was contained in this fact.

As the day wore on, it leaked out that something of import was undoubtedly to take place before its close, and that the double attack would probably commence at five or six p.m. An immense concourse of officers and men was gathered all the afternoon round the flagstaff on Cathcart's Hill,[1] and streamed along the spines of the three heights which wind towards Sebastopol from the English encampment. The fire on our side, which had continued from daybreak quietly and soberly, assumed a sudden fury about three o'clock, and was kept up from that hour to the critical moment.

The plan was for French troops to capture the Mamelon while British troops on their left mounted a diversionary attack on the Quarries, a defensive position recently thrown up by the Russians in advance of the Redan. Towards evening Lord Raglan and his staff appeared on one of the hills facing the fort.

A flagstaff was erected with threatening ostentation shortly before he came down, and a little angle of rude wall was as hastily thrown up as a breastwork. The man with the signal-rockets was in attendance, but there was a pause for a while. Sir Colin Campbell was observed to place himself on the next summit, still nearer to the enemy, commonly called the Greenhill. His appearance drew some fire, and the shells dropped and flashed close by, but without disconcerting his purpose of having a thorough good look-out place.

[1] So called from General Cathcart's habit of using it as a look-out post.

It was about half-past six when the head of the French attacking column came into view from these two spots, as it climbed its arduous road to the Mamelon. A rocket was instantly thrown up as the signal for our diversion, and as instantly the small force of our men detached for the post of honour made a rush at the Quarries. After one slight check they drove out the Russians, and, turning round the gabions, commenced making themselves snug; but interest was so entirely concentrated upon the more exciting scene, full in view upon the right, that they had to wait a good while before attention was directed to their conflict.

The French went up the steep to the Mamelon in most beautiful style and in loose order, and every straining eye was upon their movements, which the declining daylight did not throw out into bold relief. Still their figures, like light shadows flitting across the dun barrier of earthworks, were seen to mount up unfailingly – running, climbing, scrambling like skirmishers up the slopes on to the body of the work, amid a plunging fire from the guns, which, owing to their loose formation, did them as yet little damage. As an officer, who saw Bosquet wave them on, said at the moment, 'They went in like a clever pack of hounds.' In a moment some of these dim wraiths shone out clear against the sky. The Zouaves were upon the parapet firing down into the place from above; the next moment a flag was up as a rallying-point and defiance, and was seen to sway hither and thither, now up, now down, as the tide of battle raged round it; and now like a swarm they were in the heart of the Mamelon, and a fierce hand-to-hand encounter, here with the musket, there with the bayonet, was evident. It was seven minutes and a half from the commencement of the enterprise. Then there came a rush through the angle where they had entered, and there was a momentary confusion outside. Groups, some idle, some busy, some wounded, were collected on the hither side, standing in shelter, and now and then to the far corner a shell flew from the English battery facing it. But hardly had the need of support become manifest, and a gun or two again flashed from the embrasure against them, than there was another run in, another sharp bayonet fight inside, and this time the Russians went out, spiking their guns. Twice the Russians made head against the current, for they had a large mass of troops in reserve, covered by the guns of the Round Tower; twice they were forced back by the on-sweeping flood of French. For ten minutes or so the quick flash and roll of small arms had declared that the uncertain fight waxed and waned inside the enclosure. Then the back door, if one may use an humble metaphor, was burst open. The noise of the conflict went away down the descent on the side towards the town, and the arena grew larger.

It was apparent by the space over which the battle spread, that the Russians had been reinforced. When the higher ground again became the seat of action – when there came the second rush of the French back upon their supports, for the former one was a mere reflux or eddy of the stream – when rocket after rocket went up ominously from the French general's position, and seemed to emphasize by their repetition some very plain command, we began to get nervous. It was growing darker and darker, too, so that with our glasses we could with difficulty distinguish the actual state of affairs. There was even a dispute for some time as to whether our allies were going in or out of the work, and the staff themselves were by no means clear as to what was going on. At last, through the twilight, we discerned that the French were pouring in. After the interval of doubt, our ears could gather that the swell and babble of the fight was once more rolling down the inner face of the hill and that the Russians were conclusively beaten.

The fall of the Mamelon and the pursuit of the flying foe did not by any means bring the combat to an end. The Zouaves, emboldened by their success, and enraged by their losses, carried their prowess a step too far, and dreamt of getting into the Round Tower [Malakoff] by a *coup de main*. The tower itself, or rather the inglorious stump of what was once the Tower, took and gave shot and shell and musketry with the most savage ardour and rapidity. The fire of its musketry was like one sheet of flame, rolling backwards and forwards with a dancing movement, and, dwarfed as it was by the distance and seen by us in profile, could scarcely be compared to anything except the notes of a piano flashed into fire throughout some rapid tune. Our gunners, observing the duration and aim of the skirmish, redoubled their exertions, and pitched their shells into the tower with admirable precision, doing immense mischief to the defenders. The Russian defence, rather than their defences, crumbled away before this tremendous fire, but, on the other hand, the attack not being fed, as it was not designed, began to languish, and died gradually away.

Throughout the night the Russians tried again and again to recapture the Quarries in a series of murderous attacks. They also worked frantically to repair the damage done to their defences.

The sentinels outside our advanced works were near enough to hear the sound of their tools, and see the light of their tobacco-pipes. The French, on the other hand, were losing no time in the Mamelon. When morning dawned the position held by both parties was one of expectation. The French were in great force within and on the outer slopes of the Mamelon. On the right, lining a deep bay in the gorge, was dotted over half a mile of ground a French reserve with their muskets piled, attending the signal to move forward. They were partially within view of the Malakoff, and the round shot and shell came plumping down into the hollow. A lively and even pretty *vivandière* came striding up the ascent, without a symptom of acknowledgement to the racing masses of iron, and smiling as if the honour of her corps had been properly maintained.

On the 9th a white flag from the Round Tower and another on the left announced that the Russians had a petition to make. It was a grave one to make in the middle of a fierce bombardment with events hanging in the balance, and success, perhaps, depending upon the passing moments; but made it was, and granted. From one o'clock until six in the evening no shot was fired on either side, while the dead bodies which strewed the hill between the Mamelon and the Round Tower, or remained in front of the Quarries, were removed from the field of slaughter.

Apart from the military question, and the further one as to where the true humanity lay, the interval afforded another opportunity of getting a nearer look at Sebastopol, and the Mamelon, as the most important of our acquisitions, was the attractive spot whither every one who had the time and chance hastened. The rugged, channelled and shot-bruised outline of the fortress grew larger and more real as one approached; but the interior, altogether unknown till that moment, excited a more vivid feeling, and alike outside and inside attested the fierceness of the struggle and the pluck of the assailants. The surface of the ground within was cut into holes and pits – here like an old stone quarry, there like a bit of Crimean vineyard; some of these were the effect of bursting shells with well-timed fuses, some the cunning apparatus of the hardy and prolonged defence. The corpses which cumbered the earth and were in process of removal gave out faint tokens of coming putrefaction; fragments of bodies and marks of carnage were interspersed with ruined gabions and broken firelocks; Russian guns, dismounted and dented with shot-marks, lay tumbled below their embrasures; fifty or so were concealed beneath the débris, and some quantity of hidden powder was also rooted out of the subterranean recesses which abounded in the rock. These nests, excavated in the inner faces of the intrenchments, were left warm by their previous occupants – food and implements of labour were found in them, and, among other things, a bit of fishing-net in course of construction. The nearer view alone revealed the stupendous character of the earthworks, and, if astonishment had not been a stale sentiment, the eye-witnesses would have been simply astonished at the amount of labour lavished on them.

In the early part of the day there had been a popular impulse to believe that an end of the affair would be made at night by a combined assault upon the Malakoff and the Redan. That both were within scope of capture was considered in camp as proved to demonstration. But news of the suspension of arms dissipated the hope, and when the divisions got their orders for the night, it was no longer thought that aggression was likely, though defence might be.

It was understood that Lord Raglan was most anxious for the assault, and that the English officers shared his lordship's anxiety; but the French, who proved the better judges of the two, thought the fire of the place was still too powerful, and preferred erecting new batteries for its reduction.

On the 16th of June it was arranged by a Council of Generals that the assault should take place on the morning of 18th June, after three hours' cannonade from the whole of the allied batteries; but on the evening of the 17th, Marshal Pelissier sent over a despatch to our headquarters, to the effect that as the French infantry could not be placed in the trenches in the morning without the enemy seeing them, he had decided on attacking the place at daybreak, without any preliminary cannonade in the morning. Lord Raglan accepted this change of the plan of attack, although it was opposed to his private judgment, and sent orders to the divisional generals to carry it out.

It was unfortunate, to say the least, that Sir George Brown, to whom preparations for the attack were entrusted, seemed as despondent about its outcome as was his chief. The plan was for the British to capture the Redan, while the French on their right, under General d'Autemarre and General Brunet, were to capture the Malakoff. On the British left the French would mount diversionary attacks on the Quarantine and Central Bastions and on the Bastion du Mât, and on the extreme right of the line another diversionary attack under General Mayran would be made by the French on the No. 1 *Bastion and the Little Redan. It was realised that the Malakoff would be the tougher nut to crack, but the disparity in numbers between the French forces who were to make the assault, totalling* 36,000 *with* 10,000 *in reserve, and the British who were to attack the Redan –* 1,200, *with* 10,000 *in reserve – seems inexplicable on any grounds but a grave failure to appreciate the realities of the situation.*

The fire which we opened on Sunday morning (the 17th) preliminary to the assault was marked by great energy, weight, and destructiveness. Our artillery fired 12,000 rounds of the heaviest ordnance into the enemy's lines, and on the following day we fired 11,946 rounds of shot and shell.

Early on Monday morning the troops, who were under arms soon after midnight, were moved down to the trenches. Lord Raglan and his staff were stationed in the trench in rear of the Quarries Battery, which was exposed to heavy fire, but commanded a good view of the Redan. Marshal Pelissier took up his post in a battery to the rear of the Mamelon and on our right front, a considerable way from

Lord Raglan. The distance between the generals was attended with disastrous consequences. With some officers I went down soon after midnight to the Greenhill, or left attack, and remained there during the greater part of the morning. For some hours there was silence and darkness all along our front, broken occasionally by the roar and the blinding flash of a bomb.

Just as some faint tinge of light in the east announced the approach of dawn, we heard a very irregular but sharp fire of musketry on our right, close to the Malakoff. In an instant all the Russian works on the right woke up into life, and the roar of artillery, mingled with musketry, became incessant. The column under General Mayran had made a premature attack. Very injudiciously, as it appears, it was decided to give the signal by rockets, and one which was fired from the works unintentionally misled the French general, who expiated his error with his life, as he fell mortally wounded by the murderous fire with which his assault was received. In a few minutes the column, which had come in the dark right in front of the enemy's guns, was driven back with great loss. This musketry ceased, but the guns still kept up fire from the ships off Careening Creek and the works on our right. Then three rockets flew up into the gloomy sky. This was the signal for the French assault, which Mayran had anticipated with such unfortunate results. General d'Autemarre's column at once rushed out, and at the double made a dash up the ravine which separated the Redan from the Malakoff, whilst General Brunet led his men to attack the left of the work. The Russians received them with a tremendous fire, for the grey dawn just gave light sufficient to indicate the advance of these large masses of men. General Brunet fell dead. Incessant volleys of grape and musketry from the long flank of the works and from the Little Redan swept his column down in sections and it was obliged to retreat with great loss to the trenches. The other column on the right of the Malakoff was somewhat more fortunate. They dashed, in broken order, across the ditch and over the parapet of the Gervais Battery [immediately in front of the Malakoff] and drove the enemy before them. Some few got into the Malakoff itself, and certainly in the midst of the struggle, unless my eyes deceived me, I saw a flag waving in the centre of the work, which I imagined at the time to be a tricolor hoisted by the French as a signal of success. Others following, the Russians held possession of some of the houses in the suburb at the rear of the Malakoff, called the Karabelnaya, and a few French actually reached the dockyard wall.

Although it was understood that the English were not to attack until the French had carried the Malakoff, Lord Raglan resolved, at this stage of the assault, to assist the French, and the two rockets which was the signal for the advance of our men were sent up. At the moment he did so the French were fighting outside the Malakoff, but were in possession of the Gervais Battery outside it on the right flank. Brunet's column had been driven back, and a second attack on the extreme right by Mayran's column had failed completely. Our men were ready for the attack, but the Russians, warned by the assault on their left that we were about to storm their works, were equally prepared, and in the Redan they held a great force in reserve. Their guns were manned and loaded with grape, and the parapets were thickly lined with infantry.

The storming party to assault the left face of the Redan consisted of eleven officers and 400 men of the 34th Regiment, under Major Gwilt, preceded by a covering party of the Rifle Brigade and a ladder party from the Sailors' Brigade. When the signal was given for the assault, the sailors and men carrying the ladders and wool-bags rushed out of the trench; they were at once swept down by the tremendous fire of grape, musketry, and case, and Major Gwilt ordered the companies of the 34th who were near him to lie down again; but on the extreme right of the trench the men, who did not receive the order, advanced in sections at the double and the result was that the whole of the storming party made a run at the re-entering angle of the left face of the Redan. They were soon thrown into confusion, and on getting up to the abattis their disorder was increased by finding that a formidable barrier was before them. Colonel Yea came up at this moment, and complained that a considerable number of the men of his regiment were hiding in a small ditch, but it was found that these men were all either killed or wounded. Colonel Yea was killed almost immediately, and Major

Gwilt, who was about sixty yards from the abattis, was soon severely wounded, and obliged to retire. When the 34th came up, there was only one ladder at the abattis. The causes of this failure were various. The columns were too weak in number, nor was any attempt made to support them. The moment they came out from the trench the enemy began to direct on the whole front a deliberate and well-aimed *mitraille*, which increased the want of order and unsteadiness caused by the mode of their advance. Poor Colonel Yea saw the consequences too clearly. Having in vain tried to obviate the evil caused by the broken formation and confusion of his men, who were falling fast around him, he exclaimed, 'This will never do! Where's the bugler to call them back?' But, alas! at that critical moment no bugler was to be found. The gallant officer, by voice and gesture, tried to form and compose his men, but the thunder of the enemy's guns close at hand and the gloom frustrated his efforts; and as he rushed along the troubled mass of troops, endeavouring to get them into order for a rush at the batteries, a charge of their deadly missiles passed, and the noble soldier fell dead in advance of his men, struck at once in head and stomach by grape shot.

The column on the left, which had been told off for the attack of the re-entering angle and flank of the right of the Redan, was exposed to the same fire. The sailors were swept away by the enemy's grape and musketry. There were no scaling-ladders placed at the abattis, much less at the ditch of the Redan, nor could the Rifles keep down the enemy's artillery. In a few moments the whole of our assaulting columns had disappeared, and our failure to take the Redan at the first onset was painfully manifest.

Meantime, the French were driven out of the Gervais Battery because they received no reinforcements, though not till they had held it with great vigour and valour for upwards of forty minutes. Marshal Pelissier, however, did not abandon all hope, but made proposals to Lord Raglan to renew the assault as soon as the troops could be prepared for the purpose. Lord Raglan, though agreeing with the French General in the practicability of a renewed assault, was of opinion that it ought not to be attempted till the fire of the batteries and a heavy bombardment had been continued for some hours; and certainly on this occasion his lordship seems to have exhibited sounder judgment than the French General. As there was a considerable distance between them, Lord Raglan had to ride over to the station occupied by Marshal Pelissier in order to confer with him on the arrangements for the proposed assault; and during the interval which occurred, the French, who were greatly crowded in their trenches, and were suffering heavily from the enemy's fire, became dispirited by their losses and by the inaction which followed the check they had sustained. The Russians were evidently in great force at the Malakoff; and General d'Autemarre was so convinced that the assault would not succeed that he sent a pressing message to Marshal Pelissier to beg that he would not expose the men to be slaughtered in a fruitless assault. As General d'Autemarre was an officer of experience, Marshal Pelissier was obliged to yield to such an expression of opinion, and, Lord Raglan coinciding with him, the renewal of the assault did not take place and the Generals returned to their quarters.

The only gain resulting from the whole operation was the capture by the British of a small cemetery about 500 yards west of the Redan, the strategic advantage of which was hardly in proportion to the cost. The British had lost 22 officers and 247 men, and 1,285 had been wounded: the French had lost 39 officers and a total of nearly 1,700 officers and men had been wounded or captured.

Although the attack upon the Redan had been discussed at a council of war, held at the Headquarters Camp, on the 16th June, and the Engineer officers of both our attacks had been called upon to assist the Generals with their advice, the result proved that the arrangements were defective and inadequate. Our officers were outwitted by the subtlety of the Russians, who had for some time masked their guns, or withdrawn them from the embrasures, as if they were overpowered and silenced by our fire. No more decisive proof of the inefficiency of our force could be afforded than this fact – that in no case did the troops destined to assault and carry the Redan reach the outer part of the work; that no ladders were placed in the ditch; and that a very small portion indeed of the storming party reached the abattis, which was placed many yards in front of the ditch of the Redan. It cannot be said that on this occasion our men exhibited any want of courage; but so abortive and so weak was the attack, that the Russians actually got outside the parapet of the Redan, jeered and laughed at our soldiers as they fired upon them at the abattis, and mockingly invited the 'Inglisky' to come nearer.

No one hinted a doubt of the carrying of the Redan, though there was a general expression of opinion, among those who knew the case, that the force detailed for the storm was perilously small, and some few, as I heard, also found fault with the position of the reserves, and thought they were placed too far in the rear to be of service in case of a check. The detachments from the Naval Brigade consisted of four parties of sixty men each, one for each column, but only two of them went out, the other two being kept in reserve; they were told off to carry scaling-ladders and woolbags, and to place them for our storming parties. Captain Peel, who commanded, was wounded. His aide-de-camp, Lieutenant Wood, then midshipman of HMS 'Queen', displayed the greatest gallantry, though badly wounded in the arm. He got up to the abattis, and rendered himself conspicuous for a gallantry of which he had indeed given several proofs on previous occasions.[1]

The natural consequence, in civilized warfare, of such a contest is an armistice to bury the dead. It was our sad duty to demand it next day, for our dead lay outside our lines, and there were no Russian corpses in front of the Redan or Malakoff. Somehow or other, the rumour got abroad that there would be an armistice early in the day, and we hoisted a white flag in the forenoon, but there was no such emblem of a temporary peace displayed by the Russians. The advanced trenches were filled with officers and soldiers eager to find the bodies of their poor comrades; but they could not stir out of the parallels. They waited patiently and sadly for the moment

[1] Despite his arm being permanently affected, Midshipman Wood later obtained a transfer from the Navy to the army and was granted a commission in the 13th Light Dragoons. In 1858 he was awarded the Victoria Cross for bravery at Sindwaho in India, and later became Field-Marshal Sir Evelyn Wood.

when friendship's last melancholy office could be performed. Boats were at last seen to leave the roads of Sebastopol, and to meet boats from the [British] fleet at the entrance, and it became known that the Russians had acceded to an armistice and that it was to take place at four o'clock in the afternoon. To pass the weary time away, there was nothing to do but to watch the Russians at work repairing their batteries – labours which they continued during the armistice subsequently – and to make out the bodies which lay scattered about in front of the Redan and Malakoff.

It was agonizing to see the wounded men who were lying there under a broiling sun, parched with excruciating thirst, racked with fever, and agonized with pain – to behold them waving their caps faintly, or making signals towards our lines, over which they could see the white flag waving. They lay where they fell, or had scrambled into the holes formed by shells; and there they had been for thirty hours. An officer told me that one soldier who was close to the abattis, when he saw a few men come out of an embrasure, raised himself on his elbow, and fearing he should be unnoticed and passed by, raised his cap on a stick and waved it till he fell back exhausted. Again he rose, and managed to tear off his shirt, which he agitated in the air till his strength failed him. His face could be seen through a glass; and my friend said he never could forget the expression of resignation and despair with which the poor fellow at last folded his shirt under his head to await the mercy of Heaven.

The red-coats lay sadly thick over the broken ground in front of the abattis of the Redan, and blue and grey coats were scattered about or lay in piles in the raincourses before the Malakoff. I rode down with some companions into the Middle Picket Ravine, at the end of which began the French approaches to their old parallel, which was extended up to their recent conquest, the Mamelon. As we advanced, this ravine was almost paved with shot and shell. The earth gleamed here and there with bullets and fragments of lead. In one place there was a French picket posted in a bend of the ravine, sleeping under their greatcoats raised on twigs to protect them from the sun, or keeping watch over the eternal *pot-au-feu*, making delicious coffee with the rudest apparatus, smoking or talking gravely. For a wonder the men looked almost sullen, but they were merely thinking of the comrades whose bodies they would have to inter, for they were courteous and prompt to give a drink of muddy water, or a light for a cigar, or any information they could afford. By the side of this ravine – your horse must needs tread upon them, if you were not careful in guiding him – was many an humble mound, some marking the resting-place of individual soldiers, others piled over one of those deep pits where rank and file reposed in their common glory covered with lime, and marked now and then with a simple wooden cross. Close to the Mamelon the frequent reports of rifles and the pinging of the balls proved that the flag of truce had not been hoisted by the enemy. Two Voltigeurs approached, with a young English naval officer between them. They were taking him off as a spy, and he could not explain his position to his captors. He told us he was an officer of the 'Viper', that he walked up to see some friends in the Naval Brigade, got into the Mamelon, and was taken prisoner. The matter was explained to the Allies; they pointed out that the Naval Brigade was not employed on the Mamelon, that spies were abundant and clever – were at last satisfied, and let their captive go with the best grace in the world. We were then in the zig-zag, a ditch about six feet broad and six feet deep, with the earth knocked about by shot at the sides, and we met Frenchmen laden with water canteens or carrying large tin cans full of coffee, and tins of meat and soup, ready cooked, up to the Mamelon. They were cooked in the ravine close at hand, and taken up in messes to the men on duty.

I entered along with them. The parapets were high inside the work, and were of a prodigious thickness. It was evident the Mamelon was overdone by the Russians. It was filled with huge traverses and covers and excavations inside, so that it was impossible to put a large body of men into it, or to get them in order in case of an assault. The interior was like a quarry, so torn was it and blown up with shells. The stench was fearful. It arose from the dead Russians, who had been buried as they fell, and bones and arms and legs stuck out from the piles of rubbish on which you were treading. Many guns were also buried here when they had been disabled by our fire. Outside were plenty of those fougasses, or small mines, which exploded on the touch of the foot, and which the Russians planted thickly about their advanced works. A strong case containing powder was sunk in the ground, and to it was attached a thin tube of tin or lead, several feet in length; in the upper end of the tube was enclosed a thin glass tube containing sulphuric or nitric acid. This portion of the tube was just laid above the earth, where it could be readily hid by a few blades of grass or a stone. If a person stepped upon it he bent the tin tube and broke the glass tube inside. The acid immediately escaped and ran down the tin tube till it arrived close to its insertion into the case, and there met a few grains of chlorate of potash. Combustion instantly took place, the mine exploded, and not only destroyed everything near it, but threw out a quantity of bitumen, with which it was coated, in a state of ignition, so as to burn whatever it rested upon. Later in the day I very nearly had a practical experience of the working of these mines, for an English sentry, who kindly warned me off, did not indicate the exact direction till he found he was in danger of my firing it, when he became very communicative upon the subject.

The white flag was hoisted from the Redan just as I turned into the parallel where it joined the left of the French right. I walked out of the trench unmolested on the right and rear of the Quarries under the Redan, in which we had then established a heavy battery 400 yards from the enemy's embrasures. The ground sloped down from our attack for some few hundred yards and then rose again to the Redan. It was covered with long rank grass and weeds, with large stones, and with holes ranging in depth from three feet and a half or four feet, to a foot, and in diameter from five feet to seven or eight feet, where shells had fallen and exploded. The grass was seamed in all directions by grape-shot and furrowed by larger missiles, as if ploughs, large and small, had been constantly drawn over it. Sometimes it was difficult to get over the inequalities in the ground, which was naturally of a broken and uneven surface.

There was a red-jacket in the grass – a private of the 34th lying on his face, as if he were asleep; his rifle, with the barrel curved quite round, and bent nearly in two by the grape-shot which afterwards passed through the soldier's body, was under him, and the right hand, which protruded from under his chest, still clutched the stock. It was the first body I saw, and the nearest to our lines; but as we advanced and passed the sentries they lay thick enough around and before him. The bodies of many a brave officer whom I had known in old times – old times of the war, for men's lives were short in the Crimea, and the events of a life were compressed into a few hours – were borne past us in silence, and now and then, wonderful to relate, men with severe wounds were found still living and able to give expression to their sufferings by moans and sighs of pain.

A line of sentries was formed by the Russians as our burying parties came out, and they advanced so far in front of the abattis, that General Airey was obliged to remonstrate with an aide-de-camp of General Osten-Sacken, who ordered them to retire nearer to the abattis. It was observed that these men were remarkably fine, tall, muscular, and soldier-like fellows, and one could not but contrast them with some of the poor weakly-looking boys who were privates in our regiments, or with the small undergrown men of the French line. They were unusually well dressed, in clean new uniforms, and were no doubt picked out to impose upon us. Many of them wore medals and seemed veteran soldiers. Their officers had also turned out with unusual care, and wore white kid gloves, patent leather boots, and white linen. Their working parties brought out all our dead and laid them in front of their line of sentries, whence our people carried them away.

The precautions taken to prevent officers and men getting through the lines sufficed to keep any great crowd away; but the officers on duty, and some amateurs, who managed to get through the lines formed groups in front of the Redan and entered into conversation with a few of the Russian officers. In the midst of these brief interviews, beginning and ending with bows and salutes, and inaugurated by the concession of favours relating to cigars and lights, the soldiers bore dead bodies by, consigning the privates to the burial-grounds near the trenches and carrying off the wounded and the bodies of the officers to the camp. The armistice lasted for upwards of two hours, and when it was over we retired from the spot so moistened with our blood.

19

The Battle of the Tchernaya

IMMEDIATELY AFTER THE FAILURE OF THE ASSAULT, A great increase of sickness took place among our generals. It was observed by one of his staff that Lord Raglan's health was affected and on the 23rd of June this officer, writing home to his friends, remarked, 'he [Lord Raglan] looks far from well, and has grown very much aged latterly'.

General Estcourt, Adjutant-General of the Army, died on the morning of the 24th of June, after three days' illness. His death produced a profound impression of regret upon all who knew him, for a kinder or more amiable man did not exist. He was unremitting in the discharge of his duties, and no officer ever applied himself to the labours of the desk, which constituted so large a portion of the business of the department over which he presided, with more assiduity and devotion. I heard of his death as I was passing through the Headquarters camp to the ship in which I had procured a passage to Therapia, where I was going to recruit my health, and I was sensibly shocked at the intelligence. It was rumoured that no attempt would be made to renew the assault for several weeks, and I was glad to avail myself of the interval to seek the repose I so much needed.

A few days after my arrival at Therapia – on the Sunday following – the news of Lord Raglan's death was communicated to me. It was indeed most painful intelligence, for Lord Raglan possessed qualities which, if not those of a general – or at all events those of a great general – were calculated to obtain for the English army more consideration than that to which it was entitled by its numerical strength. His calmness in the field – his dignity of manner – his imperturbable equanimity – exercised their legitimate influence over the generals of the French army, although he was frequently obliged to give way to their councils in opposition to his declared convictions. On Tuesday evening, after his usual devotion to the desk, he was seized with symptoms of a choleraic character and he took to his bed, where he died on the night of the Thursday following, quietly and without pain. The generals of the English Divisions came in all haste to headquarters when the sad news was known and manifested the keenest sorrow at the loss of their General; and next day the French, the Sardinian generals, and the admirals, thronged round the bed of our departed chief and by the liveliness of their emotions attested their sense of his worth and excellence. I have never seen any reason to alter the opinion already expressed in the earlier part of this edition of my letters. That Lord Raglan was an accomplished gentleman, as brave a soldier as ever drew a sword, an amiable, honourable, kindly man, animated by zeal for the public service, of the most unswerving fidelity to truth, devoted to his duty and to his profession, cannot be denied; but he appears to have been a man of strong prejudices and weak resolution, possessed of limited information, offensively cold to those whom, like Omar Pasha, he considered vulgar or obtrusive, coerced without difficulty by the influence of a stronger will, and too apt to depend upon those around him when he should have used his own eyes. Still, there was a simplicity about his manner, something of the old heroic type in his character, which would have compensated for even graver defects, if their results had not been, in many instances, so unfortunate for our arms.

As successor to Lord Raglan, the War Office appointed his chief of staff, Lieutenant-General James Simpson: a further example, if one were needed, of the extent to which the authorities at home were still out of touch with the realities and requirements of the situation.

General Simpson opposed his own appointment, and bore testimony to his own incapacity; but the Government – or Lord Hardinge[1] and Lord Panmure – insisted, and General Simpson became Commander-in-Chief. Lord Raglan had, at all events, by

[1] Wellington's successor as Commander-in-Chief of the British Army.

the dignity of his personal character, secured a position for the troops he commanded to which they were not numerically entitled; but no one can say by what sacrifices that position was maintained till the battle of Inkerman forced us to abandon it. General Simpson was certainly not suited to resist any pressure which our Allies might think fit to apply; and he was destitute of those acquirements and personal characteristics which in Lord Raglan compensated for a certain apathy and marble calmness which his admirers extolled as virtues.

At this period of the siege I was relieved for a short time by a colleague, and I proceeded to enjoy my holidays at Therapia, in the society of my wife; but I was attacked by Crimean fever soon after my arrival and was not able to return to the camp till the beginning of August. During the time I was at Therapia, the Hotel d'Angleterre presented melancholy aspect, from the number of sick and wounded officers at the *table-d'hôte*. Old officers shook their heads, and there was a great desire among young and old to get away from the Crimea on any pretence, in order to escape for a time from the sanguinary monotony of trench duties, the harassing sounds of cannon and rifle, which beat on the ear day and night, and the contagious influence of gloomy thoughts.

The attack on the Redan was the one subject of conversation – the arrival of news from the Crimea, the one great event to be looked forward to daily. No one at that time appeared to think that we ought to have attacked the Redan, but it seemed to be imagined that, even if we could have taken it, the French would not have been able to maintain themselves inside any other part of the enemy's lines, and that we should consequently have been exposed to the whole brunt of their concentrated attacks in a very difficult position. The first great phase in the siege had been passed – we found that the Russians could resist the Allied forces with vigour, and that they were capable of acting upon the defensive with greater energy than we gave them credit for from their conduct at the Alma.

Except that the Mamelon was now in French hands, the tactical situation still showed very little change. But it was noticeable that the Russians were no longer so keen on the sorties and reconnaissances of the past, for which they had often paid such an exorbitant price.

Though delivered by the progress of the siege from Russian sorties, we were exposed to the attacks of other enemies, quite as troublesome, if not dangerous. Every nook and cranny was infested with millions of flies, which gave one no rest by day and little by night. Situated as I was in the delightful vicinity of several hundred commissariat mules, and a varied assortment of empty sugar barrels and receptacles for beef and pork, it was possible I might have had more than my share of the attentions of these pertinacious insects, which hovered on every side in clouds and settled on the most irritable parts of the face without giving a moment's relaxation. Like the Harpies, they literally 'disputed the viands', such as they were, on which we regaled ourselves, a morsel in its passage to the mouth being generally settled upon by two or more of the insects, which required a vigorous shaking before they would let go their hold. The only way to be at rest was to sit in a thorough draught, which, when surrounded by papers, was a somewhat troublesome position. As you entered your hut after a few moments' absence, they rose in dense clouds with deafening buzz from every object. Irritable sufferers pursued them desperately with towels, laying about on every side; others tried to carry on a more scientific warfare, by burning old newspapers after closing every aperture; but it was useless – in five minutes the place was full with a fresh and more hungry swarm. The only respite was at night, when the invaders retired to rest on the ceiling in enormous black patches; but even then the introduction of a candle roused them to all the playfulness of noon. They were an unexpected and most troublesome visitation, especially irritating to the poor sick fellows in the hospital marquees, whom they prevented from getting any repose the live-long day, and kept in a constant state of nervous restlessness. A cargo of 'ketch-'em-alive' papers at Balaklava, would have found sale at exorbitant prices. We should have papered our huts and tents with them, and still despaired of exterminating our tormentors.

On the night of the 14th July the Russians made a sortie from the

Malakoff on the trenches and parallels in advance of the Mamelon. The affair took place about ten o'clock, and lasted nearly an hour, ending, as usual, in the repulse of the Russians and their retreat to their works, after having inflicted some damage upon those of the French.

The French had now pushed their works almost to the abattis of the Malakoff, and were so near that a man might throw a stone into the Russian position. It began to be understood by all engaged that the real point of attack would be the Malakoff, the capture of which would render the Redan untenable, and make the surrender of the south side of the place merely a question of time. No firing of the Russians, good or bad, slight or heavy, could impede the progress of the works. The surface of the ground in the neighbourhood of the Malakoff and the Redan presented every day a more checkered appearance. It was one mass of trenches, traverses, rifle-pits, and batteries – a perfect maze, so that it required a strongly developed organ of locality, or else many days' practice of trench duties, to enable one to find one's way. The opinion was at this time pretty general that no very long period could elapse before another attack was made upon the Malakoff. I was told by a French officer of artillery that Pelissier, on being asked when offensive siege operations would be again resumed, said, 'Well, I don't know: the Russians are losing every day 300 or 400 men by sickness. If we wait a week, they will have lost a brigade; if we wait a month, they will have lost a *corps d'armée*.' But if the Russians lost many men by sickness, they managed to replace them somehow or other. Numbers of stories were in circulation about the formidable forces which had come, and kept coming, and apprehensions of an attack upon the Tchernaya line gained ground daily.

However improbable all these apprehensions about an attack of the Russians might have been, there was one advantage connected with them – they imparted a certain amount of life and activity to the armies occupying the Tchernaya line. Without some such stimulant, the men would have been overpowered by *ennui*; moreover, these flying reports acted as a kind of corrective against sickness. In winter, the troops engaged in the trenches suffered much more than illness than those in the rear on the heights beyond Balaklava; now the reverse was the case, and the troops in the trenches were in better health than those at the Tchernaya. Of course, inactivity was just as fatal to a body of troops as over-work. The Turks alone formed an exception.

It will be observed that all this while the Turks never took part in the siege. It is a singular thing, that while the French and British troops consider their most harassing work to be the duty in the trenches, the Turks, who are equally interested in the event of the war, and will be the most benefited by its success, do not take any share in actual siege operations and amuse themselves with the mere pastime of foraging, or actually sitting in indolence for hours together, following the shadows of their tents as they move from west to east, smoking stolidly, or grinning at the antics of some mountebank comrade. Omar Pasha goes hither and thither without object, merely that his army may seem to be employed; its actual services are of little importance. If the Ottoman troops be so excellent behind fortifications, there can be no objection to their relieving their hard-worked allies in some of the less important positions; or they might at least be employed in some more active manner than merely moving to and fro occasionally, as if for the purpose of impressing the mind of Europe with a false idea of activity.

Early in August, the report of an approaching attack upon the Malakoff gained ground and was credited in the camp. False reports were so numerous that people paid little attention to the current rumours, save when various indications, more than general expectation, gave them an appearance of probability. At an early hour on the morning of the 7th, General Simpson went round the lines, examining the works. On the 9th, General Jones[1] did the same. A council of war was held on Wednesday evening, the 8th, at the British headquarters. A more positive symptom than these of approaching action was the fact that some of the principal medical officers of Divisions had received orders to clear the hospitals, to send to Balaklava such patients as could safely be moved, and to complete

[1] Sir Harry Jones, who had succeeded Sir John Burgoyne as Chief Officer of the Royal Engineers.

the customary preparations for the reception of wounded men. This might not mean that an assault was immediately to be made, as some short time was necessary to make arrangements and procure the stores required. An idea of the quantity of these may be formed from the fact that, on receiving this order, the chief medical officer of one Division, consisting of rather more than 6,000 effective men, at once sent in a requisition for about six tons' weight of various articles. Such a mass of drugs, lint, plaster, bedding, wine, and other hospital necessaries and comforts, was painfully suggestive of what might probably occur, and of how many stout and brave fellows were expected to go down in the approaching serious operation against the tenacious foe. But at the point to which things had then come, success was not to be hoped for without heavy loss, and if the former was rendered complete, the latter might have endured, if not cheerfully, at least without repining.

It was said that after a bombardment very numerous forces would be sent in to attack. Some talked of a combination of French and English troops against the Malakoff, and even designated our First Division (Guards and Highlanders) as the British contingent that was to co-operate with our Allies. It was the opinion of some that Sebastopol would never be ours until we regularly invested the whole place. There were various opinions, in both the French camp and the English, as to the impregnability of the Malakoff. Some believed that if we succeeded in storming the outer works, we should find within them a second line of invincible strength. Others thought the strength of the inner works had been exaggerated. If we could but have obtained possession of the Malakoff, little doubt was entertained that the south side would have been speedily ours; whether it would have been found tenable under the fire from the forts on the north was another question. The Russians once driven out, however, and the fleet destroyed, we should have been at liberty to busy ourselves with the northern forts, or to move inland, as might have been decided upon.

Late in the evening of the 13th of August orders were given for the troops to be under arms by three in the morning. Of course, Malakoff was immediately the word, and most persons supposed that the long-talked-of assault was to be made. This, however, was soon found not to be the case. An attack was expected to take place along the whole line. Without tap of drum or sound of bugle, the camp was afoot at the prescribed hour, the troops forming up in profound silence. The entire army was out, including the cavalry and artillery from Balaklava. The first grey of morning found a number of officers and amateurs assembled on Cathcart's Hill, the best point of observation. There was unusually little firing the day before and during the night, and all expected that this tranquillity was quickly to be broken by the din of an engagement. The interest of the situation grew stronger as the morning advanced, and as the scarlet columns became visible, massed along the lines, motionless and expectant. Superior officers, with their staff, moved to and fro; aides-de-camp traversed the heights with orders; here and there, through the still imperfect light, which began to be tinged with the first red flush of sunrise, waved the pennons of a Lancer escort. With broad day, the brief excitement ended. Before the upper edge of the sun's disc rose above the hills, the troops were marching briskly back to their tents. In serried columns, looking hardy, active, and cheerful, and up to any work, the Crimean army regained its canvas quarters. For the day, the danger was over – to commence again, it was believed, at night. From certain orders that were given with respect to ammunition, mules, etc., I inferred that the army would again be under arms early the next morning. The officers were warned to be ready at a moment's notice.

Movements of large numbers of troops in the neighbourhood of Sebastopol, the unanimous reports of deserters, of whom several came in every day, and information gained from Tartars, had given us intimation that the Russians, having received part of the reinforcements which they were expecting, intended to try their luck once more in an offensive operation. Although, at first, the line of the Tchernaya suggested itself as the point which the Russians would most probably attack, a supposition which was moreover confirmed by all the deserters, as large numbers of newly-arrived troops were seen concentrated in and about the Russian works, apprehensions were entertained that perhaps the Russians might attempt something against the positions of the allied armies before Sebastopol, and the chief attention was consequently directed to that point.

Nevertheless, General Pelissier assembled 40,000 men along the line of the Tchernaya, which was perhaps the most vulnerable part of the Allies' position. It can hardly be supposed that the Russians had not got some idea of the strength of these forces, yet events were to show that in this they made a grave miscalculation. Their mistake, however, was not the only one.

Several deserters came in on the 15th, and spoke with the utmost certainty of an intended attack on the Tchernaya; but no particular attention was paid to their reports, and no special orders were given to the troops, except to be prepared; and this had been so often repeated that it made no impression. No additional precautions were taken on the Tchernaya line and the advance was scarcely less a surprise than that of Inkerman. The first news of an actual assault was brought about daybreak by some French Chasseurs, who, forming part of a patrol, fell into an ambuscade of the Russians and narrowly escaped, while their comrades were taken prisoners. Soon afterwards the outposts across the Tchernaya were driven in, and about daybreak the cannonade began.

The river valley at this point has a number of rather complex features, the position of which needs to be understood in order to appreciate the events that now took place. The Tchernaya, after leaving a narrow gorge above the Baidar valley, follows a winding course between a succession of hillocks. Two of these hillocks, on the extreme left of the point at which the river emerges from the gorge, were occupied by Turks. The Sardinians' position, which was of paramount importance in the defence of the Tchernaya, rested on a mountain stream (which was the left-hand limit of the Turks' position) and a large hillock above the road leading from Tchorgun to Balaklava. In front of this hillock and separated from it by an aqueduct was a small stone bridge. On this bridge the Sardinians had set up a defence post which was guarded by a detachment of infantry. They also had outposts on the other side of the river. The last three hillocks, on the Sardinians' left, were occupied by the

French. The first was separated from the others by a wide road leading to the Traktir Bridge: the last, on the extreme left, was protected by a reservoir formed by the waters of the aqueduct, and was separated by about three-quarters of a mile of open ground from a ridge of hills to the north, the Sapoune Heights.

The first movement of the Russians was against the outposts of the Sardinians on the opposite bank of the river. Corresponding to the hillocks on this side of the Tchernaya were three plateaux upon the opposite bank. These plateaux were, therefore, first to be secured, for from them the guns could command not only the hillocks opposite occupied by the Sardinians and Turks, but likewise the plain which opens towards the French position. A company of infantry of the line and a company of Bersaglieri formed the Sardinian outposts. They were attacked at dawn by the Russians. As the troops [on the western bank of the river] were not then under arms it was necessary to hold this position for a while, and General Della Marmora sent over a company of Bersaglieri to reinforce the two companies already there. They crossed the aqueduct and the river and went up the plateau; but, when they arrived on the crest, the two companies had just left the epaulement behind which they had until then defended themselves gallantly against the overwhelming numbers of the enemy, but which had become untenable, as it was swept by the guns which the Russians had brought up on the two other plateaux, and, besides, was exposed to be taken in the rear. So the troops retired in good order across the river and went to reinforce the post which occupied the second hillock on the banks of the aqueduct.

In the meantime the cannonade on both sides had commenced. The Russians left us not long in doubt where they would attack, for scarcely had the cannonade opened when three compact masses of infantry were seen advancing towards the plain opposite to the French position. The points chosen were the [Traktir] bridge and the hillock to the right.

The French outpost beyond the bridge consisted of a company of Zouaves. The other *avant postes,* to the right of the Zouaves up to the

Sardinian outposts, were furnished by the 20th *léger* [Light Infantry] and the 22nd of the line. The *réveillée* had not yet gone in camp, but some of the men were already busy preparing their coffee, when the sentinels in advance were alarmed by hearing close at hand the tramp of men, whose forms were yet invisible in the darkness. Discharging their muskets, they ran in to the posts, who had not time to stand to their arms ere they were engaged with overwhelming masses of the enemy. They were driven across the river; but the desultory firing which took place in this preliminary skirmish had given timely warning to the main guards and to the camps, and the men turned out just as a storm of round shot began to rush over the ground, upsetting camp-kettles, dashing our fires, and destroying tents in its career.

The masses, which in the morning sun looked like glittering waves, protected by the fire of their artillery, moved in excellent order down to the river side, notwithstanding the heavy fire of artillery which greeted them in front from the French and in flank from the Sardinians. At the river the first column detached itself from the rest, and dividing into two parts crossed the river, which is easily fordable in summer. Men carrying moveable wooden bridges preceded; but in the first rush the Russians, without waiting for bridges, went over wherever they could, and dispersing like a swarm of bees, rushed forward in columns, some against the bridge and others against the hillock on the right.

The continual apprehension of an impending attack had at last allayed the interest for it, and notwithstanding the signs which seemed to indicate some movement on the part of the Russians, everybody slept as soundly as possible until awakened by the Russian guns. Before the troops were properly under arms the Russians were at the bridge and at the foot of the hillock. The 20th *léger* and the Zouaves had to stand the first shock, and they certainly stood it gallantly. The rush of the Russians was splendid. Without losing their time in firing, they advanced with an *élan* scarcely ever seen in Russian troops. But their ardour was soon checked. They could not carry their point, and were, after a short trial, repulsed both on the bridge and the hillock.

The battle had been raging for an hour ere I reached the line of the French works. From the high grounds over which I had to ride, the whole of the battle-field was marked out by rolling columns of smoke and the irregular thick puffs of the artillery. All our cavalry camps were deserted; but the sun played on the helmets and sabres of the solid squadrons which were drawn up about two miles in advance of Kadikoi, and just in rear of the line of hills which the French and Sardinians were defending, so as to be ready to charge the Russians, should they force the position.

The aqueduct which supplied the Turks, and which ran close to the foot of the hillock, formed the chief defence of the French. About nine or ten feet wide and several feet deep, its skirts the steep hills so close that it is nearly in all places supported by a high embankment, offering considerable difficulties for an advancing force, and exposing it, as soon as it reaches the top of the embankment, to musketry fire from the heights. Notwithstanding this difficulty, the Russians crossed it on the right, and were beginning to scale the heights, when, taken in flank by the Sardinian batteries, they were swept down wholesale and rolled into the aqueduct below.

This first rush did not last more than ten minutes. The Russians fell back, but they had scarcely gone a few hundred yards when they were met by the second column, which was advancing at the *pas de charge* to support the first, and both united and again rushed forward. This second attempt was more successful than the first. At the [Traktir] bridge they forded the river on the right and left, and forced its defenders to fall back. Scarcely was the bridge free, when two guns of the 5th Light Brigade of Artillery (Russian) crossed it and took up a position on the opposite side, in an open space which separates two of the hillocks, and through which the road leads to the plain of Balaklava. While those two guns passed the bridge, a third crossed the river by a ford, and all three began to sweep the road and the heights. The infantry in the meantime, without waiting for the portable bridges, the greater part of which had been thrown away during the advance, rushed breast-deep into the water, climbed up the embankment, and began to scale the heights on both sides. They succeeded in getting up more than one-half of the ascent, but by the time they arrived there the French were fully prepared and met them in the most gallant style. Notwithstanding the exertions and the perseverance of the Russians, they were by degrees forced back and driven, after an obstinate resistance, across the bridge, carrying away their guns.

While this conflict took place on the bridge, the other column again attacked the French right. This time they came on in such a swarm that they could neither be kept back by the aqueduct, nor cowed by the Sardinian guns, which were ploughing long lanes through their ranks. On they came, as it seemed, irresistible, and rushed up the steep hill with such fury that the Zouaves, who lined the sides of it, were obliged to fall back for a moment before the multitude. The officers might be seen leading the way and animating their soldiers. One gallant fellow, at least twenty yards in advance of the whole column, was the first to cross the aqueduct and was afterwards seen on the side of the hill. This furious rush brought the advancing column in an incredibly short time to the crest of the hillock, where it stopped to form. But the French had not been idle during the time that the Russians were ascending the hill. The Zouaves had only fallen back from the side of the hillock to the main body, which had been drawn up behind the top. Scarcely did the column of the enemy show its head, when the guns opened upon it with grape, and a murderous fire was poured amongst its ranks by the French infantry. This immediately stopped the advance of the column, which began to waver; but the impetus from those behind was so powerful that the head of it, notwithstanding the unexpected reception, was pushed forward a few yards more, when the French, giving one mighty cheer, rushed upon the advancing enemy, who, shaken already, immediately turned round and ran down, if possible, faster than they had come up. But the mass was so great that all the hurry could not save them, and more than 200 prisoners were taken on the spot, while the hill-side, the banks of the aqueduct, the aqueduct itself, and the river-side were filled with dead and the wounded. The Sardinian and French artillery poured, moreover, a murderous cross-fire into the scattered remains of the column, and

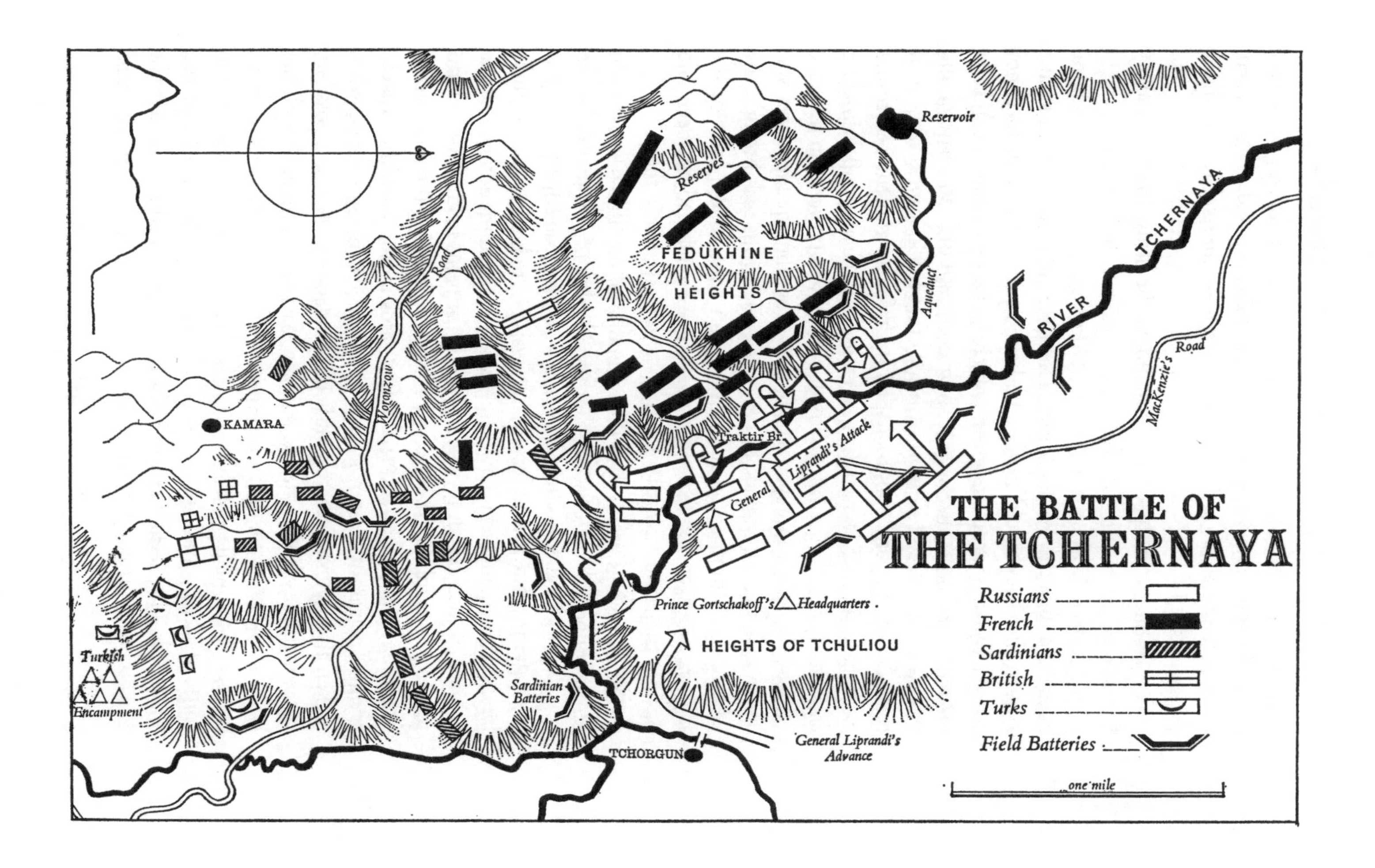
THE BATTLE OF
THE TCHERNAYA
Russians
French
Sardinians
British
Turks
Field Batteries
one mile
Reservoir
Reserves
FEDUKHINE
HEIGHTS
Aqueduct
RIVER TCHERNAYA
MacKenzie's Road
Woronzow Road
KAMARA
Traktir Br.
General Liprandi's Attack
Prince Gortschakoff's Headquarters
HEIGHTS OF TCHULIOU
Turkish Encampment
Sardinian Batteries
TCHORGUN
General Liprandi's Advance

scarcely a shot missed. It was a complete rout. The French rushed down the hill-side and drove them far across the plain. This defeat so completely depressed them that nothing more was attempted against this side.

Not so on the bridge. Notwithstanding the heavy loss suffered by the second attack, the Russians once more concentrated all their forces, collected the scattered remains of the column which had been routed on the right of the French position, and brought up all their reserves to attempt one more attack. They again crossed the river, and the aqueduct too, and tried to take the heights – but in vain; the French were now thoroughly prepared, and the tenacity of the Russians only served to augment their losses. They were soon seen fleeing in all directions, followed by the French. This last attack was decisive, and immediately the usual Russian preparation for retreat – namely, the advance of the artillery – showed that the Russians acknowledged themselves defeated and were on the point of retiring. Three batteries, each of twelve guns, which during the greatest part of the attack had been nearly silent, began to open their fire while the scattered remains of the infantry columns rallied behind a rising ground leading up towards Mackenzie's Height.

The Sardinians, who, with the exception of the little outpost fight on the opposite side of the Tchernaya, had confined themselves to support the French by their admirable artillery, which entirely subdued the Russian fire on the opposite plateaux, began now to move across the aqueduct. The Russian riflemen, after the last defeat on the right, had retired behind the banks of the Tchernaya, whence they kept up a brisk but ineffective fire. A battalion of Piedmontese, preceded by a company of Bersaglieri, advanced in beautiful order as if on parade, and soon drove these riflemen from their position. It even advanced some way towards the plateaux; but as it was not intended to force the heights, it contented itself, supported by other troops, with following the enemy, who was already in full retreat.

The guns which the Russians had brought up to cover their retreat suffered so much by the fire from our side that they made off in a hurry. Scarcely a shot was thrown away, and so admirable was the practice, that all the shot fell at or close to the guns, which we could plainly distinguish, as a slight breeze carrying off the smoke left a beautiful view over the whole battle-field. But the Russian guns returned only for a moment under cover and opened their fire, but only for a short time, and at half-past nine or ten o'clock the dust on the Mackenzie Road and the black lines moving off were the only traces which remained of the so long threatened attack of the Russians.

Everybody now rushed to the battle-field, and one look was sufficient to convince them that the Allies had won a real battle. Although not quite so obstinate and sanguinary as the battle of Inkerman, which this affair resembled in many points, it was a pitched battle. The Russians, as in the battle of Inkerman, gave up manœuvring, and confided entirely in the valour of their troops. The essential difference was in the manner of fighting. At the Inkerman the great mass of the Russians fell under the file firing and the bayonets of the infantry, while on the Tchernaya it was the guns which did the greatest execution. Most of the wounded and dead showed frightful traces of round-shot, grape, shell, and canister, so that, as a battle-field, one could scarcely imagine anything more terrible. Nearly all the wounds were on the legs and the head. On the banks of the aqueduct particularly, the sight was appalling; the Russians, when scaling the embankment of the aqueduct, were taken in flank by the Sardinian batteries, and the dead and wounded rolled down the embankment, sometimes more than twenty feet.

The French made every possible despatch to collect the wounded. They were laid on the open space about the bridge until the ambulances arrived. According to the account of the prisoners, and judging from the straps on the shoulders of the wounded and dead, three divisions were engaged in the attack. A soldier belonging to the last battalion of the reserves said that before the attack began, General Gortschakoff, who commanded in person, had a letter from the Emperor read before them, in which he expressed a hope that they would prove as valorous as last year when they took the heights of Balaklava; and then there was a large distribution of brandy. There was not a soldier who had not his bottle lying empty near him, and good-sized bottles they were, too. This brandy distribution was, however, only for the infantry, whom they wished to excite to madness. The artillery got only the usual rations.

The march of the Russians continued till late in the day – their last column gained the plateau about two o'clock. It must have been a terrible march for them – not a drop of water to be had; and even when they gained their arid camp, it is only too probable that they had nothing to drink; indeed, the prisoners told us the men were encouraged to the attack by being told that if they gained the Tchernaya they would have abundance of water – the greatest inducement that could be held out to them. I rode down towards the *tête-du-pont*. In order to get a good view of the retreat, I descended to the bridge, which was covered with wounded men. Just as I gained the centre of it, a volley of shells was pitched right upon it, and amid the French, who, with their usual humanity, were helping the wounded. Some burst in the shallow stream, the sides of which were crowded with wounded men; others killed poor wretches who were crawling towards the water – one in particular, to whom I had just an instant before thrown a sandwich; others knocked pieces out of the bridge or tore up the causeway. As the road was right in the line of fire, I at once turned off the bridge and, pulling sharp round, dashed under an arch just as the battery opened on us a second time, and there I remained for about ten minutes, when the Russians gave us a respite for a few moments. The next time they fired was with round shot; and as I retreated up the road to obtain shelter behind one of the hills, one of these knocked a wounded Zouave to pieces before my eyes. In the rear of the hill there was a party of about five hundred Russian prisoners *en bivouac*. Many of them were wounded; all were war-worn, dirty, ill-clad – some in rags, others almost bootless. The French sentries who guarded them seemed to commiserate the poor fellows; but two or three of their own officers, who sat apart, did not look at them, but smoked their cigars with great nonchalance, or talked glibly to the French officers of the fortune of war, etc.

In a short time I returned to the front, and saw General Simpson and a few staff-officers descending from the Sardinian position, whence they had watched the battle. The aspect of the field, of the aqueduct, and of the river, was horrible beyond description; the bodies were closely packed in parties, and lay in files two and three deep, where the grape had torn through the columns. For two days the bodies rotted on the ground which lay beyond the French lines, and the first Russian burying party did not come down till the 18th, when the stench was so very great that the men could scarcely perform their loathsome task.

20

The Malakoff Falls

THE TCHERNAYA BECAME, IN CONSEQUENCE OF THE attack, a point of attraction for all curiosity-seeking persons, whose name was legion, in the Allied armies. Officers and soldiers, although numerous enough, were few in proportion to the merchants, sailors, suttlers from Balaklava and Kamiesch, and other nondescript camp-followers, who formed a class of themselves, and were as sure to appear after an action was over as vultures. They had little chance of getting hold of medals, amulets, and crosses, and other more valuable spoil, for these disappeared marvellously; but they were not particular. The greatest mania seemed to prevail for muskets – nevertheless, cartridge-boxes, swords, bayonets, etc., were taken *faute de mieux*. But the getting of the arms was not always the most difficult part of the business; it was the getting them away, for there were gendarmes prowling about who confiscated all arms, whether paid for or not, as, according to the regulations of the French army, they ought to have been collected on the battle-field by the Artillery – a thing which was never done. There were some excellent rifles with sword-bayonets, which were in great request; they were, as was usually the case with all valuable things, picked up by the Zouaves, who certainly had the best right to them, having won them by their bravery. The Zouaves sold them, and the gendarmes took them away again, leaving the purchaser free to single out the Zouave who sold the rifle and to get back his purchase-money.

The more the particulars of that affair became known, the more it grew in importance. The ground where the attack took place being extended and very much broken up, one could not at first fully appreciate the amount of the loss of the Russians, but after a time it was officially known that the French had 2,200 Russians wounded and prisoners, the number of unwounded prisoners amounting to 400. For the burial of the dead an armistice was concluded, during which the French buried all those upon our side of the river, while the Russians buried those in the plain beyond. Of course the number of those buried by the Russians can never be ascertained, but their number must have been prodigious, for large spaces were cleared in the dense columns by grape and shell; besides, the Russians fired with grape into their own people from behind. I heard so from many people, and I saw it myself.

In the expectation of a new attack, the French and the Sardinians set about strengthening their defences along the line of the Tchernaya. The Turks, however, in spite of the Sardinians – their left-hand neighbours – urging them to do the same, made no such efforts: they had other matters to attend to.

The Turks celebrated their Korban Bairam and there was no end of sweetmeats and visiting. The solemnity of the occasion seemed to have acted powerfully on their religious feelings: for in passing through their camp at the hours of prayer, whole battalions might be seen going through their prayers and prostrations. Each battalion had a space cleared for the purpose, and it was provided with the few arrangements which their simple worship required. Some of them had only a stick planted in a south-easterly direction; others went much further, and made enclosures of earth or wickerwork pulpits, and in one place even a minaret was erected in a most primitive way – it consisted of nothing but slender poles interwoven with branches of brushwood. By coming in contact with Europeans the Turks did not seem to have lost any of their zeal for their religion; and although no one was forced to take part in the prayers, there were but few absentees from service, particularly in the evening.

The state of tension in which we were kept by the daily and almost hourly expectation of an attack, although every precaution was taken against surprise, was somewhat relaxed towards the end of August. Everybody was afoot or in readiness to turn out at an instant's notice, and dusty and disgusted enough some of the Staff appeared, after knocking about all night in anticipation of a fight that did not come off.

For the moment, hostile activity along the front showed signs of slackening, though not of ceasing altogether. Both sides seized this as an opportunity to repair and reconstruct their defences. Time was also found in the British camp for a certain amount of gaiety. An evening entertainment, presented in strange surroundings for such an occasion – the 'amputating house' of the Naval Brigade – was given by the sailors.

THEATRE ROYAL, NAVAL BRIGADE

On Friday Evening, 31st of August, will be Performed

DEAF AS A POST!

To be followed by

THE SILENT WOMAN

The whole to conclude with the laughable Farce, entitled

SLASHER AND CRASHER

Seats to be taken at SEVEN o'clock. Performance to commence precisely at EIGHT o'clock.

God save the Queen! Rule Britannia!

The scenes were furnished from the 'London', the actors from the Brigade. There was an agreeable ballet girl, who had to go into the trenches to work a 68-pounder at three o'clock in the morning, and Rosa was impersonated by a prepossessing young boatswain's mate. Songs there were in plenty, with a slight smack of the forecastle, and a refrain of big guns booming down the ravine from the front; but they were all highly appreciated, and the dancing was pronounced to be worthy of Her Majesty's.

There were at this period many rumours of peace. We had a peace party in camp, who reasoned that the Russians could sustain the contest no longer, owing to the want of water and the difficulty of obtaining supplies; their final attempt had been made in the action of the 16th, and, having been repulsed with heavy loss at the point which they had selected on account of its seeming to offer most chances of success, they would not risk another battle to raise the siege. According to these authorities, in a couple of months the British army was to go home again. The hopefulness of youth, and a certain vivacity of imagination, doubtless qualify a man to produce rose-tinted sketches of this kind, and there certainly could be no manner of question as to the immense superiority of a merry Christmas in England to a muddy one on the heights of Balaklava, any more than there could be of the smoking sirloin and tenderly-fed turkey being preferable to lean kine of the Crimea and fowls that refused to be fattened. But there is no magic in wishes any more than in words, and these prophets of peace underrated the tenacity and endurance of the Russian government and people. The enemy's position was no doubt a difficult one, but they evinced through this contest a dogged, passive courage, which is the very quality that enables generals to hold difficult positions.

As the crisis of the siege approached, many an anxious eye was cast upon the Russian position, for it was confidently affirmed that the enemy were about to try the chances of war once more, and that in one grand attack along the whole of our line they intended to assault the Allies with 90,000 men at three or four points between Baidar and the gorge of Inkerman, and at the same time to make a general sortie in great force from Sebastopol on the left, centre, and right of our works. The mass of the Russian forces was concentrated on the cultivated plateau between Kamishli and Kalankoi, on the south side of the Belbek, supported by divisions echeloned on the road to Bakschiserai.

The disposition of these forces suggested that if the Russians were to attack, they would do so across the Tchernaya.

Nothing would have given such universal satisfaction to the whole army as another attempt by the enemy to force our position. If the Russians descended into the plain we were sure of success, and the prospect of a sanguinary engagement gave positive pleasure to both officers and men, alike weary of the undistinguished, if not inglorious, service of the trenches.

With nearly 3,000 English cavalry and upwards of 5,000 French sabres we should have made signal examples of our defeated foes in their retreat; and our field guns, all in high efficiency and order, together with the admirable batteries of the French, would have annihilated any artillery which the Russians could have placed in position to check pursuit or cover the flight of their infantry. As to their cavalry, they were inferior in number to our own, and in dash and pluck they could not have matched the men who charged at Balaklava.

The condition of the army, notwithstanding the existence of a considerable amount of sickness, of some discontent, and of an element of weakness in the youthful recruits, was, on the whole, satisfactory. The Sardinians, acclimatized, flushed with triumph, and anxious for another opportunity to try their steel, formed a fine corps of about 8,000 effective bayonets, and the Turks could turn out about 13,000 strong. The French, notwithstanding their enormous losses by sickness, their sufferings in the capture of the Mamelon, in the assault on the 18th June, and, above all, in the trenches, where they had on an average 150 *hors de combat* on 'quiet nights', and perhaps twice as many when the enemy were busy, could present 55,000 bayonets to the enemy. The Allied cavalry was just 9,000 sabres strong, and our field artillery was overpowering. In a word, while the siege works were advancing steadily, and with very few checks, the Allies could present on any side a front which was quite strong enough to hold its own against whatever numbers the Russians could bring up. There was no ground for them to attack in large masses; there was no room to deploy the men if they had had them; and they had discovered that in attacking by masses of columns successively surging against us, their slaughter was increased, and the confusion of their repulse very much aggravated.

It was, in the end, the Allies who took the initiative.

On the morning of the 5th of September, the Allied batteries opened fire for the sixth time on Sebastopol, and the last bombardment commenced. The air was pure and light, and a gentle breeze from the south-east, which continued all day, drifted over the steppe and blew gently into Sebastopol. The sun shone serenely through the vapours of early morning and wreaths of snowy clouds, on the long

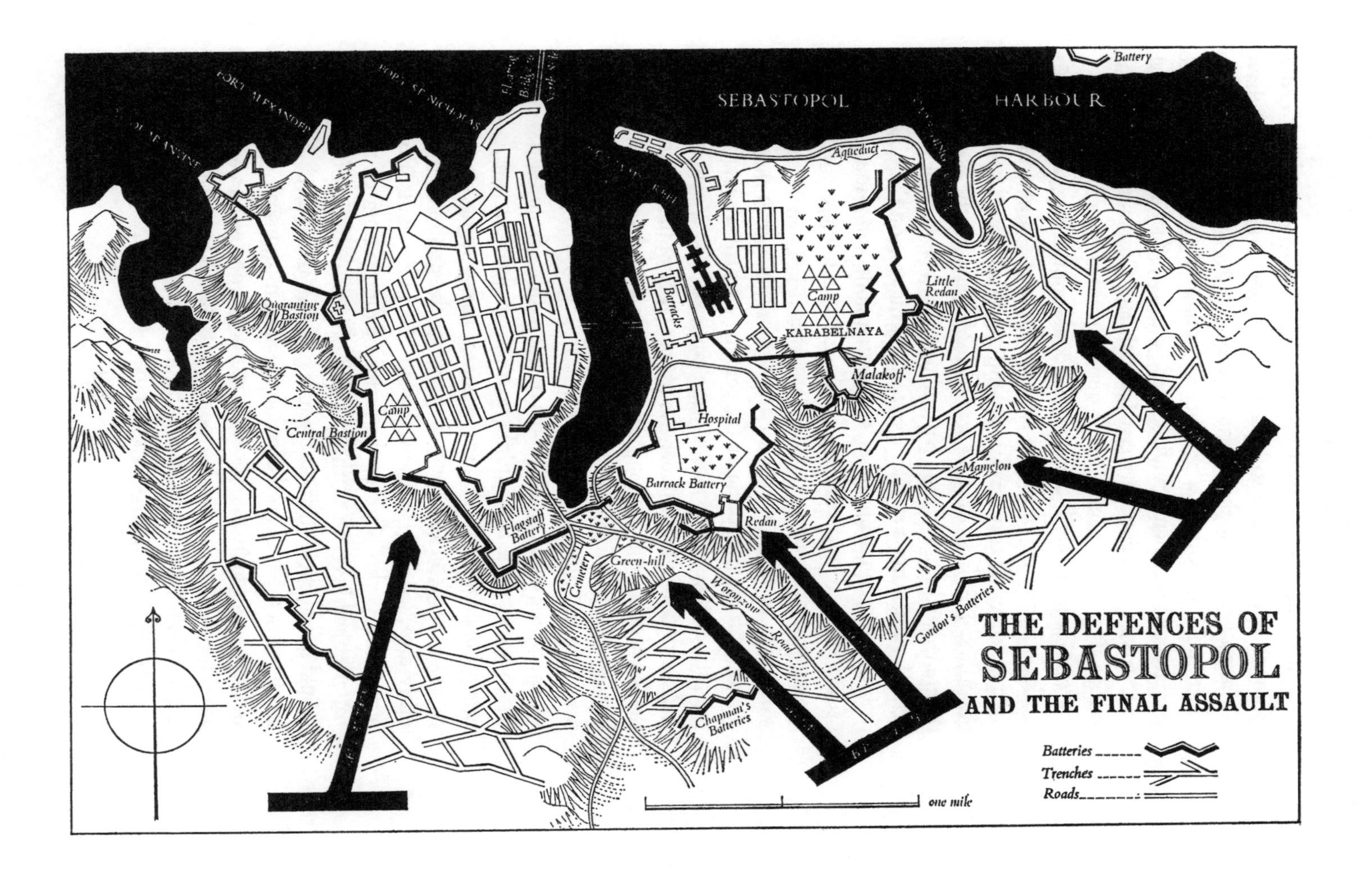
THE DEFENCES OF
SEBASTOPOL
AND THE FINAL ASSAULT
SEBASTOPOL
HARBOUR
Battery
FORT ALEXANDER
Quarantine Bastion
Camp
Central Bastion
Flagstaff Battery
Cemetery
Green-hill
Woronzow Road
Chapman's Batteries
Barracks
Hospital
Barrack Battery
Redan
Aqueduct
Camp
KARABELNAYA
Little Redan
Malakoff
Mamelon
Gordon's Batteries
Batteries
Trenches
Roads
one mile

lines of white houses inside those rugged defences of earth and gabionnade which have so long kept our armies gazing in vain on this 'august city'. The ships floated quietly on the waters of the roads, which were smooth as a mirror, and reflected the forms of these 'monarchs of the main', while outside our own fleet and that of the French were reposing between Kazatch and Constantine as idly as though they were 'painted ships upon a painted ocean'.

From Cathcart's Hill the spectator could see the Flagstaff Batteries works – the suburb of ruined houses, or rather the sites of cottages and residences, all that was left of long streets destroyed by the fire of our Allies. This mass of ruins was enclosed between the Flagstaff and the crenellated sea wall, and beyond this might be seen the civil town behind, presenting a stately appearance as it rose on the hillside tier over tier, displaying churches, stately mansions, and public buildings of fine white or red sandstone, with gardens interspersed and trees growing in the walks.

The line of the first parallel and the hill on which it was placed concealed from the spectator the cemetery which we occupied after the 18th of June. They also hid the course of the Woronzow Road and the ravine in front under the proper right of the Redan. Behind the Redan was seen the long line of the dockyard and arsenal buildings, and the barracks, which had been rendered uninhabitable on the near side by our fire. From Cathcart's Hill, one could gain an admirable view of certain points of the position from the sea on the left to our extreme right at Inkerman. That advantage was, however, rarely obtainable when there was any heavy firing, as the smoke generally hung in thick clouds between the earthworks, not to be easily dispelled, excepting by the aid of a brisk wind. If one of the few persons who were in the secret of the opening of the French batteries had been on Cathcart's Hill on the morning of the 5th he would have beheld then, just before half-past five o'clock, the whole scene marked out in keen detail in the clear morning air. The men in our trenches might have been sitting down behind the traverses, or strolling about in the rear of the parapets. Small trains of animals and files of men might have been continually observed passing over the ground between the trenches and the camp, and the only smoke that caught the eye rose from the kettles of the soldiery, or from the discharge of a rifle in the advanced works. On the left, however, the French trenches were crowded with men, and their batteries were all manned, though the occupants kept well out of sight of the enemy, and the mantlets and screens were down before the muzzles of some of their guns. The men beneath the parapets swarmed like bees. A few grey-coated Russians might have been noticed repairing the works of the Flagstaff Battery, or engaged in throwing up a new work, which promised to be of considerable strength, in front of the second line of their defences.

Suddenly, close to the Bastion du Mât three jets of flame sprang up into the air and hurled up as many pillars of earth and dust, a hundred feet high, which were warmed into ruddy hues by the horizontal rays of the sun. The French had exploded three fougasses to blow in the counterscarp and to serve as a signal to their men. In a moment, from the sea to the Dockyard-creek, a stream of fire three miles in length seemed to run like a train from battery to battery, and fleecy, curling, rich white smoke ascended, as though the earth had suddenly been rent in the throes of an earthquake and was vomiting forth the material of her volcanoes. The lines of the French trenches were at once covered as though the very clouds of Heaven had settled down upon them and were whirled about in spiral jets, in festoons, in clustering bunches, in columns and in sheets, all commingled, and uniting as it were by the vehement flames beneath. The crash of such a tremendous fire must have been appalling, but the wind and the peculiar condition of the atmosphere did not permit the sound to produce any great effect in our camp. The iron storm tore over the Russian lines, tossing up, as if in sport, jets of earth and dust, rending asunder gabions, and 'squelching' the parapets, or dashing in amongst the houses and ruins in their rear. The terrible files of this flying army extending about four miles in front, rushed across the plain, carrying death and terror in their train, swept with heavy and irresistible wings the Russian flanks, and searched their centre to the core. A volley so startling, simultaneous, and tremendously powerful, was probably never before discharged since cannon were introduced.

The Russians seemed for a while utterly paralysed. Their batteries were not manned with strength enough to enable them to reply to such an overlapping and crushing fire; but the French, leaping to their guns with astounding energy, rapidity, and vigour, kept on filling the very air with the hurling storm, and sent it in unbroken fury against their enemies. More than 200 pieces of artillery of large calibre, admirably served and well directed, played incessantly upon the hostile lines. In a few moments a great veil of smoke – 'a war-cloud rolling dun' – spread from the guns on the left of Sebastopol; the cannonade now pealed forth in great irregular bursts, now died away into hoarse murmurs, again swelled up into tumult, or rattled from one extremity to the other of the line like the file-fire of infantry. Stone walls at once went down before the discharge, earthworks yawned to receive shot and shell alike. So swift and incessant was the passage of these missiles through the embrasures and along the top of the parapets that the enemy had to lie close and scarcely dare show themselves in the front line of their defences. For a few minutes the French had it all their own way and appeared to be on the point of sweeping away the place without resistance. This did not last long, as after they had fired a few rounds from each of their numerous guns, the Russian artillerymen got to work and began to return the fire. They made good practice, but fired slowly and with precision, as if they could not afford to throw away an ounce of powder. The French were stimulated rather than restrained by such a reply to their astonishing volleys and sent their shot with greater rapidity along the line of the defences and among the houses of the town. Our admirable Naval Brigade and our gallant siege train were just working their guns at a quiet rate, but they maintained their usual destructive and solid 'hammering' away at the faces of the Redan and of the Malakoff, and aided our invaluable Allies by keeping up a regular shell practice on the batteries from the Creek to the Redan.

Our Quarry Battery, just 400 yards below the Redan, plied the suburb in the rear of the Malakoff vigorously with bombs and kept the top of the Redan clear with round shot and grape. Redan and Malakoff were alike silent, ragged, and torn. At most the Redan fired three guns, and the adjoining batteries were equally parsimonious. The parapets were all pitted with shot and shell and the sides of the embrasures greatly injured, so that the gabions were sticking out and dislodged in all directions. There was no more of that fine polishing and of that cabinet-maker's work which the Russians bestowed on their batteries; our constant fire by night, the efforts of our riflemen, and incessant shelling, having rather checked their assiduous anxiety as to external appearance.

After two hours and a-half of furious firing, the artillerymen of our Allies suddenly ceased in order to let their guns cool and to rest themselves. The Russians crept out to repair damages to their works, and shook sandbags full of earth from the banquette over the outside of their parapets. At ten o'clock, however, having previously exploded some fougasses, as before, the French re-opened a fire if possible more rapid and tremendous than their first, and continued to keep it up with the utmost vigour till twelve o'clock at noon, by which time the Russians had only a few guns in the Flagstaff Road and Garden Batteries in a position to reply. From twelve to five o'clock p.m. the firing was slack; the French then resumed their cannonade with the same astounding vigour as at dawn and at ten o'clock and never ceased their volleys of shot and shell against the place till half-past seven, when darkness set in, whereupon all the mortars and heavy guns, English as well as French, opened with shell against the whole line of defences.

There was not one instant in which the shells did not whistle through the air; not a moment in which the sky was not seamed by their fiery curves or illuminated by their explosion; the lines of the Russian earthworks of the Redan, Malakoff, and of all their batteries, were rendered plainly visible by the constant light of then inumerable explosions. The Russians scarcely attempted a reply.

On the night of September 6th a steady fire was kept up all along the front, with the view of preventing the Russians from repairing damages. At ten p.m., orders were sent to our batteries to open the following morning as soon as there was a good light, but they were limited to fifty rounds each gun. At 5.30 a.m. the whole of the batteries from Quarantine to Inkerman began their fire with a grand crash. There were three breaks or lulls in the tempest; one from half-past eight till ten; another from twelve till five; and the third from half-past six till seven – during these intervals the fire was comparatively slack.

The agitation in the town was considerable throughout the day, and the enemy seemed to be greatly distressed. They were strengthening their position on the north side – throwing up batteries, dragging guns into position, and preparing to defend themselves should they be obliged to leave the city.

The bombardment was renewed on Thursday night at sunset, and continued without intermission till an hour before daybreak on Friday, and the musketry fire was most tremendous and unremitting. The orders to the trench guards were to keep up a perpetual fusillade on the face of the Russian works, and about 150,000 rounds were expended each night after the opening of the bombardment. On Friday at daybreak the cannonade was re-opened and continued as before – the Russians made no reply on the centre, but their Inkerman Batteries across the harbour fired briskly on the French Right Attack and distressed our Allies considerably. A strong wind from the north blew clouds of dust from the town, and carried back the smoke of the batteries, so that it was very difficult to ascertain the effect of the fire, but now and then the veil opened, and at each interval the amount of destruction disclosed was more evident and appalling. At mid-day, a council of generals was held at our headquarters, at which General Pelissier and General Della Marmora attended. After the council broke up, orders were sent to the surgeons to clear out the hospitals of patients and prepare for the reception of wounded.

The contest on which the eyes of Europe had been turned so long – the event on which the hopes of so many mighty empires depended – was all but determined. A dull, strange silence, broken at distant intervals by the crash of citadels and palaces as they were blown into dust, succeeded to the incessant dialogue of the cannon which had spoken so loudly and so angrily throughout an entire year. Tired armies, separated from each other by a sea of fires, rested on their arms, and gazed with various emotions on all that remained of the object of their conflicts.

On the morning of the 8th it became bitterly cold. A biting wind from the north side of Sebastopol blew intolerable clouds of harsh dust into our faces. The sun was obscured and the sky became of a leaden wintry grey. Early in the morning a strong force of cavalry received orders to move up to the front and form a chain of sentries in front of Cathcart's Hill and all along our lines. No person was allowed to pass this boundary excepting staff officers or those provided with a pass. Another line of sentries in the rear of the camps was intended to stop stragglers and idlers from Balaklava, the object of these arrangements being in all probability to prevent the Russians gathering any intimation of our attack, from the unusual accumulation of people on the look-out hills.

It was arranged that the French should attack the Malakoff at noon, and as soon as their attack succeeded, we were to assault the Redan. Strong columns of French were to make a diversion on the left, and menace the line of the Bastion du Mât, Central and Quarantine Bastions. The cavalry sentries were posted at 8.30 a.m. At 10.30 a.m., the Second and the Light Division moved down to the trenches, and were placed in the advanced parallels as quietly and unostentatiously as possible. The French trenches were crowded with men as close as they could be packed, and we could, through the breaks in the clouds of dust, which were most irritating, see our troops all ready in their trenches. The cannonade languished purposely towards noon, but the Russians, catching sight of the cavalry and troops in front, began to shell Cathcart's Hill and the heights, and the bombs and long ranges disturbed the equanimity of some of the spectators by bursting with loud 'thuds' right over their heads, and sending 'the gunners' pieces' sharply about them. After hours of suspense, the moment came at last.

At five minutes before twelve o'clock, the French, like a swarm of bees, issued forth from their trenches close to the Malakoff, scrambled up its face, and were through the embrasures in the twinkling of an eye. They crossed the seven metres of ground which separated them from the enemy at a few bounds – they drifted as lightly and quickly as autumn leaves before the wind, battalion after battalion, into the embrasures, and in a minute or two after the head of their column issued from the ditch the tricolor was floating over the Bastion. The musketry was very feeble at first – indeed, our Allies took the Russians by surprise and very few of the latter were in the Malakoff; but they soon recovered themselves, and from twelve o'clock till past seven in the evening the French had to meet and repulse the repeated attempts of the enemy to regain the work, when, weary of the fearful slaughter of his men, who lay in thousands over the exterior of the works, and, despairing of success the Muscovite General withdrew his exhausted legions, and prepared, with admirable skill, to evacuate the place. The French attack on the left, if intended in earnest, was not successful and caused great loss to our Allies.

As soon as the tricolor was observed waving through the smoke and dust over the parapet of the Malakoff, four rockets were sent up one after another as a signal for our assault upon the Redan. They were almost borne back by the violence of the wind and the silvery jets of sparks they threw out on exploding were scarcely visible against the raw grey sky.

The wind was not the only impediment to the British. Considering the cost at which failure had been bought in the previous attack on the Redan, it might have been expected that the lessons taught by that disaster had been well and truly learnt. But General Simpson was a backward pupil. The forces now allocated by him to attack the Redan consisted of equal numbers drawn from the Light and Second Divisions, 'a portion of each being virtually in reserve and not engaged in the affair at all'. In other words, the force deployed for the actual attack numbered 1,380 men. For their assault on the Malakoff, the French had assembled the same number of divisions as before, when 36,000 had been thrown into the battle, and, as before, 10,000 were to be held in reserve.

As the Light Division rushed out into the open, they were swept by the guns of the Barrack Battery and by several pieces on the proper right of the Redan, loaded heavily with grape, which caused considerable loss amongst them ere they reached the salient or apex of the work at which they were to assault. They crossed the abattis without difficulty; it was torn to pieces and destroyed by our shot, and the men stepped over and through it with ease. The Light Division made straight for the salient and projecting angle of the Redan and came to the ditch, at this place about fifteen feet deep. The men, led by their officers, leaped into the ditch and scrambled up the other side, whence they scaled the parapet almost without opposition; for the few Russians who were in front ran back and got behind their traverses and breastworks and opened fire upon them as soon as they saw our men on the top.

The storming columns of the Second Division issuing out of the fifth parallel rushed up immediately after the Light Division. The first embrasure to which they came was in flames, but, moving on to the next, the men leaped into the ditch and, with the aid of ladders and of each other's hands, scrambled up on the other side, climbed the parapet, or poured in through the embrasure, which was undefended. The salient was carried at once, and the men entered the stronghold, which is a work traced on a most obtuse angle, requiring a large mass of men to assault it, not only at the salient, but at the same moment on both flanks, so as to turn them and to enable the salient storming party to advance down the interior space at once, taking the defenders in front and flank, and indeed in rear, at the same moment. In consequence of attacking the salient only, no front could be formed, on account of the small interior space at that point; the men were forced to advance by driblets.

To this dangerous handicap another was now added. At the base of the Redan and a little in advance of it there was a protective breastwork from behind which a number of Russians now began to fire up at the men who had got through the embrasure and were crowding the parapet of the salient. Inside the salient they were met by ferocious efforts to repel them and from this stream of cross fire the attackers suffered heavily.

As the alarm of an assault circulated, the enemy came rushing up from the barracks in rear of the Redan, increasing the force and intensity of their fire, while our soldiers dropped fast. In vain the officers, by voice and act, by example and daring valour, tried to urge our soldiers on to clear the work. The men, most of whom belonged to regiments which had suffered in the trenches, and were acquainted with the traditions of June 18th,[1] had an impression that the Redan was extensively mined and that if they advanced they would all be blown up; yet, to their honour be it recorded, many of them acted as became the men of Alma and Inkerman, and, rushing confusedly to the front, were swept down by the enemy's fire. The officers fell on all sides, singled out as a mark for the enemy by their courage. The men of the different regiments got mingled together in inextricable confusion. The 19th did not care for the orders of the officers of the 88th, nor did the soldiers of the 23rd heed the commands of an officer who did not belong to the regiment. The officers could not find their men – the men had lost sight of their own officers. All the Brigadiers, save Colonel Windham, were wounded, or rendered unfit for the guidance of the attack.

Every moment our men were diminishing in numbers, while the Russians were arriving in swarms from the town, and rushing down from the Malakoff, which had been occupied by the French. Thrice did Colonel Windham despatch officers to Sir W. Codrington,[2] who was in the fifth parallel, to entreat of him to send up supports in some order of formation; but all these three officers were wounded as they passed from the ditch of the Redan to the rear, and the Colonel's aide-de-camp, Lieutenant Swire, of the 17th, a gallant young officer, was hit dangerously in the hip as he went on his perilous errand. Supports were, indeed, sent up, but they advanced in disorder, from the fire to which they were exposed on their way, and arrived in driblets on the parapet, only to increase the confusion and the carnage. The narrow neck of the salient was too close to allow of any kind of formation; and the more the men crowded into it, the worse was the disorder, and the more they suffered from the enemy's fire. This miserable work lasted for an hour. The Russians had congregated in dense masses behind the breastwork, and Colonel Windham resolved to go to General Codrington himself. He crossed

[1] The day on which the Redan had been previously assaulted.

[2] Successor to Sir George Brown as commander of the Light Division.

the parapet and ditch, and succeeded in gaining the fifth parallel, through a storm of grape and rifle bullets, in safety; standing on the top of the parapet he again asked for support. Sir W. Codrington asked him if he thought he really could do anything with such supports as he could afford, and said, if he thought so, 'he might take the Royals,' who were then in the parallel. 'Let the officers come out in front – let us advance in order, and if the men keep their formation the Redan is ours,' was the Colonel's reply; but he spoke too late – for at that very moment our men were seen leaping into the ditch or running down the parapet of the salient and through the embrasures out of the work into the ditch, the Russians following them with the bayonet and with heavy musketry, and even throwing stones and grape-shot at them as they lay in the ditch.

The struggle that ensued was short, desperate, and bloody. Our soldiers, taken at every disadvantage, met the enemy with the bayonet too, and isolated combats occurred in which the brave fellows who stood their ground had to defend themselves against three or four adversaries at once. In this melée the officers, armed only with their swords, had but little chance; nor had those who carried pistols much opportunity of using them in such a close and sudden contest. But the solid weight of the advancing mass, urged on and fed each moment from the rear by company after company, and battalion after battalion, prevailed at last against the isolated and disjointed band, which had abandoned that protection which unanimity of courage affords and had lost the advantages of discipline and obedience. Bleeding, panting, and exhausted, our men lay in heaps in the ditch beneath the parapet, sheltered themselves behind stones and in bomb craters in the external slope of the work, or tried to pass back to our advanced parallel and sap, having to run the gauntlet of a tremendous fire. Many of them lost their lives or were seriously wounded in this attempt.

The scene in the ditch was appalling, although some of the officers have assured me that they and the men were laughing at the precipitation with which many brave and gallant fellows did not hesitate to plunge headlong upon the mass of bayonets, muskets, and sprawling soldiers – the ladders were all knocked down or broken, so that it was difficult for the men to scale the other side – and the dead, the dying, the wounded, and the uninjured, were all lying in piles together. The Russians came out of the embrasures, plied them with stones, grape-shot, and the bayonet, but were soon forced to retire by the fire of our batteries and riflemen, and under cover of this fire a good many of our men escaped to the approaches.

General Pelissier observed the failure of our attack from the rear of the Malakoff, and sent over to General Simpson to ask if he intended to renew it. The English Commander-in-Chief is reported to have replied that he did not then feel in a condition to do so. All this time the Guards and Highlanders, the Third and Fourth Divisions, and most of the reserves, had not been engaged. They could, indeed, have furnished materials for making another assault; but the subsequent movements of the Russians render it doubtful whether the glory of carrying the Redan and of redeeming the credit of our arms would not have been dearly purchased by the effusion of more valuable blood.

As soon as we abandoned the assault, the firing slackened along our front; but in the rear of the Malakoff there was a fierce contest going on between masses of Russians, released from the Redan or drawn from the town, and the French inside the work; and the fight for the Little Redan, on the proper left of the Malakoff, was raging furiously. Clouds of smoke and dust obstructed the view, but the rattle of musketry was incessant and betokened the severe nature of the struggle below. Through the breaks in the smoke there could be seen now and then a tricolor, surmounted by an eagle, fluttering bravely over the inner parapet of the Malakoff. The storm of battle rolled fiercely round it and beat against it; but it was sustained by strong arms and stout hearts, and all the assaults of the enemy were vain against it. We could see, too, our noble Allies swarming over into the Malakoff, from their splendid approaches to it from the Mamelon; or rushing with speed towards the right, where the Russians, continually reinforced, sought to beat back their foes, and to regain the key of their position.

General Simpson remained in the Green Hill Battery till six o'clock, at which hour General Pelissier sent to inform him that the

Malakoff was perfectly safe, and to ask him what the English intended to do with respect to the Redan. General Simpson had by this time, it is said, formed the determination of attacking it the following morning at five o'clock with the Guards and the Third and Fourth Divisions. The difficulty of obtaining accurate information of the progress of an action cannot be better exemplified than by this fact, that at three o'clock one of our Generals of Division did not know whether we had taken the Redan or not. Towards dusk, the Guards, who had been placed in reserve behind our Right Attack, were marched off to their camp, and a portion of the Highlanders were likewise taken off the ground.

21

The Fate of Sebastopol

THERE WAS A FEELING OF DEEP DEPRESSION IN CAMP ALL night. We were painfully aware that our attack had failed. The camp was full of wounded men; the hospitals were crowded; and sad stories ran from mouth to mouth respecting the losses of the officers and the behaviour of the men.

Fatigued and worn out by excitement, I lay down to rest, but scarcely to sleep. About eleven o'clock my hut was shaken by a violent shock as of an earthquake, but I was so thoroughly tired and worn out that it did not rouse me for more than an instant; having persuaded myself it was 'only a magazine', I was asleep again.

When I rose before daybreak and got up to Cathcart's Hill, there were not many officers standing on that favourite spot; and the sleepers, who had lain down to rest doubtful of the complete success of the French, and certain of our own failure, little dreamt that Sebastopol was ours. About twelve o'clock, the silence having attracted the attention of our men, some volunteers crept up an embrasure of the Redan, and found the place deserted by all save the dead and dying. Soon afterwards, wandering fires gleamed through the streets and outskirts of the town – point after point became alight – the flames shone out of the windows of the houses – rows of mansions caught and burned up, and before daybreak the town of Sebastopol – that fine and stately mistress of the Euxine, on which we had so often turned a longing eye – was on fire from the sea to the Dockyard Creek. Fort Alexander was blown up early in the night, with a stupendous crash that made the very earth reel. At sunrise, four large explosions on the left followed in quick succession, and announced the destruction of the Quarantine Fort, and of the magazines of the batteries of the Central Bastion and Flagstaff Fort. In a moment afterwards the Redan was the scene of a very heavy explosion, which must have destroyed a number of wounded men on both sides. The Flagstaff and Garden Batteries blew up, one after another, at 4.45. At 5.30 there were two of the largest and grandest explosions on the left that ever shook the earth – most probably from Fort Alexander and the Grand Magazine. The rush of black smoke, grey and white vapour, masses of stone, beams of timber, and masonry into the air was appalling, and then followed the roar of a great bombardment; it was a magazine of shells blown up into the air, and exploding like some gigantic pyrotechnic display in the sky – innumerable flashes of fire twittering high up in the column of dark smoke over the town and then changing rapidly into as many balls of white smoke, like little clouds.

All this time the Russians were marching with sullen tramp across the bridge,[1] and boats were busy carrying off *matériel* from the town, or bearing men to the south side, to complete the work of destruction and renew the fires of hidden mines or light up untouched houses. Of the fleet, all that remained visible were eight steamers and the masts of sunken line-of-battle ships. As soon as it was dawn, the French began to steal from the trenches into the burning town, undismayed by the flames, by the terrors of these explosions, by the fire of a lurking enemy, or by that of their own guns, which kept on slowly discharging cannon-shot and grape into the suburbs at regular intervals, possibly with the very object of deterring stragglers from risking their lives. But red breeches and blue breeches, kepi and Zouave fez, could soon be distinguished amid the flames, moving from house to house. Before five o'clock there were numbers of men coming back with plunder, such as it was, and Russian relics were offered for sale in camp before the Russian battalions had marched out of the city. The sailors, too, were not behindhand in looking for 'loot', and Jack could be seen staggering under chairs, tables, and

[1] The pontoon bridge across the harbour which connected Sebastopol with the northern shore.

lumbering old pictures, through every street and making his way back to the trenches with vast accumulations of worthlessness.

As the rush from camp became very great and every one sought to visit the Malakoff and the Redan, which were filled with dead and dying men, a line of English cavalry was posted across the front from our extreme left to the French right. They were stationed in all the ravines and roads to the town and trenches with orders to keep back all persons except the generals and staff and officers and men on duty, and to stop all our men returning with plunder from the town and to take it from them. As they did not stop the French or Turks or Sardinians, this order gave rise to a good deal of grumbling, particularly when a man, after lugging a heavy chair several miles, or a table or some such article, was deprived of it by our sentries. It so happened that as the remnants of the French regiments engaged on the left against the Malakoff and Little Redan marched to their tents in the morning, our Second Division was drawn up on the parade ground in front of their camp, and the French had to pass their lines. The instant the leading regiment of Zouaves came up to the spot where our first regiment was placed, the men, with one spontaneous burst, rent the air with an English cheer. The French officers drew their swords, their men dressed up and marched past as if at a review, while regiment after regiment of the Second Division caught up the cry, and at last our men presented arms to their brave comrades of France, the officers on both sides saluted with their swords, and this continued till the last man had marched by.

Mingled with the plunderers from the front were many wounded men. The ambulances never ceased – now moving heavily and slowly with their burdens, again rattling at a trot to the front for a fresh cargo – and the ground between the trenches and the camp was studded with cacolets or mule litters. Already the funeral parties had commenced their labours. Moving down on the right flank of our cavalry pickets, a small party of us managed to turn them cleverly, and to get out among the French works between the Mamelon and Malakoff. The ground was here literally paved with shot and shell, and the surface was deeply honeycombed by the explosions of bombs at every square yard. The road was crowded by Frenchmen returning with paltry plunder from Sebastopol, and with files of Russian prisoners, many of them wounded and all dejected, with the exception of a fine little boy in a Cossack's cap and a tiny uniform greatcoat, who seemed rather pleased with his kind captors. There was also one stout Russian soldier, who had evidently been indulging in the popularly credited sources of Dutch courage, and who danced all the way into the camp with a Zouave.

Such light-hearted incidents were few. The interior of the Malakoff was dark and foul. Crammed with debris and with corpses, it was a hideous sight.

The Russians lay inside the work in heaps, like carcasses in a butcher's cart; and the wounds – the blood – the sight exceeded all I had hitherto witnessed.

Descending from the Malakoff, we came upon a suburb of ruined houses open to the sea – it was filled with dead. The Russians had crept away into holes and corners in every house, to die like poisoned rats; artillery horses, with their entrails torn open by shot, were stretched all over the space at the back of the Malakoff, marking the place where the Russians moved up their last column to re-take it under the cover of a heavy field battery. Every house, the church, some public buildings, sentry-boxes – all alike were broken and riddled by cannon and mortar.

Of all the pictures of the horrors of war which have ever been presented to the world, the hospital of Sebastopol offered the most heartrending and revolting. The building used as an hospital was inside the dockyard wall and was peculiarly exposed to the action of shot and shell bounding over the Redan; it bore in sides, roof, windows, and doors, frequent and distinctive proofs of the severity of the cannonade.

Entering one of these doors, I beheld such a sight as few men, thank God, have ever witnessed. In a long, low room, supported by square pillars arched at the top, and dimly lighted through shattered and unglazed window-frames, lay the wounded Russians. The wounded, did I say? No, but the dead – the rotten and festering corpses of the soldiers, who were left to die in their extreme agony, untended, uncared for, packed as close as they could be stowed, some on the floor, others on wretched trestles and bedsteads or pallets of straw, sopped and saturated with blood which oozed and trickled through upon the floor, mingling with the droppings of corruption. With the roar of exploding fortresses in their ears – with shells and shot pouring through the roof and sides of the rooms in which they lay – with the crackling and hissing of fire around them, these poor fellows, who had served their loving friend and master the Czar but too well, were consigned to their terrible fate. Many might have been saved by ordinary care. Many lay, yet alive, with maggots crawling about in their wounds. Many, nearly mad by the scene around them, or seeking escape from it in their extremest agony, had rolled away under the beds and glared out on the heart-stricken spectator. Many, with legs and arms broken and twisted, the jagged splinters sticking through the raw flesh, implored aid, water, food, or pity, or, deprived of speech by the approach of death or by dreadful injuries in the head or trunk, pointed to the lethal spot. Many seemed bent alone on making their peace with Heaven. The attitudes of some were so hideously fantastic as to root one to the ground by a sort of dreadful fascination. The bodies of numbers of men were swollen and bloated to an incredible degree; and the features, distended to a gigantic size, with eyes protruding from the sockets and the blackened tongue lolling out of the mouth, compressed tightly by the teeth which had set upon it in the death-rattle, made one shudder and reel round.

The Great Redan was next visited. All the houses behind it a mass of broken stones – a clock turret, with a shot right through the clock; a pagoda in ruins; another clock-tower, with all the clock destroyed save the dial, with the words, 'Barwise, London', thereon; cook-houses, where human blood was running among the utensils; in one place a shell had lodged in the boiler and blown it and its contents, and probably its attendants, to pieces. Everywhere wreck and destruction. This evidently was a *beau quartier* once. Climbing up to the Redan, which was fearfully cumbered with the dead, we witnessed the scene of the desperate attack and defence which cost both sides so much blood. The ditch outside made one sick – it was piled up with English dead, some of them scorched and blackened by the explosion, and others lacerated beyond recognition. The quantity of broken gabions and gun-carriages here was extraordinary; the ground was covered with them. The bomb-proofs were the same as in the Malakoff, and in one of them a music-book was found with a woman's name in it, and a canary bird and vase of flowers were outside the entrance.

The day after the city had fallen, attempts were made to sink by gunfire nine Russian warships that were still in the harbour, but although some were damaged, none was destroyed. It was therefore decided, as a precautionary measure, to set up a battery to cover the entrance to the harbour. The site chosen was beside the remains of Fort St Paul, which had stood at the head of the Dockyard Creek until the Russians had blown it up during their retreat. Orders were issued for men of the Naval Brigade to carry out the work during the night, with a covering party standing by to keep a look-out.

The men had been working some time when it was observed that one of the enemy's steamers had left the north side and was slowly and noiselessly dropping down to the very spot where the sailors and the covering party were at their labours. The night was dark, but they could clearly make out the steamer edging down upon them and coming closer and closer. Every moment they expected the guns to open upon them with grape and canister. The men, therefore, lay down upon their faces and kept as near to the ground as they could, and the steamer came over gently till she was within about a hundred yards of the very spot where they had been working. They heard her anchor splash into the water, and then the rattle of her cable as it ran through the hawsehole. Now, certainly they were 'going to catch it'; but, no – the Russian opened no port and showed no light, but seemed to be making himself comfortable in his new quarters.

Captain Villiers, of the 47th, who commanded the covering party, ordered his men to observe the utmost silence, and the same injunction was given to the seamen. About 2.30 in the morning, when she had been an hour or so in her novel birth, a broad light was perceived in her fore hatchway. The leading steamer on the opposite side in a second afterwards exhibited gleams of equal brightness, and then one! two! three! four! five! – as though from signal guns the remaining steamers, with one exception, emitted jets of fire from their bows. The jets soon became columns of flame and smoke – the wind blew fresh and strong, and the night was dark, so that the fire spread with rapidity along the vessels, and soon lighted up the whole of the northern heavens. The masts were speedily licked and warmed into a fiery glow and the rigging burst out into fitful wavering lines of light, struggling with the wind for life: the yards shed lambent showers of spark and burning splinters upon the water. The northern works could be readily traced by the light of the conflagration, and the faces of the Russian soldiers and sailors who were scattered about on the face of the cliff shone out now and then, and justified Rembrandt. The work of destruction sped rapidly. The vessels were soon nothing but huge arks of blinding light, which hissed and crackled fiercely and threw up clouds of sparks and embers; and the guns, as they became hot, exploded, and shook the crazy hulls to atoms. One after another they went down into the seething waters.

The cavalry out on the plains wondered what great conflagration had broken out anew in the town. At daybreak only one steamer remained. A boat pushed alongside her from the shore. They boarded her, and after remaining below about ten minutes, returned to their boat and regained the shore. Very speedily the vessel began to be seized with a sort of internal convulsion – first she dipped her bows, then her stern, then gave a few uneasy shakes, and at length, after a short quiver, went down bodily, cleverly scuttled. The Russians preferred being agents of their own destruction and did not give the conqueror a chance of parading the fruits of his victory. We could not delight the good people of Plymouth or Portsmouth by the sight of Russian liners and steamers. We could only drive the enemy to the option of destroying or of doing the work for him, and he invariably preferred the former. He led his battalions in narrow files across a deep arm of the sea, which ought to have been commanded by our guns, and in the face of a most powerful fleet. He actually paraded them in our sight as they crossed, and carried off all his most useful stores and munitions of war. He sank his ships and blew up his forts without molestation; nothing was done to harass him in his retreat, with the exception of some paltry efforts to break down the bridge by cannon-shot, or to shell the troops as they marched over.

His steamers towed his boats across at their leisure, and when every man had been placed in safety, and not till then, the Russians began to dislocate and float off the different portions of their bridge, and to pull it over to the north side.

The Russians, so far from flying in discomfort over boundless wastes, calmly strengthened their position on the north side. The face of the country bristled with their cannon and their batteries. Day and night the roar of their guns sounded through our camp, and occasionally equalled the noise of the old cannonades, which we hoped had died into silence for ever. There was no sign of any intention on their part to abandon a position on which they had lavished so much care and labour. In their new position they had placed between themselves and us a deep arm of the sea, a river, and the sides of a plateau as steep as a wall. We permitted them to get off at their leisure, and looked on, while the Russian battalions filed over the narrow bridge, emerging in unbroken order out of that frightful sea of raging fire and smoke which was tossed up into billows of flame by the frequent explosion of great fortresses and magazines.

At what moment our generals woke up and knew what was going on I cannot tell, but it is certain they did not, as a body, distress themselves by any violent efforts to get a near view of the enemy's movements *early* in the morning.

Why did not the English move? Orders and counter-orders were sent day after day – requisitions on Captain This to know how many mules he had to carry ball cartridge, orders to Captain That to turn out his battery for the purpose of taking the field at daybreak next morning; counter-orders in the evening recountered and retracted at night, till it was hard to say what was to be done; and if the men who gave the commands were in half as confused a state of mind as those who received them, they were indeed in a pitiable plight. The work of the army was actually that of preparation, not for motion, but for stagnation.

New roads were laid down from Balaklava to the front, new drainage systems built, 'the railway assumed an appearance of great solidity', huts, food, clothing and fuel were brought up in abundance. And all for what? No one seemed to know: or if they did, no hint was given to those whom such preparations were most likely to concern, the men of the British army, nor was the press kept any better informed. Meanwhile, with time on their hands, officers and men alike found there was not much to be done with it.

Even Cathcart's Hill was deserted, except by the 'look-out officer' for the day, or by a few wandering strangers and visitors. Road-making occupied some leisure hours, but the officers had very little to do and found it difficult to kill time, riding about Sebastopol, visiting Balaklava, foraging at Kamiesch, or hunting for quail, which were occasionally found in swarms all over the steppe and formed most grateful additions to the mess-table.

In spite of the frightful damage that had been done there, Sebastopol, too, was a favourite placing for 'foraging'.

Sebastopol gradually came up piecemeal to the camp. Doors, windows, locks, hinges, fire-places, stoves, pictures, chairs, tables, beams of wood, roofing, ceiling, flooring, sheet-lead, rolled copper, cut stone, crockery, and innumerable articles of every description, were brought up by carts, horses, ponies, and by men, every day in great quantities, and were found most useful in the construction and ornamentation of our huts. There were very few officers who had not got some trophies; arms of various descriptions, great-coats, and helmets, pictures of saints, often embellished by the finders with grotesque adornments of moustachios, short pipes, and eye-glasses, and portraits of the late Czar, which had not quite escaped the spirit of improvement manifested by our soldiery, were very common. Many articles of English workmanship abounded, and canary birds sang and flowers bloomed amid all the murky horrors of these blood-stained casemates.

22

Armistice

Almost a month went by before there was any further allied activity of any consequence. In the meantime it was decided that a base should be secured for operations against Nicolaev, the great shipyard, dock area and naval arsenal on the estuary of the River Bug, some sixty miles east of Odessa. Access to the river mouth from the Black Sea was through a narrow opening into Kherson Bay. It had been discovered that on either side of the opening, which was not more than a mile and a half wide, there was a small fort at Oczakoff on the north side and a larger one at Kinburn on the south side. On October 7 a combined fleet of some eighty ships set sail with the object of capturing and occupying the forts. By half-past eight the next morning, the fleet was nearing Odessa.

By degrees a white lighthouse, a guard-house, a white telegraph-house and station, white farmhouses, white villas embowered in green trees, pagodas, minarets, domes, and church spires appeared in view and clustered together, till we had a day-dream of Constantinople and Naples together with a dash of Boulogne in it, and Odessa came in sight. There stood an extensive city, built on the curve of a high sea-shore, with descending terraces and broad flights of steps to the beach, which was enclosed by broad quays and the walls of ports and casemated batteries, all shining brightly in the morning sun. Broad esplanades, or boulevards, lined with trees towards the sea-front, ran along the top of the bank, with a background of stately mansions, worthy of the best 'rows' near the Regent's Park, and we could see a numerous and gaily-dressed crowd of men and women passing along the promenade. Behind and in continuation of this esplanade are splendid residences with pillared porticoes and ornamented peristyles, magnificent public institutions, barracks, palaces, rising in front of a confused but graceful mass of domes, columns, steeples, and spires. One huge dome is of an intense ultra-marine blue and is topped by a gilt cupola; another is of bright green, surmounted by a golden star; here is a Greek temple, there a Tartaresque-looking mosque; there a Byzantine church; again, an Eastern minaret-like spire; further on, an indubitable Sir Christopher Wren steeple: and, next to it, a grand dome and cupola, which at once remind you of St Peter's or St Paul's.

The city was as peaceful as a drop-scene at the theatre, but the operations of war were going on, nevertheless, and little could we tell what alarm, confusion, terror, and dread, dwelt within that beautiful capital on which we gazed so placidly.

As the first ship of the English squadron cast anchor, a long line of dust was observed rising over the hilly coast to the north of Odessa and by the beach, which is lined with trees and a thick hedge of bushes, and we soon made out bayonets glistening in the sun and a strong body of Russian infantry with field-pieces and baggage, consisting of some five or six thousand men, marching in all haste towards the city.

Throughout the night the fleet remained at anchor. When morning came, it brought with it 'clouds, fog, and vapours'.

The fleet must have presented a spectacle full of grandeur and menace to the Odessans. It extended for five miles in front of their town – a dense array of hulls and masts, yards and rigging, which, from shore, looked as if it were one unbroken network of ships resting on the water.

Fog settled down on the water about three o'clock, slowly descending from the sky above, and distilled itself into drops of rain which ran down the masts and fell from spars and rigging. Before it became very thick, our only amusement had been watching a considerable force of cavalry and horse artillery drawn up on the cliffs about six miles from Odessa and three miles from our anchorage. These were evidently intended to act as a flying column of observation, and to march on any part of the coast which might be threatened by our troops.

On the 10th of October the fog continued and was worthy of the best efforts of the London atmosphere in November. It was not so rich in colour, so yellow, or so choky, but it was equally thick and clammy. In colour it was white and sometimes the sun stamped a moonlike imitation of his orb upon it, and in favourable moments one could see a faint indication of his existence above. Now and then you caught a dark outline of a vessel looming through the mist; you strained your eyes to make out your neighbour, but as you looked the vision disappeared. The water flowed with a heavy oily roll, and the only noise to be heard was the plash of the lazy waves against the paddle-wheels, the bumping of the rudder, and the creak of an odd timber, as he rubbed against his fellows. The rolling of drums – the beat of paddle-wheels as a solitary steamer changed her berth with caution – the striking of the bells of the ships, and the reports of guns at long intervals, were the only evidence that a great fleet was lying all around us. All communication between the ships ceased, for no one could tell where his next neighbour was.

At 3.30 p.m. the fog began to clear away and one after another the ships of the fleet appeared in sight, as if coming out in a dissolving view. Cutters and gigs glided about in all directions, visits were paid from ship to ship, and some boats swept in to have a nearer look at the shore.

All was quiet during the night. On the 11th of October the sun rose unclouded. Odessa looked more beautiful than ever. Wherever there was a good view of the fleet to be had a crowd of people collected, and the esplanades and terraces, and even the housetops and parapets of the batteries, were occupied by spectators. The cavalry on the hill to the north of the town were visible at early dawn, each man dismounted at the side of his horse. The flagship, at 8.30 a.m., signalled to the fleet to 'Prepare three days' provisions for troops to land with.'

The evening of the 11th was unsettled. On the 12th, the weather was unfavourable; and on the 13th it blew briskly, sending in a heavy surf; but the wind abated towards night and orders were given to prepare to weigh at dawn next morning. On the morning of October 14th, the fleet weighed and stood along shore. The weather was beautiful, and we could at our leisure admire the numerous clean-looking, snug villages, the immense flocks and herds, and well-filled farmyards, which met the eye along the coast. The fleet anchored, at three o'clock, three miles west of Kinburn Fort, and on the 15th the troops landed without the smallest opposition, or even the appearance of an enemy, about four miles below the fort.

It was too rough the next day for the fleet to open fire, but on the following morning the weather had changed once more.

It was a dull, grey dawn, with wind off the shore, and the sea quite calm. The fleet was perfectly still, but the mortar-vessels, floating-batteries, and gun-boats were getting up steam, and before nine o'clock they might be seen leaving the rest of the armada, and making for the south side of the fort. The floating batteries opened with a magnificent crash, at 9.30 a.m., and one in particular distinguished itself for the regularity, precision, and weight of its fire throughout the day. The enemy replied with alacrity, and his batteries must have been put to a severe test, for the water was splashed into pillars by shot all over them. At 11.10 a fire broke out in the long barrack, and speedily spread from end to end of the fort, driving the artillerymen from their guns. Small explosions of supply ammunition took place inside.

At 11.15 the Russian Jack was shot away, and was not replaced. Admiral [Sir Houston] Stewart, in the 'Valorous', and the French Admiral (second in command), in the 'Asmodée', followed by eleven steamers, came round into Kherson Bay, delivering broadsides and engaging the batteries as they passed, and they were preceded by the 'Hannibal', which ripped up Kinburn with her broadsides. The fire raged more furiously, fed by constant bombs and rockets, and at 12.35 a fresh conflagration burst out in the fort. At the same time the 'Valorous', 'Asmodée', and steam-frigates opened their broadsides, and the nine line-of-battle ships approached in magnificent style and took up their position at the seaward face of the fort, already seriously damaged by the tremendous fire of the floating-batteries, gun-boats, and mortar-vessels.

At length a flag was waved from the parapet, and two boats, each bearing a flag of truce, pushed off, one from the English and another from the French Admiral, and at the same time Sir Houston Stewart proceeded to land near the battery, where he found the French General advancing to parley with the Governor. Major-General Kokonovitch advanced with a sword and pistol in one hand and a pistol in the other. He threw down his sword at the officer's feet, and discharged his pistols into the ground, or at least pulled the triggers with the muzzles pointing downwards, in token of surrender. He was moved to tears, and as he left the fort turned round and uttered some passionate exclamation in Russian, of which the interpreter could only make out, 'Oh, Kinburn! Kinburn! Glory of Suvorov and my shame, I abandon you,' or something to that effect. As the garrison marched out they were ordered to pile their arms, but many of them threw them on the ground at the feet of the conquerors, with rage and mortification depicted on their features.

It appears that the second in command, a Pole by birth, inflamed by courage and its Dutch ally, declared he would not surrender, and that he was prepared to blow up the magazine before the enemy should enter. In this he was supported by the officer of engineers and by the officer of artillery. Amid the crash of falling buildings, the explosions of mortars, the thunder of the fleet, and the smoke and flame of their crumbling batteries, the Russians held a hasty council of war, at which it was put to the vote whether they should surrender or not. In vain the fanatic Pole, the artilleryman and the engineer tried to persuade the Governor and the majority to persist in the madness and folly of continuing their passive resistance. The white flag was hoisted, much to the satisfaction of every humane sailor in the allied fleet, who could feel no pleasure in destroying a brave enemy. Kokonovitch wept as he threw down the pen with which he signed the articles of surrender, but he had no reason to be ashamed of his defence.

By the terms of the capitulation the garrison were permitted to retire with everything except their arms, ammunition, and guns; the officers were allowed to wear their swords, the men to carry off their knapsacks, clothing, regimental bugles, church property, relics, and pictures. The officers bore their misfortune with dignity, but felt it deeply, as was evident from their grave demeanour and stern countenances. Few of them wore decorations and only one was dressed in full uniform. A Chef de Bataillon or Major, wearing a long light-blue cloak with red collar, who limped along with difficulty, had a good deal of influence over those around him and kept the drunken soldiers in awe by his look, and a sergeant in a long green frockcoat with yellow facings and stripes, aided him in repressing the mirthful disposition of some of the bacchanalians on the line of march. The Russians, with their usual incendiary propensity, set fire to the fort below Oczakoff on the 18th, and retired after blowing up the magazines, which went into the air with two heavy explosions, at six o'clock.

Before we weighed in the morning, a French boat left the Rear-Admiral's ship with a flag of truce for Oczakoff. She carried the reply to a request sent by the Russian general the previous day, and informed him that forty-five wounded Russians were in the French ambulances [at Kinburn]. As the boat neared the beach, an officer, followed by two soldiers, came from the town to meet them. One of the men bore a tremendous flag of truce – a large tablecloth suspended from a long pole, under the weight of which he staggered as he walked. The boat touched the beach, and, with much formal bowing and martial civilities, the missive was handed to the Russian, who retired with his tablecloth waving behind him up the hill and was lost to sight amid the houses. Two old priests scrambled down to the ruins of the fort, and, with their flowing robes and long beards, seemed like ancient prophets invoking maledictions – as no doubt they were – upon the fleet. At last we reached the mouth of the Bug.

A short reconnaissance of the estuary was made by units of the two fleets, but presently they were met by gunfire from shore batteries, and as it was clear that progress towards Nicolaev could not be made without further support, the ships returned to their anchorage.

Kinburn having been secured against the attack of any forces the enemy could bring against it, covered completely by the guns of the formidable flotilla we left to protect it, the greater portion of the fleet sailed for Balaklava and Kamiesch.

It was virtually the last move in the bitter, bloody and long-fought struggle. Already there was a feeling of anti-climax, of unreality about the routine duties, the inspections and the parades which were all that the allied armies now had to occupy them. General Simpson was replaced as Commander-in-Chief by Sir William Codrington, but the change came too late to excite much enthusiasm. The Allies began the systematic destruction of Sebastopol's docks, but to men who had borne the bombardments of March and April and June, the engineers' detonations seemed hardly more than a drum-beat.

The extraordinary fineness of the weather all this time afforded a daily reproach to the inactivity of our armies. We enjoyed a season of exceptionable mildness. Storms lowered over us and passed away; dark skies threatened us and melted into floods of golden sunbeams. The mornings and nights, however, began to warn us that winter was impending.

It was now November. More than three months went by, and then –

The morning of February 28th brought us news of the conclusion of an armistice. The Russians had it first, by telegraph from St Petersburg, and the mail from Constantinople brought its confirmation to the Allies.

There was a lively and novel scene at ten o'clock on the morning of February the 29th at Traktir Bridge. At its further end the white flag was hoisted, and just beyond it some five and twenty Cossacks halted, who had escorted thither the Russian General Timvoieff and his staff. The Generals, who met to arrange the details of the armistice, occupied two tents, pitched on a strip of greensward in the rear of the bridge. At a few minutes past ten General Barnard and some staff officers rode down through the ravine between the two hills on which the battle of the Tchernaya was fought and crossed to the other side of the river. There were, perhaps, half-a-dozen other English officers, about as many French, and a much larger number of

Sardinians. All these went over the bridge and a sort of fraternization ensued between them and some Russian officers – that is to say, there was a good deal of civility, and some ill-treatment of the French and German languages.

As the conference went on, more and more spectators arrived from the allied camps and began to walk about near the bridge or across to the other side, where by now there was a considerable gathering of Russian officers.

Some of them were strolling by in twos and threes in the field, at a short distance beyond, and when these were descried there was usually a regular charge down upon them by the allied officers, eager to make their acquaintance. Their manner was generally grave and rather reserved, but they conversed readily and all had the tone and appearance of well-bred men. Some of them were very young. There was one youth of eighteen, who named to us the regiment of Hussars in which he was an officer and seemed knowing about horses, pointing out the English ones from among the French, Italians, and Arabs that stood around. All – cavalry as well as infantry, and the General and his staff – wore the long uniform greatcoat of a sort of brown and grey mixture, and seemed to have no other insignia of rank than the different colours and lace of the shoulder-strap. The Staff wore white kid gloves, and I noticed some of them with smart patent leather boots – elegancies rarely seen in our part of the Crimea.

There was nothing else of any interest to observe, and most of the persons whom curiosity led to the spot soon grew tired of standing at the edge of a ditch and gazing at a distant handful of Muscovites; so they turned their horses and tried to warm themselves by a canter back to the camp.

Meanwhile, the conference continued and many of the spectators continued to wait.

Then cocked hats and feathers were seen moving among the horses near the tents; orderlies and escorts mounted; the Cossacks did the same, and presently English, French, Sardinian, and Russian generals and staff rode over the bridge and between a double line formed by the spectators. General Timvoieff, a soldierly-looking man of agreeable physiognomy, rode first, and smilingly returned the salutes with which he was received. The *cortège* proceeded a short distance into the plain. and then the allied portion of it took leave of *nos amis les ennemis*, and retraced their steps to the bridge.

So far as Sebastopol was concerned there was little for the Russians to gain by covering it with the thin cloak of an armistice. Had fire been rained down from Heaven upon the devoted city its annihilation could not have been more complete. The stranger who halted to survey it from the neighbouring heights, deceived by the white-washed and plastered walls of the houses, might think that Sebastopol was still a city; but when he walked through its grass-grown, deserted streets, formed by endless rows of walls alone, of roofless shells of houses; when he beheld great yawning craters, half filled with mounds of stone heaped together in irregular masses; when he gazed on tumuli of disintegrated masonry – once formidable forts; when he stumbled over the fragments of imperial edifices, to peer down into the great gulfs choked up with rubbish, which marked the site of the grand docks, and beheld the rotting masts and hulls of the sunken navy which had been nurtured there; when he observed that what the wrath of the enemy spared was fast crumbling away beneath the fire of its friends, and that the churches where they worshipped, the theatres, the public monuments, had been specially selected for the practice of the Russian gunners – he would no doubt have come to the conclusion that the history of the world afforded no such authentic instance of the annihilation of a great city. Had we taken Sebastopol at the outset, we must have been prepared, with our small army, to meet those *corps d'armée* which lost tens of thousands in their hasty march to relieve the place, but who, in the event of its capture, would have closed slowly round us, and the same incapacity which prevented our reaping the fruits of our *coup-de-main* in attempting the Crimean expedition might have led to more serious evils in a protracted campaign in the open field against a numerous and well-handled, if not a daring, enemy. Success was indeed obtained, but its cost has been great.

ARMISTICE

The war had drifted to an end. For nearly three months scarcely a shot had been fired by either side. Now it seemed too late for rejoicing. A feeling of anti-climax had blunted the edge of expectation. It was time to begin counting the cost.

How great that cost was in terms of personal suffering and material destruction is brought home more vividly by Russell's despatches than by any other contemporary account. Not even Kinglake's monumental survey, nor any of the researches of later historians – and few wars in which the British army has fought have been reported in greater detail – give so sharp an impression of what it must have been like actually to take part in the campaign.

Journalism, however, is not history. The first requirement of the historian is a sense of perspective. But to a journalist, dealing as journalists must with events as they happen from day to day, a sense of perspective may seem almost a handicap, for it implies a lack of that sense of immediacy that is imperative for a good journalist. Russell was not writing for posterity, he was writing for the readers of The Times, *but perhaps was not unmindful of Sir Walter Raleigh's saying that 'We may gather out of history a policy no less wise than eternal: by comparison and application of other men's forepassed miseries with our own like errors . . .'*

Index

INDEX